THE JESUS
FAMILY
TOMB

THE JESUS FAMILY TOMB

The discovery that will change history forever

SIMCHA JACOBOVICI & CHARLES PELLEGRINO

HARPER
element

HarperElement
An Imprint of HarperCollins*Publishers*
77–85 Fulham Palace Road,
Hammersmith, London W6 8JB

The web address is www.thorsonselement.com

and *HarperElement* are trademarks of
HarperCollins*Publishers* Ltd

First published in the USA by HarperCollins Publishers 2007
This edition published by HarperCollins*Publishers* 2007

1

A catalogue record for this book
is available from the British Library

HB ISBN 0-00-724567-X
HB ISBN-13 978-00-724567-3
TPB ISBN 0-00-724568-8
TPB ISBN-13 978-00-724568-0

Printed and bound in Great Britain
by Clays Ltd, St Ives plc

This book is proudly printed on paper which contains wood
from well managed forests, certified in accordance with
the rules of the Forest Stewardship Council.
For more information about FSC,
please visit www.fsc-uk.org

Mixed Sources
Product group from well-managed
forests and other controlled sources
www.fsc.org Cert no. SW-COC-1806
© 1996 Forest Stewardship Council
FSC

Contents

Foreword

What if Jesus didn't exist at all? Today many experts are saying exactly that. The theory is that he was a conflation of pagan god-man and death/Resurrection myths with first-century Jewish messiah traditions and that he had no more historical substance than Zeus.

In various pagan mystery religions predating the first century C.E. (A.D.), Osiris, Attis, and Dionysus were all god-men who died around the time of Easter (the spring equinox) and were resurrected after three days. And all three of these deities predated Jesus by centuries. Christmas itself is thought by most scholars to be an adoption of the pagan tradition of celebrating the winter solstice. With many of the basic narrative points of the Jesus story, such as the virgin birth and the Resurrection, predating his supposed existence by hundreds of years, a compelling case has been made that he never existed at all but was a myth created to fulfill a specific need. In the absence of a single particle of physical evidence that Jesus Christ actually lived, this recent movement among historical scholars could not be factually refuted.

But now, with this stunning book, Simcha Jacobovici and Charles Pellegrino have delivered not just a particle of evidence but a veritable avalanche of it. Their investigation proves, I believe, beyond any reasonable doubt that a first-century Jewish tomb found in Talpiot, Jerusalem, in 1980 is the tomb of Jesus and his family. What's even more electrifying is what the physical evidence from within the tomb says about Jesus, his death, and his relationships with the other family members found in the same burial site.

This book chronicles a three-year investigation of the most stunning archaeological find of the last century. With systematic rigor, Simcha and Charlie analyze the physical evidence, cross-referencing it with clues from both the canonical and the apocryphal Gospels to fill in the first complete picture of the Jesus family. It reads like a gripping detective novel, and one has to pinch oneself to remember that it is real. Absolutely real.

Once I was asked by an interviewer who was getting bored talking about my films, "If you could meet any person from history, who would it be?" What if there were a time machine that could enable one to go back and look into the eyes of an individual who lived centuries ago? Newton, Ben Franklin, Julius Caesar – how fascinating it would be to see what they were really like. Maybe I would choose Hatshepsut, the only woman in three thousand years of Egyptian history to reign as a Pharaoh, because I've always loved stories of strong women.

But what I blurted out in reply was "Jesus." Though I am not religious, I have always assumed that a real, flesh-and-blood, historical Jesus existed and that he was at the very least a man of extraordinary charisma and personal power.

Whether you believe that Jesus was the Son of God or that he was merely a man, it is beyond question that he was one of the most important men who ever lived; arguably, he is the man whose life continues to have the single greatest impact on our world.

But we don't have a time machine, and the physics suggests that we never will. We must rely on history and its sister discipline, archaeology. So what do we truly know, historically and archaeologically, about this Jesus? One and a half billion Christians – more than one-fifth of the world's population – believe they know exactly who Jesus was. But what do we really know for sure?

Until now, there has been *zero* physical evidence of his existence. No fingerprints, no bones, no portraits done from life, nothing. Not a shred of parchment written in Jesus's own hand. There are, of course, the famous holy relics, such as the Piece of the True Cross and the Shroud of Turin, but these all have questionable provenance and have been dated to centuries later. Most archaeologists dismiss them.

As Jesus and his followers walked through first-century Judea, there were no cameras, no tape recorders, no court stenographers. No impartial written records come down to us that might give independent proof, such as the minutes of Roman court proceedings. We don't have even the most basic census records noting his birth.

Most of what we know, or think we know, comes from the four great Gospels of Matthew, Mark, Luke, and John. But what exactly are these Gospels? To the deeply and unquestioningly faithful, they are the direct and absolute word of God, recorded by the most saintly of men. Historians, however, now view them as composite works, each created by several authors and based in turn on oral traditions carried on for decades, possibly half a century, after Christ's actual ministry. There is no historical evidence that any of the authors, if in fact they were individuals, actually heard the words of Jesus from his own lips.

Though I'm not a historian by training, I have loved history and archaeology since I was a child. But I grew up with the illusion that history, as it was taught to me, was sacrosanct, because it was all "written down somewhere." My first foray into a historical/archaeological investigation proved that notion wrong.

For my motion picture *Titanic,* I made a detailed study of that disaster, an event that took place merely a century ago, was described in detail by hundreds of eyewitnesses, and was immediately recorded by an already hypertrophied print media. Despite this, I found the testimony to be spotty and contradictory, and some witnesses clearly colored their testimony to fit personal or corporate agendas. As a result, huge gaps in our understanding of the event persist. The

oceanographer Robert Ballard surprised historians by finding the *Titanic* broken into two pieces on the seafloor, despite
an "official" history that had the ship sinking in one piece.
Even after my thirty-three dives to the site and fifty hours of
flying robot cameras through the interior, I still do not have a
complete picture of what happened. As a result of this twelve-
year investigation, I have come to realize that history is a con-
sensus hallucination. It is a myth upon which we all agree to
agree. The truth is a moving target: new evidence must always
be weighed, and "the truth" updated. Historical records must
always be questioned, and the agenda or perceptual context
of those doing the recording must always be considered.

But we learned many surprising things at the wreck site
that confirmed some historical "facts" and challenged others. The steel, the physical evidence lying twelve thousand
feet down on the seafloor, cannot lie. Its message cannot be
bent by human agendas. The story that Simcha and Charlie
tell of the Jesus family tomb is pieced together from hard
physical evidence, evidence that cannot lie. It simply is what
it is. But the physical evidence must nevertheless be interpreted in a historical context, and that interpretation
depends heavily on the sparse details about Jesus and his
family that can be gleaned from historical sources. How does
the new evidence support or contradict what the historical
record has been telling us for two millennia?

The Gospels as we know them today have been retran-
scribed and rewritten many times and translated from one

language to another – from Aramaic to Greek to Coptic to Latin to various forms of English – with corresponding losses in nuanced meaning. They have been edited by Church fathers, centuries after the original words were spoken, to conform to their subsequent vision of orthodoxy. And yet, in the absence of the tiniest scrap of concrete physical evidence, they were our only record of the life and times of Jesus.

Complicating matters are the *other* Gospels: the apocryphal texts such as the Gnostic Gospels of the Nag Hammadi Library found in the Egyptian desert in 1945. Buried in an earthen jar to keep them from the Christian orthodoxy of the fourth century, which sought to eradicate all the so-called heresies, these precious and astonishing books show the rich diversity of early Christian thought and give clues to the historical story not available in the Big Four of Matthew, Mark, Luke, and John.

In the Gospel of Mary and the Acts of Philip, for example, Mary Magdalene is known as the "Apostle to the Apostles," an important teacher and partner in Jesus's ministry whom Jesus favored even over Simon Peter. She is described as Jesus's "companion," and she even kissed him on his "mouth" (the word many supply for what is a missing word in the Gospel), to the chagrin of the other disciples. What was this all about? Magdalene is a cryptic figure in the canonical Gospels: mentioned more than any other woman except Jesus's mother, Mary, she is present at both the Crucifixion and the Resurrection. Why is she so important?

Through both brilliant scholarly research and forensic lab work, Simcha and Charlie answer that question resoundingly. And the results of their analysis of the other contents of the Talpiot tomb are equally profound. Even though I was executive producer of the documentary film that enabled this investigation and was involved in every step of the process, I found that reading this book, with all the evidence and its ramifications presented in one organized argument, was utterly gripping.

Using the same rigorous approach that he has used in investigations at the *Titanic* wreck site, at Ground Zero in New York City, at the ruins of Pompeii and Herculaneum, and at the Minoan ruins at Akrotiri, Charlie has pieced together a compellingly detailed picture of the reality behind the Gospels. The conclusions he and Simcha are able to draw are virtually irrefutable, and yet they are stunning in their implications.

Our society has a schizophrenic relationship to the concept of empirical proof. We rely on a complex science of criminal forensics in our justice system. We use advanced instrumentation to analyze minute samples of blood, fiber, and DNA evidence, all with the purpose of determining the fate of individuals, sometimes with life-or-death consequences. And yet, according to recent polls, 45 percent of Americans don't believe in evolution. Almost half of this rational, show-me-the-proof society is capable of ignoring two hundred years of scientific investigation – science performed with the same rigor and the same instrumentation used to judge a man's life.

Faith and forensics make uneasy bedfellows. There are those who will find the results of the investigation revealed in this book to be too challenging to their belief system. For these readers, no amount of scientific proof would be sufficient, and our conclusions will always remain nothing more than another alarming heresy. There are others who will find the results intriguing, even inspirational, and not challenging to the essence of their faith. Instead, they will find that this book illuminates with fascinating new detail the story that has been central to their belief system their whole lives. They will take comfort in a more complete understanding of Jesus, Mary, Mary Magdalene, and the other figures who have remained for two millennia only lightly sketched and somewhat enigmatic archetypes, not real, fully fleshed-out people. Until now.

Even non-Christians will find this investigation fascinating for what it reveals about the living, breathing individuals who had such a resounding effect on the course of Western civilization.

I have known Charlie Pellegrino for ten years, and we have worked together many times investigating subjects as diverse as the *Titanic* wreck, the ruins of Pompeii, and extremophile bacteria at hydrothermal vent sites. We share a passion for history and science and we suffer from the same curse of curiosity that has killed many cats and explorers.

Charlie introduced me to Simcha with much cloak-and-dagger secrecy – including the signing of confidentiality agreements – and the two presented their evidence to me. Though it was early in the investigation, I found their story – especially the statistical argument – compelling. Could it be true? Had they really found the bones of Jesus, Mary, Mary Magdalene, and even what appeared to be a *son* of Jesus?

The investigation was to take many twists and turns over the subsequent two years and would reveal surprises beyond our imagining at the time, but even then I was hooked. I told Simcha, "Stories don't get bigger than this."

Though I had absolutely no credentials as a biblical scholar, I wanted in. I was a documentary filmmaker, and this was an archaeology story, a detective story – I had done those. I would learn what I needed to learn in order to be a useful member of the team. Ultimately what I supplied, I think, was a healthy dose of layman's perspective. Simcha and Charlie knew way too much about the subject, whereas I knew only what I remembered from Sunday school. It became my job to remind them that the vast majority of viewers and readers would not be versed in the complexities of first-century Judaic practices or early Christianity with all its fractious sects, and many might not even have heard of the Gnostic Gospels.

If I was the "coach" of our team, Simcha was the "quarterback." He was the real-life Indiana Jones whose quest to solve this mystery drew the rest of us in. He led the on-site investigation and was the hub of all the activities. Simcha also directed the film that enabled this investigation in the first place. The film was financed by Discovery USA, Vision TV in Canada, and Channel 4 in the United Kingdom, and its budget allowed for repeated expeditions in search of the lost tomb, DNA tests, robotics, patina fingerprinting, and so on – scientific techniques that are beyond the scope of most archaeologists. I found Simcha to be funny, passionate, vastly knowledgeable, and absolutely relentless in tracking down the truth. We became instant friends.

This story scared us. It was big – lightning in a bottle. It was going to be controversial. There would certainly be people so unsettled by the findings that their denial would manifest as anger.

Did I really want this in my life? And yet, how could I turn away from the greatest archaeology story ever? How could I call myself a documentary filmmaker if I let fear deter me from such an important investigation? I decided to throw myself into this and let the chips fall where they might. But I had certain rules that I believed we needed to follow if I was going to join the team, because I knew that one day I would have to stand behind our results. Even though our forensic work was going to be very preliminary, limited as it was by the budget of a Discovery Channel two-hour documentary, it had to follow extremely rigorous procedures regarding the provenance of the samples and subsequent chains of evidence. We had to use proper control groups to eliminate false positives. We had to enlist the aid of impartial and well-credentialed researchers to perform the forensic and statistical analyses. And we had to have a period of peer review to vet our conclusions, just as we would do with a scientific paper. Charlie, with his background as a published scientist, would be able to apply the required rigor to the process. And Simcha, with his extensive contacts in the worlds of archaeology and biblical scholarship, could enlist a world-class team of expert advisers.

Some of the most respected experts in biblical history and archaeology have contributed to this investigation. Even so, our results will be challenged – as they should be. That is the scientific process that drives toward an accepted truth. Our investigation must be followed by others to examine the evidence in greater detail (and with better budgets), and this larger investigation and peer-review process should take years, perhaps decades. But I believe that the results of Simcha and Charlie's initial investigation are extremely convincing.

As I write, it is Christmas Eve. The world is as torn by war as ever, and those wars are centered more in biblical lands than they have been for almost a millennium. A few months ago, the last part of our film production was delayed because Lebanese Katusha rockets were falling too close to our locations in Nazareth. Jesus's cry for compassion among men is as desperately needed a message today as it ever was. At Christmas we celebrate the birth of a man who called to the spark of goodness that exists within all of us, a man who gave the world hope two thousand years ago. His words, thoughts, and deeds have echoed down through the centuries undiminished.

But who was this Jesus?

Read on. You're about to meet him.

James Cameron
December 24, 2006

1

Vault of the Ages

The most famous death in history was the Crucifixion of Jesus of Nazareth.

Two millennia ago, in Jerusalem, Jesus was scourged and executed by Roman soldiers. The Gospels tell us that his body was taken down from the cross, shrouded in cloth, and placed in a family tomb belonging to one of his followers, Joseph of Arimathea.

On the third day, Mary Magdalene, Jesus's trusted disciple, found the tomb empty – a moment that marks the origin of the Christian belief in the Resurrection.

Out of all the millions of words and thoughts devoted to this event, how many people have ever asked why Jesus's body was placed in a tomb carved out of stone in the first place, and not simply buried in the ground?

According to ancient Jewish laws still in effect today,

bodies had to be interred in the ground before sundown on the day of death. Family tombs, cut into rock, qualified as "in the ground." In most places, the bedrock of Jerusalem lay barely more than a few inches below the ground surface. For this reason, the dead were placed in preexisting tunnels, dug into local hillsides. During much of the first century C.E., most of Jerusalem's tombs were man-made caves, hewn from solid rock and located just outside the city walls. Usually a tomb consisted of two chambers. In the outer chamber, the body was anointed with perfumes, spices, and oils, then shrouded in cloth. Archaeological evidence from hundreds of first-century tombs excavated in the Jerusalem hills is perfectly consistent with descriptions of Jesus's burial as described in the four Gospels. According to both archaeology and the Gospels, the tomb would have been sealed by rolling a large stone in front of its entrance. Behind the seal stone, lying in state in its white shroud, the body was ordinarily given a full year to decompose. After the flesh had vanished, the shrouded bones were collected from the outer, temporary burial chamber and placed in a small limestone box called an ossuary. Occasionally an occupant's name would be inscribed on one side of the ossuary, which was then placed for permanent burial in a small niche deep within the tomb. Eventually ossuaries representing three or more generations from the same family might be sealed, one after another, in a tomb's innermost niches.

No one knows why the practice of using ossuaries began just prior to the birth of Jesus. Some archaeologists and theologians suspect that the Jewish belief in a bodily Resurrection led to the gathering of bones, to be preserved for the Day of Judgment.

Regardless of the reason, the Gospels attest to great concern among Jesus's followers about shrouding his body and placing it in a tomb. Because he died late on a Friday afternoon, they needed to bring him to a tomb quickly, before the arrival of sunset and the holy Sabbath. Joseph of Arimathea's newly hewn family tomb was nearby, and it would serve Jesus's family until the body could be moved to a permanent resting place.

The Gospels also say that on Sunday, before he could be moved, Jesus conquered death, left the tomb empty, and later, on several separate occasions and in several forms, appeared before his disciples.

But the Gospels also hint at an alternative explanation for Jesus's empty tomb. Matthew says there was another story circulating in Jerusalem after the Crucifixion of Jesus. Although Matthew calls it a lie, according to the rumor, Jesus's disciples secretly came by night and stole away with their Master's body. As Matthew tells it, the story persisted among Jews for a very long time (Matthew 28:11–15).

If the disciples took the body, there is only one thing they could have done with it. They would have reburied it.

If Jesus was reburied, his family would have waited for his flesh to disappear and then stored his bones in an ossuary, sealed away forever deep in the recesses of his family tomb.

Spring 1980

About eleven o'clock on the morning of March 28, 1980, with the Christian season of Lent already a month old and almost over, first light entered a tomb, beneath the treads of a bulldozer. On this exceptionally beautiful Friday, the entire south face of the tomb's antechamber fell away to reveal what looked for all the world like a doorway; carved above it was a symbol that none of the construction crew had ever seen before.

No one really understood what an array of dynamite detonations and a bulldozer mishap had revealed until the next day, after the Sabbath had arrived, the dust had settled, and a little army of diabolical schoolboys had discovered a collection of strange, new playthings in the ground.

That is how it began.

And that is how it almost ended.

If not for Rivka Maoz and a couple of engineers who revered the past, the damage might have known no end until the losses became epic, without anyone's ever suspecting what had been lost.

Rivka's family lived within a few meters of the construction site. She happened to be studying archaeology as part of her certification to become a tour guide in Jerusalem. Rivka was a newcomer to Israel and to Judaism. She had emigrated from France. And so it happened that every night her eleven-year-old son, Ouriel, who quickly became fluent in

Hebrew, read Rivka books about the Old City, its Temple, and its tombs.

On that Friday the boy had come running home after lunch, begging his mother to come see what he was certain could be nothing other than an ancient tomb, newly exposed. But when Rivka called the Department of Antiquities (later the Israel Antiquities Authority, or IAA), she was told that the afternoon was already half over and that, in preparation for the Sabbath, all the offices were closing down.

Rivka tried to make the IAA understand that she had seen the tomb entrance. There was no doubt in her mind that an important discovery had been revealed. She urged them to send someone to guard the tomb lest antiquities dealers, or their henchmen, come by night and steal away with the entire contents of the cave; the best that anyone could promise, however, was to issue a command to halt all dynamiting near the tomb and to send archaeologists to the site early Sunday morning, after the Sabbath was over.

Then, on the morning of the Sabbath, Rivka's son came running home a second time.

"Mom!" he called. "Come quick. The kids have found some skulls outside the tomb, and they're playing soccer with them!"

Enough was enough, Rivka decided. Road-cuts and condominium foundations were being blasted and carved along the entire hillside, turning the western region of her neighborhood into a giant, open-pit mine. There was no means of knowing how many tombs had already been blown apart and bulldozed into road-fill. All Rivka knew for certain was that ossuary fragments and ancient teeth were becoming a minor constituent of local gravel beds. A quarter-century later, she would recall that it had seemed only by a miracle that the "Tomb of Ten Ossuaries" survived at all while so many others in these hills simply disappeared.

Brandishing large black plastic bags and yelling, Rivka and her husband confronted the "children of the skulls," who scattered and ran, leaving the ground strewn with brow ridges and chips of fractured jaws. At least two of the skulls had shattered when kicked, like clay pots struck by buckshot.

Rivka and her family collected the skulls and skull fragments in the plastic bags and brought them home for safekeeping until they could pass them over to the archaeologists. Rivka would record for historians years later that it was actually "kind of fun" having the ancients reside in her basement. She and Ouriel felt a measure of pride in having honored these ancestral people through the Sabbath.

*   *   *

During the many centuries since the tomb had first been decorated and sealed, the Temple high priests, the Romans, and the Temple itself had fallen. And now a new civilization was piling up around the Temple Mount and spreading outward to the tallest hill of East Talpiot. The area had been renamed Armon Hanatziv.

The year 1980 was a high-tide mark for tourism, immigration, and construction in the Jerusalem hills. It was also a time when construction companies throughout Israel were accidentally discovering new archaeological sites at the rate of a dozen every month – and in a particularly bad season, a dozen every week. By law (albeit a law only rarely obeyed), all finds had to be reported immediately, and all construction had to be halted until the archaeologists were finished, which might be days or weeks later, depending on the size and importance of the find. By some calculations, the crossroads of civilizations dating back more than four thousand years contained thousands of archaeological sites not yet recorded on the maps of the Israel Antiquities Authority. By these same calculations, any attempt to create an irrigation line, a basement, or a foundation for an apartment complex was a gamble that could go wrong with every shovelful of earth.

The site that was eventually to be cataloged "IAA 80/500–509" – according to the year of its discovery and the order in which its major artifacts were cataloged – had already brought some small notoriety and no small amount of grief to an engineer named Efraim Shochat who had been directing bulldozers in the clearing of freshly dynamited ground for the Solel Boneh Construction Company. Naturally, there was nothing unusual about exposing an old, forgotten crypt, especially if the company happened to be

7

clearing acres of land in preparation for the building of a new suburb. Many of Shochat's colleagues, striving to avoid expensive construction delays, were in the habit of averting their eyes from interesting new cavities in the ground and occasionally sacrificed a tomb, especially if it happened to be small and appeared to consist of, say, only one or two ossuaries. But Shochat, as an Orthodox Jew bound by biblical law not to desecrate the resting places of the dead, could not look away from even a small tomb. And what one of his bulldozers almost fell into was anything but small.

There had been an outer courtyard in front of the tomb facade, carved into the local limestone and chalk and buried under ages of red mud and weed growth. The courtyard alone was nearly five meters (almost fifteen feet) wide. Just north of the courtyard's remains, an entire wall had collapsed under a combination of dynamite and bulldozer assault. When the engineer climbed inside, he discovered that what at first glance had looked to him like a damaged but still reasonably intact underground chamber was really just an antechamber, with an entrance carved into the bottom of its north wall. Its stone seal looked like a partly opened door pointing the way down into a rather larger chamber. Clearly, IAA 80/500–509 was not a small tomb. Although pieces of skull were mixed in with the rubble of the antechamber, there was not even a recognizable fragment of the stone ossuaries that were so common to this region. Unlike the people of the tomb, those whose skulls were found in the antechamber had not been buried according to first-century Jewish burial practices. When Shochat climbed out of the tomb antechamber, he said, with both regret and excitement in his voice, "We have to shut down. I'm afraid we have something interesting. Something important."

It was about this time, on that first Friday, that Ouriel went running home to his mother. Behind him, Shochat shut down all demolition and excavation in a two-acre radius around the antechamber and then began making phone calls, almost simultaneously with Rivka Maoz. Thus it came to pass that, about 1:00 P.M., Jerusalem time, on an otherwise un-historic Friday, IAA 80/500–509 first came to the attention of the archaeologists.

The IAA, housed at the Rockefeller Museum, assured Shochat and Maoz that archaeologists would begin to move at the end of the Sabbath and would be on-site before dawn on the first day of the new week.

Those in charge of the IAA knew that they had to live up to their promise to have scientists on-site before dawn on Sunday, before the beginning of the workday. To halt construction and then to delay responding, with workers standing idle for a day or two, "with the money clock ticking," would create a bad reputation that the IAA could not afford and that sooner or later would cause a major find to be plowed under or paved over, unreported.

Eliot Braun was a professional archaeologist who happened to be living near the construction site, so he was the first to be dispatched, toward dawn on the third day after the tomb's discovery. His task was to drive Yosef Gat to the site. Gat, an antiquities inspector assigned to the Talpiot tomb, did not drive. Gat's boss, a Jerusalem District archaeologist and Ph.D. student named Amos Kloner, soon joined the team.

This should not still be here, Gat thought as he stood with Kloner on a new road bed, overlooking the damaged patio and antechamber. For a long time the three men said nothing. They just stood above the cave in a predawn breeze, trying to piece together this little acre of history. The day had not yet begun for the builders, but in the evidence of those last few hours of their work – in those last few *minutes* of activity – Gat could see even in the faint morning glow, and by flashlight, just how close a shave this had been. The entire landscape around the entrance was scarred deeply with bulldozer tracks and huge piles of rocky debris mixed with reddish soil.

At construction-site discoveries such as this, the archaeologist's role was like that of a firefighter during a rescue operation in a burning building. Everything has to be done quickly. This was not, by the greatest stretch of anyone's imagination, going to be a careful, best-of-conditions archaeological excavation. They called it "salvage archaeology." They would be allowed mere days instead of weeks.

There was nothing to be done except remove every object and map every structural detail inside. Toward this purpose, a student named Shimon Gibson was assigned to sketch the tomb and map precisely the contents of its chambers. Although quite young, Gibson was a natural, and already known for his exceptional ability.

Shimon Gibson would not be arriving until well after sunrise, Kloner announced, and on this Sunday morning of March 30, 1980, there was no time to waste. So Gat led the way, over the tomb's all-but-obliterated patio and into the half-obliterated antechamber. At the north wall, his flashlight illuminated what at first viewing resembled a decorative, V-shaped gable, carved above the door. On closer inspection, it became a decorative stone relief sculpture – a chevron or upside-down V or Y, deliberately carved. It measured more than a meter wide, with a prominent circle placed in its center. The men puzzled over it briefly.

Beneath this symbol, just wide enough for a man to squeeze through on his belly and elbows, was the passage to a lower chamber. The air in the tunnel was stagnant and almost certainly unhealthy, with a slight scent of damp chalk laced with stale and moldy earth.

After a mere two-meter backslide or belly crawl through the opening, they were able to stand up inside. They were standing ankle-deep upon drifts of red mud. It must have taken centuries to accumulate. This was a distinctive, ancient agricultural soil with its own scientific name: *terra rossa*. The *terra rossa* mud had seeped in from the antechamber, but the rubble in the antechamber appeared to have fallen onto a floor that had been relatively clean when the bulldozers arrived. Something had drained the soil – nearly all of it – down here past where the seal stone had once been. In places it had piled up more than knee-deep.

Like Gat, Shochat and Kloner did not think it made sense that pieces of human skull should have been deposited outside the tomb, in the antechamber. In other tombs of this kind two thousand years before, people had left oil lamps, perfume bottles, and what might be regarded as ceremonial meals outside the central chamber. One occasionally found bowls and cups or spices and perfumes in fine Roman glass, but Jews of the first century c.e. did not leave the remains of their elders outside the tomb to rot on the wrong side of the seal stone. IAA 80/500–509 was becoming rich with contradiction. Even the air was a contradiction: at once oppressively damp and oppressively dry. The archaeologists' slightest movements stirred up particles of dust that, driven by breaths of air, flashed like swarms of microscopic fireflies wherever their searchlamps grazed them.

Amos Kloner would never be able to forget this place, though from time to time during the years following he would claim not to remember it. The curious symbol over the antechamber door would grace the cover of his book on Jerusalem tombs,* and yet in 2005 he would three times deny, on camera, that the tomb meant anything special.

*Kloner, Amos, and Boaz Zissu, *The Necropolis of Jerusalem in the Second Temple Period.* Yad Izhak Ben-zvi, The Israel Exploration Society, 2003.

Those who understood the rest of the story would never blame him.

The two scientists crawled around IAA 80/500–509 over meter-deep mounds of the "rose earth" and discovered the tops of six burial niches radiating outward into three of the chamber's four walls. Inside the niches they could count ten ossuaries. Pawing the soil away with his hands and shining lights down each of the niches, Gat quickly determined that five of the chamber's six niches, known in Hebrew as "kokhim" and in Latin as "loculi," contained ossuaries. The *terra rossa* flood tides had not overflowed the tops of the ossuaries and sunk them completely in mud. In antiquity – clearly no one had entered this tomb recently – someone had removed the five seal stones that should normally have walled up the kokhim. Displacement of the seals and removal of the stones were sure signs that looters or vandals had entered the tomb at some point ahead of the entry of the red soil. And yet the ossuaries remained, in apt and self-contradictory fashion, with their lids undamaged and perfectly in place, as if the intruding looters or vandals had been interested in neither looting nor vandalism.

Little about this tomb was measuring up to expectation – except perhaps the architecture. Above the ossuary niches, untouched by the *terra rossa* tides, two arched "arcosolia," or primary burial shelves, were cut into the north and west walls. Like everything else in the chamber, the altarlike shelves were carved from the solid rock of the Jerusalem hills. Gat examined the workmanship on the two shelves and admired the attention to detail. "It's a good-sized tomb, carved with great care under the direction of someone not lacking funds," he observed. "Important people were buried here."

Yosef Gat was one of archaeology's most unflappable personalities, so there was no excitement in his voice as he stepped forward into history with perhaps one of the greatest understatements ever uttered. As he crouched nearer the two shelves, withdrawing a small magnifier from his pocket and aiming his flashlight from a low angle, he noted matter-of-factly that the shelves had provided a poor environment for preservation of the tomb's occupants. Only fragmented and powdered limbs remained, but in the still-buried ossuaries themselves, awaiting technology that had not yet been invented, lay biological wonders that Gat, Kloner, and Braun did not dream possible.

"Let's get started," Gat said, and began handing out spades and shovels.

At first there was no discussion of the names emerging with the ossuaries. Gat's main concern was digging the artifacts out of the mud without scratching or damaging them. Gat and Kloner were too focused on mounting the ossuaries on wooden boards and sledding them up through the narrow entrance intact to be paying much attention to whose bones might be in them or what might be written on them. Indeed, the first two ossuaries, at the niche entrances, had been so encrusted with the red earth that there was no opportunity even to search for inscriptions, much less read them. Gat would know more about what the objects actually said once they had spent an hour or two outside baking in the sun. Then a simple brushing might reveal what, if anything, was written beneath.

About 20 percent of Jerusalem's ossuaries had inscriptions on them. So, with luck, these ten might reveal something interesting.

Not until two of the ossuaries were above him in the sunlight and gentle breezes and three more ossuaries were out of their niches did Gat break for a drink of water in the central chamber and begin to take a closer look. He angled his flashlight to deepen the shadows of a peculiar rosette pattern, carved by a skilled hand; no name could be read, however, apart from a partial "Jes," inscribed in Aramaic, a sister language to Hebrew. A second ossuary bore, in what appeared to be Hebrew letters, the name Mary, but written as it is pronounced in Latin. And a third ossuary, insofar as could be seen in the dark with an incomplete brushing away of the red soil, seemed to speak of a "Mara," this time in Greek. *Unusual,* he thought. *A lot of languages for one tomb.*

Meanwhile, a worker, carefully digging a cross-sectional trench along the floor to bridge the opening of one ossuary niche to another, found a human skull where it had no business being: not on a shelf ("arcosolium") or in an ossuary, but on the very floor of the chamber. Puzzled, Gat continued trenching – a little more vigorously now – sending up buckets full of earth through the antechamber tunnel, one after another. They soon found on the floor a second skull, and then a third, and recorded them on the map.

About this time, Rivka Maoz had retrieved her two bags of bones from their Sabbath resting place in her home and was walking along the new road-cut in the direction of the tomb. A strengthening breeze – now almost a wind – blew sheets of shifting chalk dust over her clothing and into her eyes. The hills were a hive of heavy vehicles. Rivka had heard rumors of even grander tombs – tombs with huge stones that were once used to block their entrances, tipped impartially into vast rubble pits, along with ossuary fragments and granulated bedrock.

It seemed altogether anticlimactic and unfair to Rivka that after traveling twenty centuries to her time, the ancients should find the future so indifferent to them.

Shimon Gibson had gotten off to a late start on the road toward what was reportedly a pretty large but otherwise not particularly extraordinary tomb. Still, the sun was more than halfway up the sky and the workday for everyone else was already well under way, as the tolling of church bells from the Christian quarter made crystal clear.

The first thing Shimon noticed was the giant hill in the center of Talpiot, being demolished by its predators. The machines were accomplishing a very precise and orderly job of demolition, smoothing out roads that had been marked out practically to the square centimeter. About fifty meters (or yards) uphill of the place toward which Shimon was heading, the builders were planting the first steel beams of a new suburb.

The second thing Shimon noticed, whenever the clouds of dust allowed a clear view, was the hole in the side of the hill, where the tomb had been revealed. From a distance, even if the area had not been roped off, with the trucks and bulldozers steering away from the perimeter, and even if a little knot of people had not already gathered there, the entrance would have stood apart from the landscape.

The third thing Shimon noticed was the symbol carved over the doorway of the tomb: a circle within a large chevron. (He would record later in his on-site field report that the pyramid-like chevron had a little "chimney" on top.)

Immediately, Shimon had two equal and opposite theories about the tomb symbol. By one theory, the symbol could be explained away quickly as a decorative carving left unfinished. The circle, or letter O, would thus have been a wreath intended to be detailed later with carved leaves and fruits. If so, no one would ever know whether or not it really was a wreath, because the tomb's builders merely left behind a rough draft protruding from the wall, like a blank coin awaiting the final stamp.

Shimon Gibson's second theory was that this had in fact been the final draft of what the tomb's builders meant to say.

The surveyor's personal belief was that the symbols, as mysterious as they might appear, had been completed and were displayed exactly as intended. In this case, no one would ever know beyond dispute whether or not the circle was a wreath – which in ancient Jewish and Roman tradition represented a royal bloodline, as in the golden wreath of leaves worn by emperors since the time of Julius Caesar. The Gospels record a distinctly Roman mockery in which the golden laurel of kingship was substituted by a crown of thorns and pressed onto the head of Jesus.

Shimon was convinced that the circle – whether or not it was a wreath or laurel – was more than merely an unfinished blank. It was the evidence trail of other first-century tombs that convinced him. The Roman destruction of Jerusalem in 70 C.E. had stopped the construction of all tombs-in-progress and thus preserved the construction sequences at various stages of completion – as if the engineers' handiwork had been frozen in midstride. This symbol was different. It *had* been finished. Later, he would remark that an elaborate facade such as this on a tomb that otherwise had no decorations whatsoever was very unusual indeed.

By the time Shimon Gibson reached the tomb's patio, there was a flurry of excitement around the contents of two black bags, and Yosef Gat was waving at him with an expression that said, *we have something interesting.*

"You're certain these were found here in the antechamber?" Gat was asking Rivka Maoz, pointing to a skull and bones.

"Yes," said Rivka. "It was under this carved circle – the place where the children found the bones."

This seemed to explain the tiny pieces of bone mixed in with the rubble of the antechamber. But it did not entirely make sense, to either Gat or Gibson. Bodies had never before been found *outside* an antechamber. This did not fit ... unless Rivka was mistaken and the children had found bones from a second tomb and simply discarded them here.

Everyone was excited, except Yosef Gat. Shimon always considered himself "Mr. Enthusiasm." Gat was the opposite. Shimon was fascinated by Gat's uniquely unemotional nature. The man was archaeology's own Mr. Spock, including the unusually elongated ears, but unlike Spock, Gat wore huge horn-rimmed glasses. Shimon had once asked Gat, "What would you do if we found, I don't know, something that was clearly too exciting, like the Ark of the Covenant or the Holy Grail?"

And Gat replied, "Well, it's archaeology. It's sometimes interesting, but it is a nine-to-five job."

For Shimon Gibson, archaeology would always be more than "nine-to-five."

Before he slid on his back down the entrance to the tomb, Shimon had had a chance to inspect the piles of gravel-sized rubble on the antechamber floor. Brushing the pebbles away, he and Gat had found traces of the original floor surface, as it had existed before the arrival of the bulldozer. Here the rose earth appeared to have accumulated barely ankle-deep before flowing downhill into the tomb. There were traces of human bone, but no fragment or hint of the cups and bowls normally left by family members in tomb antechambers. It was as if whoever piled the human remains outside the entrance to the chamber had taken the cups and bowls away. But for what reason? For souvenirs? Or because bowls and cups were suddenly needed somehow – were suddenly of new importance?

Yosef Gat was beginning to have his first doubts that the bones in the antechamber really belonged to natives of Jerusalem during the first century C.E.. Judaism had a very long memory and some very old traditions. The cups and bowls used during a meal of remembrance at the door to a tomb were never meant to be used for any other purpose after having been in such close proximity to the remains of the dead.

The very first things Yosef Gat showed Shimon – speaking with what was the closest semblance of excitement Shimon would ever see in Gat – were the three precisely marked locations of the skulls he had found in his trenches.

"You must put these on your drawing at once," Gat emphasized. "I found them here – here – and here, exactly. They were on the very bottom of the sequence, uninterrupted. And I think they're important."

The very bottom of the sequence, Gat said, uninterrupted. This meant that the significance of the skulls could not be
diminished or explained away by supposing, for example,
that another group of children had found another damaged
tomb and that instead of taking the bones home, as Rivka
Maoz did, another parent had dug three holes and buried
each of the skulls in IAA 80/500–509's central chamber.

Gat had enough experience of archaeological sites to
know an uninterrupted sequence of soil or rock strata when
he saw one. After the first layer of soil flowed into the tomb,
many weeks, months, or years passed before the next layer
formed. During this interval, the mud had time to settle and
compact, and a fine silt began to form on the soil surface, a
silt made mostly of deteriorating chalk topped with a thin
mineral patina of microscopic apatite crystals. When a new
inflow of mud occurred, it spread over an older mud surface
that was of a different texture. In this manner, successive layers were easily discernible, even without the aid of a magni-
fying lens. They were as discrete as the individual strata of a
layer cake. And much like a layer cake with a scoop taken
out of it, if someone had dug down through the layers of *terra rossa* during the past three days and interrupted the
sequence to bury something underneath, then the holes, once
filled, would have stood apart from the sequence like an
archaeological alarm bell. In cross-section, the three skulls
would have been found at the bottoms of three shafts, filled
in with soil that – in a complete mismatch of the centuries-

old layer-cake pattern on either side of the fill – would have displayed no layering at all.

In the parlance of archaeological investigation, "it was all layer cake" – all around and all the way to the floor beneath the skulls.

"It's cake," Gat had concluded, meaning that it was real.

Gat's trenches had so far revealed no pelvic bones, femurs, or other large remains adjacent to the skulls. Gibson's initial and lasting impression was that some sort of ceremony had been held here, involving the intentional placement of three skulls in the main chamber of the tomb.

The arrangement of the skulls on the floor made the impression of ceremony all but inescapable, once Shimon had mapped them. They formed a sort of isosceles triangle whose base was oriented toward Jerusalem's Temple Mount.

Gat asked himself: *Would first-century Jews do this?*

No, Gat decided. *This could never have happened during the lifetimes of the tomb's builders. But if this was a religious arrangement of human remains, what was the ceremony?*

Shimon examined a pair of exposed ossuaries still in their niches, then looked around. All before him was discovery. For the first time in all these centuries, IAA 80/500–509 knew the footsteps of living human beings. The surveyor was touching things that no one from his time had ever touched until this day. He had experienced the joy of discovery at other sites, so he had expected it, but he was glad to say that he had not really become accustomed to it. He hoped that, no matter how many decades he worked at this job, mysteries would always feel so new.

He was still brooding over the mystery of the skull triangle when Gat reminded him that there was no time to waste and that they had to start photographing, drawing, and mapping the ossuaries.

There were ten ossuaries all told.

One of them, IAA 80/509, would become a mystery in its own right: it vanished before it could be photographed or properly scrutinized for insignias, decorations, or inscribed names, but *not before* it had been cataloged.

As the limestone objects were bound securely against breakage and passed, one by one, up the entrance, through the antechamber, and onto the demolished patio, Amos Kloner reached a conclusion. To him, despite what might be signified by the skull triangle on the floor or the chevron and circle inscribed outside, the objects in the tunnels were typical Jewish ossuaries of the first century C.E. Nevertheless, atypically, no fewer than six of the ten showed signs, through lightly brushed mud, of having been inscribed with people's names. This was an exceptionally high ratio compared to other known ossuary clusters, whose occupants were mostly anonymous.

Whatever its origin, the custom of building limestone ossuaries had provided archaeologists with a dating system at least as accurate as finding a coin memorializing a particular emperor's name. Jewish law had always dictated that a deceased person be buried by sundown. In Jerusalem, where in most places the soil was only a few inches deep before the spade struck bedrock, a special dispensation had been made around 430 B.C.E.: temporary burial in a cave, or in a tunnel carved into rock, counted as burial in the earth. By the time of Jesus and the apostles, about 30 C.E., bodies in Jerusalem were wrapped in linen or woolen shrouds and placed on shelves inside man-made caves. After the bones were finally collected and placed in ossuaries, they in turn were sealed in *kokhim*. The burning of Jerusalem in 70 C.E. had killed the increasingly popular ossuary tradition before it could spread more widely, thus rendering the mere existence of an ossuary tomb as datable as carbon-14. There was nothing particularly exotic or controversial about the supposition that the people who constructed the Tomb of Ten Ossuaries, who mourned in the antechamber and courtyard and whose remains were sealed in the niches of the innermost chamber, had lived either just before, or during, or shortly after the time of Jesus.

Deep inside a Jerusalem hill the archaeologists carefully now excavated the rose earth, while on the courtyard above them the drying ossuaries began shedding their thin veneers of mud and the inscriptions started to reveal themselves.

Ossuary number 80/505 was inscribed with the name Maria, a Latin version of the biblical Miriam, written in Hebrew letters. This was extremely unusual. Shimon would recall that when he first saw the name, it was possible to believe that here lay a Jewish woman who just happened to have been known to many Gentiles and Jews by the Latin version of her Hebrew name, Mary.* Next to her, ossuary number 80/503, as the hardened soil fell away from it, was revealing the name Joseph. To judge from the names alone, it seemed possible that this was a typical family tomb and that the Maria and Joseph named on these two ossuaries were married.

In large Hebrew letters, ossuary number 80/502 proclaimed MATTHEW. At this point, the family tomb began to seem perhaps less typical. In some Christian traditions, Matthew the Evangelist was Matthew the Disciple who walked with Jesus and recorded prophecies, sermons, and revelations.

Young Shimon Gibson was not about to let himself jump up excitedly, or even break into a noticeable sweat, in the presence of this growing concentration of New Testament names. No, this would not happen. Allowing excitement to take root in front of Yosef Gat, or in front of the almost equally unflappable Amos Kloner, would simply be in bad taste.

Ossuary number 80/506 had suffered significant mineral evaporation while it slept within the earth, and except for a large, cross-shaped mark on one side, any scratches in the chalky limestone had been rendered illegible. Ossuary

---

* To date, out of thousands of ossuaries that have been found, only eight others bear the name Maria in Hebrew letters.

number 80/504, however, had "Yosa" or "Yose" (or "José" in English) etched on one side – a name that Kloner and Gat recognized as a contraction of Joseph.

If Amos Kloner wondered about a Jesus connection at all, he did not show it. Indeed, the unique way of saying the name Joseph was, for Kloner, a simple reflection of the fact that more than one way to say "Joseph" was needed in this family. For Kloner, two Josephs in this family was nothing special.

At some point (no one would remember precisely when), the explorers went back to ossuary number 80/503, to the *other* Joseph ossuary, and looked a little closer. Thin scratches, barely legible before the word JOSEPH, had been (and always would be) mostly obscured by thick layers of ancient mineralization called patina. When the ossuary was moved into the shade and bright flashlight beams were aimed at just the right angles, the complete Aramaic inscription could be read: YESHUA BAR YOSEF – Jesus, son of Joseph. And then they noticed that the first name was preceded by a large cross-mark, taller than the name itself.

This time, though no one would ever specifically recall it, someone must have uttered an expletive.

"We will look like fools if we go down this path," concluded Amos Kloner. "These are common names, and that X is a mason's mark, not a cross. It's just a coincidence."

All four were in agreement on this, at least officially.

"But just the same," Gat added, "I would feel better if we

could find in here one or two ossuaries that have no connection to the Jesus story."

Gat and Kloner had withdrawn ossuary number 80/501 from its niche and pushed it up through the opening into the glare of midafternoon. A smoothly polished ossuary, 80/501 was decorated with carved rosettes set in carved frames. Its inscription, written in Hebrew, was engraved with more care than the others, as if by a skilled calligrapher who worked his art in stone and wanted it to be read.

After he read the inscription, Kloner summed up the whole ossuary assemblage in one word: "Preposterous."

He had hoped and expected to find someone named Daniel or Jonathan. He had hoped to find something different from the pattern they had been seeing – even an ossuary inscribed "Sue" would do – but instead the letters spelled out "Yehuda bar Yeshua" – Judah, son of Jesus.

No one remembers whether it was Gat or Kloner who mentioned that a "Mara," or another Mary, had been brought out of the tomb.

That ossuary, number IAA 80/500, was larger than the rest – nearly seventy centimeters long – and beautifully ornamented with petaled rosettes. The archaeologists had to brush away the drying earth to expose the whole inscription. The words were written in Greek.

Kloner's first brushstrokes revealed letters of the second name, and there was indeed an *M* and an *A*.

"In Greek?" said Gat. "They wrote her name in Greek?"

This *was* fascinating. From the same tomb had come a Mary whose name was pronounced in Latin. And now another Mary whose name was written in Greek. For Amos Kloner, the idea that this could be the Jesus family tomb wasn't even in the picture. As for Gibson, he did not want to begin and end his career with the bones of Jesus. *And if this Mary of number 80/500 was supposed to be Magdalene, then what? Were 80/500 and 80/503 – this Greek-inscribed "Mary" and "Jesus, son of Joseph" – married? And if these two were married, then was "Judah" their son?*

"Creating such a group," Kloner would later say, "and suggesting that this is the actual Jesus and that he had a son – and that these are the two Marys with him – is a very far speculation with very far-reaching consequences. This is a line we should be very careful not to cross."

For Shimon Gibson, there was already excitement enough in the unusual carvings on the antechamber wall and in the positioning of the skulls within the chamber itself.

Twenty-five years later, Shimon would suggest that a period of time needed to elapse before a "reassessment" could be made. "There is no doubt about it in my mind: it is a tomb that has been retained in my memory over these decades because of certain elements. By now I'm no longer a student, and I've grown a few gray hairs. I can look at things differently. I'm still not convinced we have a tomb connected with the family of Jesus, but I'm not discounting that. However, I would need something a bit more convincing than just these common names."

Improbably, as time and chance seemed to dictate, a quarter-century was to pass before something more convincing came up when someone took a closer look at the Mary of ossuary number 80/500.

Inscription specialist Tal Ilan would reveal in December 2005 that part of the second Mary's inscription – "Mara" – had two possible meanings. It could be read simultaneously as "Master" and "Lord."

"Mara" was preceded by a Greek symbol that means "also known as." So what was her name, this woman, who was also known as Master?

On the ancient patio outside the Talpiot tomb, the only question of significance was whether or not brushing the rest of the inscription would reveal the name Magdalene.

Amos Kloner certainly did not believe this could be so. Yosef Gat and Shimon Gibson did not believe so either.

So no one was surprised when the *M* and the *A* turned out to be followed by an *R* instead of a *G*. This, on top of the surprising inscription "Judah, son of Jesus," was, for Kloner, the second and more lethal blow against a Jesus connection, and it brought an inner sigh of relief. Kloner really did not like TV cameras or "pop culture science of the Carl Sagan and Steven Spielberg kind." Even *National Geographic* made him nervous and stuttery, and scientific symposia gave him "a touch of the stage fright." Like most of his colleagues, he preferred a quiet life devoted to learning, and his ambition was to keep a low profile. So he truly was relieved after a careful brushing away of dry mud revealed an *R* in letter number three's spot. He breathed easier still after seeing that the number four, five, and six spots were occupied by the letters I, A, and M. The second Mary in the tomb was not "the Magdalene." She was a woman named Mariamene or Mariamne, a Greek version of the Hebrew Miriam.

Now Amos Kloner and his colleagues could box the ossuaries, shelve them away in a warehouse, and forget about them for the rest of their lives. For Kloner especially, the emerging assemblage of names had seemed to bring a momentary embarrassment, as if he were personally affronted by it. Though he would privately admit to being impressed by the inscriptions on the ossuaries, his attitude toward the words from the tomb would officially remain total indifference, if not contemptuous denial.

For Shimon Gibson, the sense of relief brought an equal and opposite sense of disappointment.

"If it had said 'Mary Magdalene,'" he would recall much later, "then of course all the bells would have started ringing even then, when I wasn't particularly interested in early Christian history. Even then, I would have said, 'Well, this is something very special, something unusual.' And I would have looked at it in greater detail. But as it turned out, when I saw the inscriptions, all I sort of understood was that these were common Jewish names of the first century on these ossuaries. And that was it. Nothing else."

"Mariamne," on top of "Judah, son of Jesus," became

the crux of contradiction. There was no Mariamne in Jesus's life, and he didn't have a son. For Kloner and Gat, the contradiction was so blazingly apparent that it had eliminated, almost from the very first moments, any connection between Jesus, son of Joseph, in ossuary number 80/503 and the historical Jesus. It was another Jesus. It was a different Mary.

"These words – these names – are not statistically improbable at all," Kloner concluded. "Why, a quarter of the women in Jerusalem were named Mary. There's no story here."

Shimon was not about to disagree with Gat and Kloner. Still, climbing out of a hole in the ground with news of a Jesus family tomb would have been quite interesting. It could not help but be the most exciting adventure of his young career, and perhaps of his entire career. Yet he was not inclined to violate rule number one in academia: never attract more attention than your department chairman. Shimon Gibson had been around long enough to know that ivory towers are dangerous places.

"No story here," a wise young man said, and they all agreed.

But history, like time itself, was bound sooner or later to have its say. Even blazingly apparent contradictions sometimes have a way of being more apparent than real.

By sunset on Good Friday, during the week of Passover, it was all over. The archaeologists had systematically removed

31

every ossuary, every bone fragment, and every cubic meter of *terra rossa* soil.

About four days earlier, on Tuesday, April 1, word of the new ossuary tomb and the unusual cluster of biblical names had gotten away from the archaeologists and begun to circulate. Fortunately, it was April Fool's Day, and even the Christians of Jerusalem dismissed the news that Jesus, Mary, and Joseph had all been found in the same tomb as a timely joke. But southward, on the central hill of Talpiot, the local Jewish religious authorities did not think the joke very funny. To them, news of archaeologists working at a local tomb never provoked laughter. Their collective notion was that archaeologists were plunderers of tombs who displayed no respect for the long sleep of their ancestors.

In this expectation, at least one of the archaeologists did not disappoint. Amos Kloner would recount years later that he had gone exploring twenty meters uphill from the Tomb of Ten Ossuaries and discovered a second tomb – also exposed by the builders.

He descended into the new hole and entered another large central chamber filled with ossuary niches. This chamber differed from the one in the first tomb in having all of its seal stones still intact and in never having been intruded upon by inflows of *terra rossa* soil. When he pried loose the seal stones, he found more ossuaries – at least seven of them. One was decorated with finely carved rosettes, and three others were inscribed in words of Greek. But there was no time to copy the inscriptions or even to take photographs.

"It was not possible to do more," he would record. "I don't remember exactly what happened there, but I decided that one of the small ossuaries – which was very close to the tomb entrance – might be taken."

Kloner would lament that this tiny ossuary, bearing the bones of a child, was the only one taken out of the cave and "saved" because about this time students from a nearby rabbinical school arrived and began cursing at him and spitting. Whatever Kloner's reply, their spitting quickly escalated to stone-throwing and threats of death.

More than two decades later, another side of the story could be heard around Talpiot. The religious authorities, having learned of yet another new tomb torn open by bulldozers and having heard of the archaeologists gathering there, discovered Amos Kloner in a cave and observed him spilling the ancient bones of a child out of the tiniest ossuary and onto the tomb's floor – evidently to lessen the weight of the ossuary. This, they recalled, was what provoked them to riot. Perhaps because this activity at the second tomb inadvertently diverted the attention of the religious authorities, the work at the "Tomb of Ten Ossuaries" was able to continue.

And so it came to pass that on Easter Sunday, April 6, 1980, IAA 80/500–509, a.k.a. the Tomb of Ten Ossuaries, or the Talpiot tomb, lay empty.

Soon thereafter, the religious authorities *did* find IAA
80/500–509, and in very short order the empty tomb was
sealed in a protective cocoon of steel, plastered over with a
shell of concrete.

Shimon Gibson would joke years later that the spirits
must have been displeased with the archaeologists, or at least
with their cameras. Except for Amos Kloner's single photograph of the symbol above the tomb entrance, all of their
negatives were so underexposed that their photos were
absolutely unpublishable, no matter what darkroom magic
was applied.

The only clear images from inside the tomb were recorded by Rivka Maoz sometime between Good Friday 1980 and
Shochat's final sealing of IAA 80/500–509. The pictures in
Rivka's family album show all the ossuaries gone and all the
"rose earth" gone. A meter-high stain covering the walls
almost to the tops of the empty ossuary niches – matching
precisely Shimon Gibson's drawings – shows the height to
which the *terra rossa* soil had risen on the day he first entered
the central chamber.

By the time Rivka Maoz entered the red chamber, one
ossuary had gone missing, and nine surviving ossuaries were
stored in one of the IAA's suburban warehouses. The three
skulls from the main chamber, the bones from the antechamber, and all of the skulls and bones from inside the ossuaries,
including any loose fragments from the "Jesus, son of
Joseph" ossuary, were poured out and set aside for temporary

34

study. According to an understanding between the archaeologists and the rabbis, the bones would eventually be turned over to the religious authorities for reburial. There were several large graves reserved locally for the purpose of "respectful reinterment of ancient human remains."

A year later a large housing development, complete with shops and tiled courtyards and backyards, covered the tomb's original courtyard and had spread for blocks around. During this same year, Yosef Gat died suddenly. Amos Kloner, Eliot Braun, and Shimon Gibson went on to pursue other studies, each imagining that after they left, Shochat's team had simply pounded the tomb into gravel, lime, and level ground – and made the basement of a condominium out of it.

And that was that, Kloner told himself.

Sixteen years later, in 1996, a BBC film crew came across several of the IAA 80/500–509 ossuaries on shelves in a back room of the Israel Antiquities Authority's warehouse. The British team was filming an Easter documentary about Jewish burial customs of the Jesus period. An unidentified student or warehouse employee led one of the crew to a cluster of names.

The flurry of excitement at BBC headquarters turned out to be as short-lived as the original excitement, sixteen years earlier, at the tomb itself. Amos Kloner and several other archaeologists volunteered to step before the cameras and to cut the flurry short.

"These were common names, nothing unusual," Kloner explained.

Shortly after that interview, and sixteen years after the discovery, Amos Kloner finally assembled and compiled his notes and Yosef Gat's, along with Shimon Gibson's maps. His report was published in the Israeli archaeological journal *Atiqot*, volume 29, 1996. (Shimon noticed – and he would always wonder how and why this happened – that on the way to publication someone had applied "white-out" to the prints of his maps and removed from his floor plans two of the three skulls that Gat had believed important enough to be plotted precisely.)

"And besides, this Mariamne lady does not belong to the Jesus family," Kloner told the BBC.

"Preposterous," he said again.

For the BBC, a nod from such a learned authority was as good as a shove. Thus, after a mere mention of the IAA 80/500–509 ossuaries in passing (taking up a total of five minutes during a two-hour program titled *The Body in Question*), everyone forgot about the Tomb of Ten Ossuaries.

Well, not *everyone*.

*   *   *

You may not think it a miracle, not even perhaps if you could have watched, with ageless eyes, an evolving Jewish tradition of building underground tombs filled with ossuaries being cut short before it could spread out of Jerusalem, or if you could have seen those who destroyed the tradition becoming, for archaeologists of the future, the paradoxical creators of a dating system more precise than any isotope.

It may not strike you as a miracle that, somewhere near the dividing line between C.E. and B.C.E., four thousand years of human history already lay underfoot of the men who tended vineyards and carved tombs in the Jerusalem hills. All those forgotten years of civilization had piled themselves into artificial mounds upon the Jerusalem landscape, each concealing stratum upon stratum of destruction and rebirth.

Somewhere in time, somewhere between the death of James the Just about 62–66 C.E. and the destruction of Jerusalem in 70 C.E., a tomb was sealed, not very far from the Temple Mount. The deepest of the tomb's chambers enclosed ossuaries, some containing relics in a woven shroud, and the bones themselves awaited a prophesied Resurrection.

2

Simcha:
The Investigation Begins

first met Hershel Shanks on September 11, 2002. It was an Alice-through-the-looking-glass experience. We had known each other for only a few hours when he said, "What if I told you that we've identified an ossuary in Israel that has an inscription on it that reads 'James, son of Joseph, brother of Jesus'?"

That encounter was the Big Bang of my professional life from that point forward. It was one of those defining moments that had within it the seeds of everything that would follow. First of all, there was the element of strange coincidence or divine intervention, depending on your take on these kinds of things. I met Hershel, the legendary editor of *Biblical Archaeology Review* (BAR), on a total whim. I was a fan, and like

38

some possessed groupie, and for reasons I still don't understand, I felt compelled to call him in Washington, DC, in an
attempt to arrange a meeting. Coincidentally, he was on his
way to Toronto, where I live. After I set up an interview for
him with Canada's largest national newspaper, he came to my
downtown documentary production office for breakfast.

Hershel is lanky and speaks with a bit of a drawl, a kind
of Jewish Jimmy Stewart. He's a former district attorney
with a passion for biblical archaeology. He's also a fast learn-
er. He took a quick look around our boardroom, saw the
various awards, including two Emmys for investigative jour-
nalism, sized me up, and decided to tell his story. The key
line bears repeating: "What if I told you that we've identified
an ossuary in Israel that has an inscription on it that reads
'James, son of Joseph, brother of Jesus'?"

It's a code, really. A statement that would make sense only
to a relatively small group of the initiated, and at that time I
didn't belong to the club. Along with most of the world, I
did not know what an ossuary was, and I certainly didn't
know that the Christian Gospels claim that Jesus had siblings. I now realize that the general ignorance concerning
ossuaries, and also concerning Jesus's family, is precisely
what has allowed the story of the discovery of the Jesus family tomb to linger in the shadows for nearly thirty years. But
at the time, all I could manage was, "What's an ossuary?"

As I was to learn later, scholars have no real idea how the
ossuary ritual began. But we know why it stopped. It came to

a fiery end when Roman troops destroyed Jerusalem in 70 C.E., crushing the great Jewish revolt of 66–70 C.E. and extinguishing Jewish sovereignty for nearly two millennia. Not until the rebirth of modern Israel in 1948 would there again be an independent Jewish state in the biblical land of Israel.

On the face of it, it seems that Jesus's death and reported Resurrection are intimately bound to the practice of secondary burial – the use of ossuaries – but no one seems to have noticed. In fact, if you tour the ossuaries section in the Israel Museum, the use of ossuaries is described as a "typical" form of Jewish burial from the first-century period. There is even a small quote from an early rabbinic document attesting to secondary burial. But calling it a typical form of Jewish burial begs the question. How can something be "typical" if it was practiced only by a small group of people during a very short period of time in Jerusalem and to a lesser extent in the Galilee? The Talmud doesn't record a single incidence of a Jewish sage buried in this manner. In fact, the only famous death ever recorded in ancient Jewish sources associated with the Jerusalem practice of secondary burial is the death of Rabbi Jesus.

When Hershel responded to my question, "What's an ossuary?" by explaining that Jews in ancient Jerusalem wrapped the dead in shrouds, placed them in tombs, and returned a year later to rebury the bones in limestone ossuaries, the proverbial lightbulb turned on in my head. For the first time I understood the story of Jesus's burial.

That strange story had always bothered me. If Jesus was dead for three days prior to the Resurrection, as Christian orthodoxy demands, why wasn't a grave dug and his body lowered into it? Why had his body been placed in the family tomb of one of his wealthy followers, a man the Gospels call Joseph of Arimathea (Matthew 27:15)?

According to Jewish law (and Jesus was a Jew after all), a body has to be buried *in the ground before sundown* on the very day of passing. I had always wondered what the tomb business, mentioned in all four Gospels, was all about. Now I had my answer. Ossuaries! Clearly, certain Jews of Galilee and Jerusalem at the time of Jesus's ministry practiced secondary burial. And clearly, Jesus's followers belonged to this group.

As time went on, I got my hands on every piece of literature ever published on tombs and ossuaries in Israel. In fact, I started joking that I was so fascinated with first-century ossuaries that I wanted to start a worldwide retail chain called "Ossuaries-R-Us." The reasons for my excitement had to do with the historical information packed into this custom of ossuary use. Consider this: given the narrow historical window – one hundred years – in which ossuaries were in use in the Jerusalem area, the custom is self-dating. You don't need any fancy tests to figure out that an ossuary dates to the first century, or, more precisely, that it dates to just before, during, or after Jesus's life.

Also, by and large, ossuary use did not spread to the masses. Real estate in Jerusalem, then and now, is extremely expensive. Only the religious, political, and economic elite could afford family crypts or tombs in which to store the ossuaries. The poor were buried in the ground (either by simple placement into little niches cut into the local "chalk stone" or by burial in soft earth, far beyond the city walls). The people who could afford tombs or who had a religious reason for practicing this particular form of burial were placed in ossuaries. Also, it is probable that many of the people buried in ossuaries believed in physical Resurrection – a kind of ancient cryogenics.* The faithful were buried in ossuaries rotated toward the Temple. The House of God that crowned Mount Zion served as the centerpiece of ancient Judaism and was one of the wonders of the world. Many believed that the Messiah – the longed-for redeemer of the world – would declare the "end of times" on the Temple Mount. In other words, the people buried in ossuaries had front-row seats to the Apocalypse. Jesus himself echoes this when he says he will rebuild a destroyed Temple in three days – the heart of the charges against him (John 2:19). His followers may have seen ossuaries oriented to the Temple as the quickest way to share in the Second Coming. No, there is nothing "typical" about the practice of secondary burial among Jews. But to admit

---

*It is possible that some Sadducess, i.e., the Temple cult elite, and/or some Hellenizers who did not believe in Resurrection, also engaged in the practice of ossuary use. They probably did so to emulate Roman practices of storing ashes in urns. Since Jewish law forbids cremation, bones in ossuaries were the next best thing.

that ossuary use might somehow be associated with the early Jesus movement is to admit that many of the ancient remains found in Jerusalem today might belong to Jesus's followers. In a Jewish state, this idea doesn't get you very far.

Most ossuaries have carved ornamentation on them. Many have religious symbols. Some of these symbols are recognizable, and some have not been deciphered to this day. As mentioned, 20 percent of the ossuaries found are inscribed, usually with the name of the deceased. Sometimes biographical material is written on the ossuary, such as "mother" or "father." These inscriptions would turn out to be invaluable to the detective work that would now lead to the Jesus family tomb.

From the moment I found out about them, I wondered why ossuaries were not on every New Testament scholar's lips. Also, as a longtime student of Jewish history, I wondered why ossuaries weren't at the forefront of any study of the period? Why wasn't there an "Ossuaries 101" course in every Jewish studies program and New Testament studies department? After all, because of the existence of ossuaries, we have a veritable phonebook of Jerusalem's political, economic, and religious elite dating back to the time of Jesus.

Think about it. There weren't that many people on Planet Earth at the time – only about 300 million. There were fewer people in ancient Israel than in modern Brooklyn. And the crowds attending some professional football games today would outnumber the people living in Jerusalem at

43

the time of Jesus. More than that, of the small number of people who lived in Jerusalem at that time, only a tiny fraction could afford or had the desire to be buried in tombs and laid to rest in ossuaries. As the penny dropped, I suddenly realized that connecting an inscription on an ossuary to the historical Jesus was not so crazy. In fact, it might indeed be possible to identify key players in first-century Israel and link them to their ossuaries. In other words, just as it should not come as a surprise to anyone that the mummies of pharaohs known to us from history can be found in the Valley of the Kings in modern Egypt because, after all, only ancient Egypt's elite could afford to engage in mummification, it should come as no surprise to find the bones of Jesus's followers – such as "brother James" – buried in Jerusalem. There simply weren't that many people promoting secondary burial at the time. And historically speaking, the most famous family engaged in secondary burial and living in Jerusalem in the first century was the family of Jesus.

When Hershel told me about what has come to be known as the James ossuary, I didn't think of all the possible implications of that find. I was simply excited to learn that ossuary use in ancient Israel could be dated to the time of Jesus and to no other, and that it helped to explain Jesus's burial in the tomb of Joseph of Arimathea. I was also surprised to learn that the Gospels explicitly state that Jesus had siblings. But what I couldn't understand was how Jesus could have a brother named James. Did Jesus have an Anglo sibling?

The inscription states: "Yakov bar Iosef, achui d'Yeshua," or "Jacob, son of Joseph, brother of Jesus." "James" was introduced as a translation for the Hebrew "Yakov" or "Jacob" quite recently ... during the creation of the King James English translation of the Bible in 1611. Prior to that, all versions of the synoptic Gospels – the four Gospels that tell the story of Jesus's life – stated that Jesus had four brothers: Jacob, Simon, Joseph, and Judah. Somehow, Jacob traveled through Latin, Italian, and Spanish, reaching England as James.

It seemed to me that the James, brother of Jesus ossuary was arguably the greatest archaeological find of all time. After all, here you had – literally carved in stone – archaeological proof of the existence of Jesus of Nazareth. I asked for television exclusivity to the ossuary, and I got it.

But what if it was a fake?

The simple fact is that no one has to fake an ossuary. You can buy one in the Jerusalem antiquities market for as little as $500 if it has no inscription or ornamentation. In fact, today ossuaries are experiencing a bit of a revival, but not for burial. People use them as planters – especially foreigners living in Israel. One ambassador's wife paid thousands of dollars for tiny ones that had been used for the burials of babies; she could put them on coffee tables because they did not take up much room. For $2,000, you can purchase a beautiful ossuary complete with ornamentation and inscriptions. In fact, if you look closely inside empty ossuaries on sale in various Jerusalem antiquities shops, you will see that although the bones that occupied them for the better part of two thousand years have been removed, there is often what crime-scene investigators call "human residue" at the bottoms and adhering to the sides. This too would turn out to be key in the investigation of the Jesus family tomb.

How ossuaries get into the antiquities market is an interesting story. It turns out that in the State of Israel an agreement has been struck between the religious and the archaeological communities. This agreement prevents the excavation of ancient tombs for fear of disturbing the dead. Israeli archaeologists are not happy with the deal, but the alternative involves facing rock-throwing Orthodox crowds for whom the excavation of tombs is tantamount to the desecration of graves. In modern Israel, religion is politics, and the rabbinical authorities will not cut the archaeologists any slack, even when it can be demonstrated that the dead will not be disturbed. I spoke to Rabbi Schmidl of the Atra Kadisha, an organization dedicated to preserving Jewish burial sites. It is he who is in charge of dealing with the archaeological community, and I pointed out to him that by not allowing Israeli archaeologists to enter tombs, he was giving a free hand to tomb robbers, allowing them to desecrate what he was ostensibly protecting. My logic didn't move him. What archaeologists do, he can control. What tomb robbers do is between their conscience and their god. For their part, he said, the archaeologists had it coming to them. Most of them treat the bones of the ancients with secular disdain, keeping them boxed in the basement of the Israel Antiquities Authority or dumping them in the garbage.

As a result of the archaeological status quo, today tombs can be excavated only when bulldozers uncover them in the course of construction. Ossuaries found by archaeologists in this way are stored in a large, *Raiders of the Lost Ark*–type warehouse in the city of Bet Shemesh, ancient home to the biblical Samson. Alternatively, archaeologists get to examine tombs after Palestinian youth, scouring the countryside for marketable ancient relics, raid a tomb and steal away with some of its artifacts. Bizarrely, if you're caught tomb raiding, you can be arrested and prosecuted. But if you make your way to an authorized antiquities shop, your loot automatically becomes legal and your activities are retroactively kosher. In other words, there is no reason to fake ossuaries. They can be easily had.

Yet when it comes to inscriptions, that's another matter. Very soon after the announcement of the existence of the James ossuary, several experts came out of the academic woodwork to declare that the inscription was a fake. Mind you, no one has ever argued that the *entire* inscription is forged. Rather, those who believe that it is a hoax say that the first part of the inscription, "Jacob, son of Joseph," is real, but that the second part, "brother of Jesus," is fake. According to this argument, the last two words of the Aramaic inscription* were added by a cynical forger hell-bent on pulling the wool over the eyes of the world and cashing in on what would surely be perceived as the greatest holy relic in all of Christendom.

But none of this came up in my initial conversation with Hershel. All I knew at that time was that the ossuary belonged to an anonymous private collector living in Tel Aviv and that it had been checked and authenticated by the Israel Geological Survey (IGS) and by the world-famous epigrapher André Lemaire of the Sorbonne in France, a former priest. And that's all I needed before embarking on a journey that would result in a one-hour documentary called *James, Brother of Jesus* for the Discovery Channels around the world. We made international headlines, but the elation was short-lived when the academic counterattack began. The ossuary's detractors argued that the second part of the inscription was bogus, and the world was eager to believe them without actually weighing the evidence. But for me it was already too late. By the time the James ossuary was being discredited, James had already introduced me to his family.

Amos Kloner is a small man with an impish grin. For years he worked at the Israel Antiquities Authority, becoming something of an expert on tombs in the Jerusalem area. He literally wrote the book on them, or more precisely, the

* In first-century Israel, Hebrew was largely used in liturgical settings, while Aramaic, a related dialect, was the day-to-day vernacular.

catalog. I first met Kloner in 2003 at the old IAA warehouse in Jerusalem, before they moved to Bet Shemesh. It was a small building bursting at the seams with antiquities ranging from Stone Age tools, to Crusader swords, to Turkish cannons. Every civilization has left its mark on the Promised Land, and the IAA warehouse is the repository of some of the debris they have left behind.

In the old IAA basement, which was accessed by a spiral iron staircase, you literally had to step on and over artifacts to find what you were looking for. What I was looking for were ossuaries. I was trying to contextualize the James ossuary, so I got in touch with Dr. Kloner because, as it turns out, there is only one other ossuary that mentions a "brother." It reads: "Shimi, son of [unclear], brother of Chanin [or Chanania]." The father's name hasn't been deciphered. But there is a very famous rabbi in the Talmud, a miracle worker named Chanania ben Akasha. If the Shimi ossuary could be definitively identified as the bone box of the brother of Chanania, this would create a precedent for the James ossuary. It would mean that brothers of miracle workers had their famous siblings mentioned on their coffins.

Kloner is the kind of guy who knows many facts but is loath to connect the dots for fear that they might form a picture. He doesn't like pictures. He likes dots. Kloner feels that connecting dots is unscientific speculation. For him, ossuaries are a catalog of anonymous, unknowable people. They're all Jews of the first century. That's the most we can say about them. When I asked him recently what he would say if an ossuary was found with the inscription "Mary Magdalene" on it, all he could muster was a grin and a brief comment: "I would say ... very interesting."

Standing knee-deep in ossuaries in the IAA basement in 2003, he asked me in Hebrew why I was so interested in the James ossuary.

"For one thing," I said, "this box may contain the DNA of Jesus's clan."

Kloner laughed out loud and said: "If that's the case, why focus on the brother's ossuary? Why don't you concentrate on the ossuary of the man himself – Jesus, son of Joseph?" For Kloner, this was a joke. Since no ancient "Jacob" could be linked to the New Testament James, no ancient "Jesus" could be linked to Jesus of Nazareth. As far as Kloner was concerned, Jesus, Jacob, Judah, Miriam, and so on, were all common Jewish names in first-century Jerusalem and to try to link them with the main characters of the Christian Gospels was a silly exercise from the get-go.

For my part, I asked, "You've found the name 'Jesus' on an ossuary?"

"Many times" came the reply.

As it turns out, not that many – six, in fact. But I wasn't interested in every ossuary with the name "Jesus" on it. I was interested only in any inscription mentioning a "Jesus, son of Joseph." In more than one hundred years of archaeology, only two such inscriptions have been found.

The first time an ossuary was found with the name "Jesus, son of Joseph" on it was in 1926. It made international headlines when its existence was announced on January 6, 1931, at a conference in Berlin. Several things about it were worthy of consideration. First of all, the man who identified the inscription was Professor Eleazar Sukenik of the Hebrew University, the archaeologist who in 1948 would be responsible for the discovery of the Dead Sea Scrolls. Second of all, the entire ossuary, except for the lid, had been preserved. It's still on permanent display in the Israel Museum, not as a unique find that may have once held the bones of Jesus, but as an illustration of how common names like Jesus and Joseph were in first-century Judea. The point of the exhibit is that we shouldn't get excited if New Testament names appear on ossuaries. The third interesting thing about the "Jesus, son of Joseph" ossuary identified by Professor Sukenik was the nickname inscribed on its side: "Yeshu," or Jesus. What many people don't realize is that there is no Hebrew equivalent for "Jesus." The proper name is Yeshua, or Joshua. In ancient times, some "Yeshuas" were also called Yeshu, kind of like Josh for Joshua. Jesus may have been known by the ancient equivalent of Josh. And here, on this ossuary, were both versions of the name – Yeshua and Yeshu.

When Sukenik made a big deal about this find, he was encouraged by his colleagues to shut up. As far as they were concerned, linking names on ossuaries to people in the New Testament was irresponsible at best. Sukenik sort of complied. He stopped pushing his Jesus ossuary because, though it was an oddity to be sure, it was not provenanced – Sukenik had found it in the basement of the Rockefeller Museum. There was nothing else to be said about it because the context in which it had been found was lost. Maybe the tomb in which it had rested said "Redeemer of Mankind," or maybe it said "Best Baker in Jerusalem." There was no way to know. But though Sukenik stepped back from the ossuary, he pushed forward on another related matter: the Judeo-Christians, or the Ebionites.

"Ebionites" is the name originally ascribed to some of the early followers of Jesus. The name comes down to us from early Church fathers such as Irenaeus. It is derived from the Hebrew "Evionim," or "poor ones." It most probably was a title for those who renounced worldly goods in favor of spiritual ones. Another historical name for the early followers of Jesus is "Nazarenes," and yet another is "Judeo-Christians." The former also comes down to us from early Christian writers. It's not clear what the differences were between the Ebionites and Nazarenes, but some scholars have suggested that the Ebionites were essentially Jews who believed that Jesus was Messiah while rejecting any idea of his divinity, while Nazarenes were Jews who accepted the tenets of the evolving Christian faith, including the virgin birth and the Holy Trinity. The term "Judeo-Christian" is a modern academic invention referring to both Ebionites and Nazarenes; it's a catchall term for any Jewish follower of Jesus in ancient times. Though Sukenik dropped the matter of the Jesus ossuary, he was convinced that many of the tombs being uncovered in Jerusalem, and their ossuaries, belonged to the early Jesus movement – the Judeo-Christians.

Looking at the Judeo-Christians was – and is – an exercise fraught with potential controversy. It's likely to get you into hot water with both Jews *and* Christians, because it involves shedding light in the dark corners of the so-called Judeo-Christian tradition. It's certainly not something that the Kloners of this world want to get involved with. Why should the Judeo-Christians pose such a problem? Let's start by looking at the matter from the Christian perspective.

According to most scholars, Jesus was crucified around 30 C.E. Christianity became an official state religion of the Roman Empire under Constantine in 312 C.E. Roughly three hundred years separate the Crucifixion of Jesus, as a Jew guilty of sedition against the Roman Empire, and his elevation as a supreme deity – if not *the* Supreme Deity – of that same empire. During this meteoric rise to power, his followers went from a persecuted Jewish sect to the dominant religious force of the civilized world. All this was accomplished while other Jewish Messiahs, such as Bar Kochba, were still challenging Roman authority. Think about it: selling Jesus to the Romans was like attempting to convince post–Vietnam War Americans that someone they thought was a Vietcong leader was really both a pacifist and the Son of God. A hard sell, to be sure.

One of the ways in which the early Gentile followers of

Jesus accomplished the transformation of the Jesus movement from a persecuted Jewish sect into a worldwide Gentile religion was by separating themselves from the so-called
Judeo-Christians – the Jewish followers of Jesus. Before the
destruction of Jerusalem in 70 C.E., this was all but impossible. After all, Jesus, his family, the apostles, and every single
one of his significant followers had been Jewish. The people
who touched Jesus, talked with him, broke bread with him,
and believed in his Messiahship were all Jewish. But after
his Crucifixion, a Jew named Saul, who became the apostle
Paul, rose to lead a Gentile following that threatened to over-
whelm the original group.

The struggle between Jewish and Gentile followers of
Jesus seemed irrelevant as long as Jerusalem stood. In other
words, as long as the Jewish Temple functioned, the Judeo-
Christians called the theological shots in the early Jesus
movement. Not even Paul could ignore James, "the brother
of the Lord" (Galatians 1:19) and leader of Jerusalem's
Judeo-Christians. But once the Temple was torched and
Jerusalem had been reduced to smoldering ash, the original
movement lost its power base and disappeared from official
histories. Legend has it that the Judeo-Christians fled to Pel-
la, in modern Jordan, survived for a couple of centuries, and
then were either assimilated into Gentile Christianity or
reabsorbed into rabbinic Judaism.

The Church fathers, the men who shaped Christianity,
either ignored the Ebionites and Nazarenes or dealt with

them in various polemics against heretics – in fact, these writings are often our only record of some of these groups. After all, there was no point in overly stressing their existence; given that these emphasized the historical Jesus over the theological one, doing so might lead to embarrassing questions such as, "If Mary was a virgin, how is it that Jesus had four brothers and two sisters?" That problem was dealt with, incidentally, by turning his siblings into half-brothers and half-sisters, or into cousins. But other questions were harder to deal with, such as, "If Jesus and his followers kept the Sabbath, followed kosher laws, and practiced circumcision, why don't Christians?" Of course, theological answers can always be formulated, but it was best to ignore the people who once walked with Jesus. Simply put, by continuing to be practicing Jews, the Judeo-Christians were an embarrassment to the early Church.

So the Judeo-Christians fell off the radar screens. Retroactively, they didn't exist. Even the academics who specialize in Christian movements prior to the Emperor Constantine largely ignore the Judeo-Christians. For many people, Christianity was born in Rome in the fourth century. As a result, hardly anyone expects to find earlier archaeological evidence. Since they didn't exist, how could they have left material for archaeologists to find?*

For their part, Jews have by and large gone along with the

---

* In 2006, the earliest known Christian Church was accidently discovered in the courtyard of a prison in Megiddo. The mosiac is clearly gentile Christian and therefore not controversial.

Christian blind spot. After all, for the better part of two millennia the relationship between Christianity and Judaism – Christians and Jews – was the relationship between rulers and ruled. Jews were not in a position to say to papal authorities, "By the way, Jesus was one of us. From our point of view, he is a failed messiah but one hell of a patriot, and if you don't believe us, why don't you study the Ebionites?" Thus, as Gentile Christianity evolved out of what had been a Jewish sect, rabbinic authorities drew a sharp line between Christians and Jews. From their perspective, since Christianity had become a Gentile religion, Jesus's Jewish followers had to choose between Jesus and the Jewish people. They couldn't have both.

The defining moment in the ousting of the Judeo-Christians from the synagogue came around 90 C.E. with the introduction of the "Birkat ha-Minim" curse in the Jewish prayer service.* "Minim" means "genus" or "variety" or "branch" in Hebrew. In religious terms, it implies "sect." In practical terms, it has come to mean "heretic." Interestingly, the enemies of Israel – for example, the Romans – were not mentioned. This was an internal affair. The curse could be deemed effective only if, again, in practical terms, heretics were leading the prayer service. The "Birkat ha-Minim" curse required that congregational *leaders* publicly denounce themselves if in fact they were followers of Jesus. The net effect of this change in the liturgy was to force the Ebionites and

---

* The curse was introduced in Jabneh under the patriarch Rabban Gamaliel II.

Nazarenes, many of whom *were* leading the prayer service, to pack their prayer shawls and leave the synagogue. When they did, they effectively walked out of history. They literally fell between the theological chairs. They were an embarrassment to both Jews and Christians. Jews wanted to forget that Jesus had a relatively large and growing following, and Gentiles were happy to preach that since the Jews had rejected Jesus, they were now a rejected people themselves.

The disappearance of the Judeo-Christians from history has meant that, archaeologically speaking, one cannot look for any Christian artifacts prior to the fourth century. Before that time, according to the accepted wisdom, Judeo-Christians are indistinguishable from other Jews. There can be no "material culture" – no hard evidence of their existence – to discover. According to the majority of historians and Middle East archaeologists, therefore, the archaeology of the early Christians begins with Constantine, or just prior to him at the beginning of the fourth century C.E.

Sukenik disagreed with all of this. He believed that he had found evidence of early Judeo-Christian tombs in and around Jerusalem – especially in Talpiot.* He also believed that

---

* In September 1945 in Talpiot, a tomb was found containing eleven ossuaries. Sukenik was the excavator. Architecturally, it is very similar to the "Tomb of the Ten Ossuaries." On ossuary 8, there are large cross-marks. There is also an inscription written in Greek: "Jesus Aloth." It has been suggested that this is a rendering of the Hebrew verb "Aleh," meaning "rise up." On ossuary 7, there is Greek writing drawn in charcoal. Sukenik translated it as "Jesus, woe!" On ossuary 1, a Hebrew inscription was found, "Shimon bar Saba." Barsabbas is a family name known only from Acts (1:23, 15:22).

archaeology could fill in a gap created by theology. To the general archaeological community in Israel, Sukenik's obsession with Judeo-Christianity was an eccentricity, a bizarre interest of an otherwise sound mind. They ignored – and continue to ignore – this part of Sukenik's legacy. But think about it: if Sukenik was right and you could locate early Judeo-Christian tombs, why not the tomb of the family of Jesus?

In the Christian world, Sukenik had his counterpart: Franciscan Father Bellarmino Bagatti (1905–90). Starting in the 1930s, he held a chair at the Studium Biblicum Fransciscanum in Jerusalem, where he taught, studied, wrote, and worked. Besides being a Franciscan monk, Father Bagatti, an Italian by birth, was also an accomplished archaeologist. In fact, he opened a small museum where he housed some of his many finds. His museum can still be found next to the Church of the Flagellation, the Second Station on the Via Dolorosa.

In 1953 the Franciscans were renovating their church at Dominus Flevit ("the Lord Wept") on the Mount of Olives, overlooking the Temple Mount. It was here, according to Church tradition, that Jesus saw the Temple of Jerusalem – the centerpiece of Jewish worship for one thousand years – and wept for what he rightly believed was its forthcoming destruction. It's an important episode in the history of the early Christian movement because not only did Jesus predict the Temple's destruction, he also prophesied its eventual Resurrection. Jesus promised that after its destruction, he would personally rebuild the Temple in three days. In this way, he would usher in "the end of days," the era of the Third Temple, and the advent of God's rule on earth. When that didn't happen, some of his followers concluded that they had misunderstood Jesus's words. The "temple," they said, meant his "body," and "rebuilding" it after three days was an allusion to his own Resurrection three days after the Crucifixion*. The point, after all, was to save humanity as a whole and not simply to redeem the Jewish people from Roman oppression.

For other followers, however, this did not wash. For them, Jesus was Messiah, and as the Messiah it was his job to reunite the tribes of Israel, emancipate God's people, and usher in a universal state of divine rule by reestablishing God's holy throne in Jerusalem. Since the Temple was destroyed *after* the Crucifixion, they argued, it would also be rebuilt *after* the Second Coming. When they died, many must have wanted to be buried on the Mount of Olives so that they could have a front-row seat to the Second Coming. At least that's what Bagatti thought in 1953 when he discovered what he called a "Judeo-Christian necropolis."

There, Bagatti unearthed at least half a dozen tombs and dozens of ossuaries bearing New Testament names such as "Saphira" and "Martha." Some of the ossuaries were even inscribed with crosses. Unlike Sukenik's Jesus ossuary, Bagatti's discovery of what he believed was the earliest

---

* This is how the Gospel of John explains Jesus's allusion to rebuilding the Temple (John 2:19–22).

Judeo-Christian cemetery did not make headlines. On the contrary, Bagatti's claims provoked howls of derision from both Christian and Jewish quarters, religious and secular. So he dropped the matter. He stopped the Dominus Flevit excavation, leaving tombs unexplored and graves open. Nonetheless, to this day, at Dominus Flevit there is a plaque identifying the necropolis as "Judeo-Christian" – Bagatti didn't back off that claim – and tourists can gaze at the unearthed bones of the people who, according to Bagatti, were the original followers of Jesus. They haven't been reburied, perhaps so as to avoid the controversy over whether they should be given a Jewish or Christian burial.

If Bagatti was right, the cemetery at Dominus Flevit is one of the most important archaeological finds in all of Christendom. Why was the dig abandoned and his findings ignored? There were essentially four reasons, none of them good. First, there was the circular reasoning that since Judeo-Christians cannot be differentiated from other Jews, no Judeo-Christian remains can ever be found. Second, conventional wisdom held that the cross (a symbol leaping out from the ossuaries) doesn't appear as a Christian symbol before Constantine. This was simply untrue. For example, you can find mentions of the cross as a Christian symbol in Tertullian, an early Christian writer, at least one hundred years before Constantine.*

---

* See Tertullian's "de Corona" (iii) for his view that Christians "wear out their foreheads making the sign of the cross."

The next two reasons were more political than historical. Bagatti found the Judeo-Christian necropolis at Dominus Flevit only five years after the birth of modern Israel, and only eight years after Auschwitz. The post-Holocaust Jews of the infant state had had enough of Europeanized Christianity. They were trying to reconnect with their own Jewish past. The last person they were willing to listen to was a Franciscan monk who claimed that some of the earliest tombs found in Jerusalem belonged to the followers of Jesus. "Lay off our history" was, and continues to be, the mantra of Israeli archaeologists.

One might have thought that the Church would have backed Bagatti, but there were two problems with his finds, neither of them having to do with archaeology. First of all, Bagatti was unearthing the remains of the very people the Church fathers had called heretics. Hardly a reason to celebrate them. Second of all, there was a particularly distracting find at Dominus Flevit: Bagatti had identified what was arguably the ossuary of St. Peter.

For years, the Vatican has been digging under St. Peter's Basilica in Rome, looking for evidence that St. Peter is actually buried there, as per tradition. Sure enough, there is an ancient Roman cemetery under St. Peter's, but it is a pagan cemetery. There is not one shred of credible archaeological evidence linking the cemetery under the Vatican with the apostle Peter. And yet, from time to time rumors surface that St. Peter's relics have been found. Once, bones found in the ancient graveyard, under a second-century monument said to mark the place of Peter's martyrdom, made international news until it was determined that the bones belonged to a variety of people, including women, and that there were even some ancient chicken bones thrown in for good measure. Not only is there no evidence that Peter is buried under the Vatican, there's no evidence there of a Christian, Jewish, or Judeo-Christian cemetery of any kind.

But if something were to be found, what would it look like? Well, it is doubtful that St. Peter's gravestone, for example, would even mention the name "Peter." After all, that was not his name – it was his title. The Gospels relate that Jesus turned to a disciple named Simon ("Shimon" in Hebrew and Aramaic), called him "Cepha" – which means "rock" in Aramaic ("Petros" in Greek) – and declares that he is the rock upon which the Jesus movement shall be built (John 1:42, Matthew 16:16–19). In other words, "Peter" is an anglicization of the name "Petros," which is itself a translation of the Aramaic "Cepha," which is the appellation, title, or nickname that Jesus gave one of his leading disciples.

But what is that disciple's real name? Well, there is no argument about that. The Gospels are clear that Peter's name is actually Shimon bar Jonah (Simon, son of Jonah). As it turns out, Shimon, or Simon, was the most common Jewish name in first-century Judea. Finding an ossuary with this name on it would be meaningless, since about 20 percent of all Jewish males were called Simon. The name Jonah, on the other hand, was very rare. It's a biblical name that had fallen out of use by the first century. Finding an ossuary with the inscription "Shimon bar Jonah" is a very rare event, and such a find should, arguably, make headlines everywhere. In fact, it is safe to say that if the Vatican found an ossuary under St. Peter's Basilica with the name Shimon bar Jonah on it, there would be a major press conference, the pope would conduct a special service, and the ossuary would become the holiest relic in Christendom. It would most likely be housed in St. Peter's Basilica as the centerpiece of the Vatican. Millions of the faithful would line up for hours to file past it in veneration and prayer.

And yet, an ossuary inscribed with the name Shimon bar Jonah *has* been found in an archaeological context more compelling than the pagan cemetery under St. Peter's Basilica. It was found by Bagatti in what he had identified as the Judeo-Christian necropolis of Dominus Flevit. Of the thousands of ossuaries found in the Jerusalem area, it is still the only one of its kind. In fact, the inscription is so rare that there is no precedent for it in any writings of the first century, whether on ossuaries, parchments, or something else. But because the ossuary was not found where the powers-that-be would have liked it to be, there was no press conference, no religious service, no enshrining of the ossuary and reburial of the bones. Nothing. It was spirited away to Bagatti's little museum at the Church of the Flagellation in Old

Jerusalem, where it still sits, broken and ignored. The bones were discarded, the cover was lost, two of the sides were also lost, and it was dumped unceremoniously amid some twenty other ossuaries, silent witness to what happens to artifacts that do not conform to theological or archaeological expectations. You find it. You ignore it.

In 2003, in the basement of the old IAA warehouse with Dr. Kloner, I was still months away from knowing all of this. All I knew at the time was that I was investigating an ossuary inscription with the words "Yakov (James), son of Joseph, brother of Jesus," and here was this man telling me that an ossuary with the name Jesus, son of Joseph had also been found.

"Where is it?" I asked.

"Right here," said Kloner, and he proceeded to talk to the young woman sitting at the entrance studying for her university exams. She was in her twenties, attractive, and slightly bookish. Working in the IAA basement was her part-time job. Kloner asked her to look up "Jesus, son of Joseph," and she did. There was no excitement in her eyes. Her fingers didn't tremble as she located the card in her index file. Nor did perspiration bead up on her forehead as she led me through the rows of ossuaries sitting on their shelves and lined up on the floor. "Here it is," she smiled, and pointed me to the plainest ossuary I had seen before or since. "See, here on the side is the inscription," she said.

"It's hard to read," said Kloner. "Like doctors' writings,"

he added, laughing. "Only pharmacists can read them." I shone my flashlight sideways against the script on the ossuary, and Kloner traced the letters with his fingers: "Jesus, son of Joseph."

I tried to stay calm, but something told me that this was not simply an example of an everyday occurrence. Kloner told me that he had found the ossuary in a tomb in east Talpiot, one of the boroughs of Jerusalem, on the road to Bethlehem. The tomb had been uncovered in 1980 by bulldozers during the building of high-rise apartments in the area. He had been called in with Yosef Gat, a Romanian-Israeli archaeologist, now deceased, to investigate. They had removed ten ossuaries from the tomb. This was one of them.

"Were there any other inscriptions?" I asked.

He laughed. "If I tell you, you'll run around screaming, 'I found Jesus's entire family.'"

I didn't laugh. I did manage a smile, however, and a question: "What other names were in that tomb?"

"If I'm not mistaken, there was a Matia [Matthew], Ioseph [Joseph], and two Marys," he said.

"And why is this *not* significant?" I asked.

"Because Mary, or Miriam, is the most common female name among women of first-century Israel," he said. "Stand in a marketplace in ancient times and shout, 'Miriam,' and twenty-five percent of the women will turn around. That's why there are so many Marys in the Gospels. Everyone's a Mary. Finding a Mary next to a Jesus is no big deal."

"Really," I said. "How many other times have tombs been uncovered with two Marys, a Joseph, and a Jesus in them?"

"None," Kloner answered. "But here's your problem – the second Mary has a name, and it's not Magdalene. Her name is Mariamne, which is a Hellenistic, Macabbean version of Miriam. One of Herod the Great's wives had this name. But none of the people associated with Jesus was called Mariamne. Too bad for you, Mr. Jacobovici," he said as he laughed and pushed his way past the antiquities and out of the ossuary stacks.

I lingered behind and looked at the inscription. Even my untrained eye could clearly make out the letters that translated as "Jesus, son of Joseph." I then leaned over, looked around, and, when I was sure that no one was looking, removed the lid to the ossuary. It was empty. But there at the bottom, embedded in a kind of red earth, and clearly visible amid flakes of limestone that had disengaged from the sides of the ossuaries, were human remains.

Ron Pappin is an anomaly. He hails from Timmins, a mining town in northern Ontario. He's been everything from a hardware store manager to a lighthouse keeper. He's one of those rare souls whose life arc seems to have nothing to do with his surroundings. He's become an expert on all things past. He can describe the streets of ancient Rome better than modern New York because, truth be told, he's never been out of Canada. He decided long ago that if he's going to travel only in his imagination, he'd rather visit the ancient world.

Ron was close to getting his Ph.D. in ancient studies at the University of Toronto when his much younger wife contracted Lou Gehrig's disease, or ALS, and he's been caring for her ever since. He smokes a pipe, so his teeth are dark brown and decayed. He's missing his front teeth altogether, but because all his money goes to caring for his wife, he hasn't got around to fixing them. He also wears an Ontario version of an Indiana Jones hat, and he carries a paunch of several stone. He cuts quite a figure. He's my friend and the chief researcher in our company.

When I came back from Jerusalem in the fall of 2003, I brought Kloner's published IAA report on the discovery of the tomb in east Talpiot with me. Dropping the report on Ron's desk, I said, "In 1980, they found a tomb in south Jerusalem."

"They found many tombs," he said. "What does this have to do with the James ossuary?" he asked. We were working on a film on what was destined to become the world's most celebrated bone box.

"Well," I said, "in the Talpiot tomb they found ten ossuaries, six with inscriptions. The inscribed ones include a "Matthew," a "Joseph," two "Marys," and a "Jesus, son of Joseph."

Ron raised an eyebrow. "And no one noticed?"

"Well," I retorted, "one Mary was called Maria, which merits attention, but the other was called …"

"Magdalene?" he interrupted, laughing.

"No, Mariamne," I said.

"Never heard of her. Too bad," he chuckled, and got back to work.

"Look into her," I said. "See if there's a connection between the names Mariamne and Magdalene."

"Well," Ron smiled a toothless grin, "today we have the Internet. Why don't we look into it right now?" He googled "Mariamne" and then turned slightly pale. "Look, Simcha," Ron exclaimed. Over his shoulder I peered at the screen and the article his search had led him to. "According to modern scholarship," he read out loud, "Mary Magdalene's real name was Mariamne."

3

Simcha: The Lost Tomb

Oded Golan is the most infamous collector of biblical antiquities in the world. I first met him in October 2002, right after Hershel Shanks gave me exclusive access to the story he was about to break on the cover of *Biblical Archaeology Review* (*BAR*) concerning the discovery of the bone box of Jesus's brother James. At the time, among the small circle of people in the know, the James ossuary was completely kosher, and its Israeli owner wanted to remain anonymous.

I flew to Tel Aviv to videotape one final examination of the ossuary prior to the publication of the *BAR* article. The world still didn't know about the existence of what was ostensibly the first archaeological artifact attesting to the existence of Jesus of Nazareth. Hershel told me that after this final examination, the owner might withdraw access to the ossuary. "This may be a one-shot deal," he said. I had to make the opportunity count.

On the appointed day, I left the Carlton Hotel by the Mediterranean and started driving toward Tel Aviv center. The owner was giving directions to my driver over a cell phone. I had imagined a Hollywood-style drive along the shore to a secluded villa high on some cliff. Instead, we drove a couple of blocks and stopped in front of a very nondescript Tel Aviv low-rise apartment building. My Israeli film crew and I then took a small elevator to the third floor, and I found myself in a kind of bachelor apartment, greeted by a youngish-looking middle-aged guy of medium height.

Oded Golan is a complex man. He comes from a good family. His mother is a retired professor of agriculture, his father an engineer. His brother is a publisher of educational books. Golan has been an Israeli army officer and an entrepreneur. He has a passion for Asian women, modern architecture, and classical music. The only thing that stands out in his otherwise unremarkable apartment is the white baby grand piano in the living-room. The apartment is a bit grimy but neat, a bachelor's idea of clean. It was nothing like what I imagined the home of one of the most active collectors of biblical antiquities would look like. The legendary multimillionaire Shlomo Moussaieff, probably the most famous collector of biblical antiquities in the world, has homes in Israel, the United Kingdom, and the United States, all of them renowned for their opulence and decor. Standing in the center of Golan's apartment, I felt cheated. I was expecting Moussaieff, and I got Golan.

But then Golan pressed a button, and everything changed. Shutters rose on various walls, exposing glass shelves displaying priceless artifacts from biblical times. I now felt like I was part of a James Bond thriller, not a "James, son of Joseph, brother of Jesus" documentary.

Golan is a collector. It permeates his being. As we chatted he got a call from an Arab near the town of Hebron in the West Bank, one of those territories of ancient Israel whose ownership is disputed by Palestinians and Israelis. The man at the other end of the line had Golan go to a Web site. I followed him to his computer. And there, before my eyes, was a treasure trove of Bronze Age artifacts discovered by Palestinian youths the day before: swords, knives, jewelry, pottery, and more. After a quick glance at the merchandise, Golan bought a couple of Bronze Age swords for a couple of thousand dollars. If the biblical Exodus happened in the late Bronze Age, those swords might have belonged to Israelite soldiers serving in Joshua's army.

"The IAA doesn't know this major discovery has occurred. It will never know. The Arabs are giving me what you would call a 'first look.' Whatever I don't buy will leave the country and end up in some Tokyo executive's boardroom, lost to researchers forever. I'm performing a service for this country, ensuring that at least some of our treasures stay here. And do you think I get some honorary doctorate for my efforts? Quite the contrary. Because I buy artifacts from West Bank Arabs, the Antiquities Authority treats me like a criminal engaging in illegal activities. Does this make sense to you?" Golan asked.

Actually it did not make much sense. In fact, if I were the IAA, I would try to regulate the antiquities market by buying archaeological discoveries from Palestinian youths. It would be a kind of "clean needle program" in biblical antiquities. Don't criminalize what you can't control or punish. Regulate it.

In any event, in the fall of 2002, I didn't have deep thoughts about the trade in biblical antiquities. The only thing I was concerned with was the James ossuary and the inscription on its side: "James, son of Joseph, brother of Jesus." So all day I videotaped the various tests that the experts were conducting in Golan's apartment. André Lemaire, the great epigrapher from the Sorbonne, examined the inscription one last time, evaluating the writing style, grammar, and so on. Dr. Shimon Ilani and Dr. Amnon Rosenfeld of the Israel Geological Society examined the patina, the thin film that develops over thousands of years on the walls of the limestone boxes. For his part, Hershel Shanks was reviewing what we historically knew of James, trying to match this information with the ossuary. For example, Josephus Flavius, the first-century Jewish-Roman historian, recorded that James was killed in Jerusalem, so it wasn't surprising to find his ossuary there. The story matched the archaeology. Also, the New Testament explicitly refers to James as the "Brother of the Lord" (Galatians 1:19). So finding him linked on his ossuary to his brother was consistent with what we knew about him. The ossuary matched the New Testament.

There was a great mood in the apartment. Everyone was on the same side. The inscription was good. The grammar was good. The patina was good.

The ossuary rested on a table in the middle of the room. I peeked inside and saw bone fragments. *Jesus's family DNA!* I thought. Later I learned that Golan had put the fragments in a plastic container and given them to a friend for safekeeping.

When everyone had finished, I stayed behind for a while. Golan went to the white baby grand and started playing Beethoven. It was one of those surreal moments in life. There I was in Tel Aviv, listening to German classical music played by an eccentric Israeli collector next to the bone box of the brother of Jesus.

When Golan finished playing the sonata, I complimented him on his performance and then went back to my hotel. As I walked along the beach, the sun was setting. A Barbra Streisand song wafted out of a hummus restaurant, coincidentally called Simcha's Place. I didn't stop for a meal. I kept walking, clutching the shot tapes in my hand. I had Jesus's brother in the can! The sun was a red ball, settling into the sea, and all I could think about was the fact that practically the entire world would soon be obsessed with the images captured by my camera.

On October 21, 2002, Hershel Shanks and the Discovery Channel held a press conference in Washington, DC. The next morning, the James ossuary – in full color – appeared on the front page of the *New York Times*. In fact, the story made headlines around the world, and thirty seconds of the images I shot in Golan's apartment were beamed around the globe by CNN.

On October 31, 2002, the ossuary again made front-page news, this time because it broke en route to Toronto, where it was going to be exhibited at the Royal Ontario Museum (ROM). Again I was at the center of the action, filming the broken ossuary, the restoration process, and the ossuary's first exhibition.

One hundred thousand viewers filed past the restored ossuary during its visit to Toronto. One of them was Professor James Tabor, chair of the Department of Religious Studies at the University of North Carolina at Charlotte. In fact, I captured Tabor on tape as he examined the ossuary under glass, but I did not know this at the time. He was part of a throng of academics who happened to be in Toronto because the Society of Biblical Literature (SBL), the American Academy of Religion (AAR), the American School of Oriental Research (ASOR), and the Biblical Archaeology Society (BAS) had all decided to have their annual meetings at the same Toronto hotel. It was strange. Hershel had come to me, and more than one thousand biblical scholars also came to Toronto, as did the ossuary. It was as if all the players were following me instead of the other way around.

I didn't know Tabor at the time of the ossuary's exhibition. I spoke to him for the first time a few months later, after the ossuary had returned to Jerusalem and been declared a forgery by the IAA. He rang me at home on a Sunday evening when I was trying to help my wife put our four girls and one boy to bed. "Simcha?" I heard my Hebrew name pronounced with an accent all his own, developed as an airforce brat growing up around the world.

After we got to talking, Tabor explained that the year before he and a friend, the archaeologist Dr. Shimon Gibson, had excavated a Jerusalem tomb ransacked by robbers. In it they had found what appeared to be moldy human residue. It turned out, under the microscope, to be the oldest shroud ever found in the Jerusalem area. It was a piece of a burial shroud that dated back to the time of Jesus. The shroud had once enveloped a man who died from leprosy, or Hansen's disease. The leper was the oldest case of Hansen's disease found anywhere. The discovery proved that people were suffering from actual leprosy at the time of Jesus. Recently, some scholars have theorized that when the New Testament speaks of "leprosy," it's really only talking about skin rashes. Tabor and Gibson's find put an end to that kind of speculation.

Tabor is fascinating and friendly. He is also extremely smart and erudite. At the time he was writing his soon-to-be bestselling *Jesus Dynasty*. What I couldn't figure out was why he had called me out of the blue. "I'll confide in you," he said. "I think Oded Golan's James ossuary came from our shroud tomb. I don't think he's had it since the seventies or eighties, as he claims. I think he's had it for a year. But I do think that the inscription on it is authentic."

"Why would he lie about when he purchased the artifact?" I asked.

"Because in 1978 Israel changed its antiquities laws," Tabor answered. "So if you found or purchased something prior to '78, it's all yours. If it's after, and if it's a significant find, it belongs to the state."

"Why do you think it's from your tomb?" I asked.

"Several ossuaries were stolen from there, so he could have bought it from whoever broke into the shroud tomb. There was a Maria in the tomb, and this is only one of a handful of Marias ever found inscribed on an ossuary. If James also came from the same tomb, then maybe the shroud tomb is the Jesus family tomb."

I didn't buy Tabor's theory. The timeline was too short. Golan couldn't have bought the ossuary just a year before. It was all too fast. Golan buys it. Lemaire sees it. They make the connection to the brother of Jesus, and suddenly it's front-page news. Even if Golan hadn't bought it before the antiquities rules changed, I believed that he'd had the ossuary for a long time. If not 1978 then maybe the early 1980s. Besides, I had gotten to know Golan. Maybe he fudged things a little, but as near as I could tell, he didn't make things up out of thin air. Tabor was wrong, I thought: the James ossuary didn't come from his shroud tomb.

"Where do I fit into this?" I asked.

"Well," Tabor said quickly, "we managed to extract DNA from most of the ossuaries found in our tomb. If we can get some bone fragments from the James ossuary, we can try to extract DNA from them and compare it to the DNA in our tomb. That way we'll know if it originated there. Golan trusts you. If he's managed to recover any authenticatable bone fragments, maybe he'll turn them over to you."

"Okay, James," I said. "I'll try. But I think you're barking up the wrong tomb."

When he heard my response, Tabor wanted to know why I thought what I thought. I liked him. Most biblical scholars don't care what journalists or filmmakers think. They're so full of their own ability to quote Irenaeus that they don't discuss – they lecture. But this academic wanted to know which tomb I thought the James ossuary came from. Even though I had never met him, I trusted him. So we pledged each other to secrecy, and I told him what I thought. "I think it comes from another tomb that had a Maria ossuary in it. The Talpiot tomb," I said.

There was a moment of silence at the other end. "Isn't that the one with the Jesus and the two Marys?" he said at last.

I was impressed. Most scholars had no idea the tomb existed. "Yes," I said, "that's the one."

"But the second Mary is all wrong. It's not Magdalene," Tabor said.

"Let's meet," I suggested, "and after you sign a nondisclosure agreement, I'll tell you a secret."

*   *   *

As the old song goes: what a difference a day makes. Or a year, as the case may be. In the fall of 2002, I was in Tel Aviv shooting what promised to be one of the biggest stories of the decade. By the fall of 2003, the publicity winds had shifted. In the court of public opinion, Oded Golan had morphed from reclusive collector to master forger, and the James ossuary had been dismissed by a special panel of the IAA as nothing more than a hoax.

For my part, I stood by my documentary *James, Brother of Jesus*. It had aired Easter 2003 on Discovery Channels worldwide. Hershel Shanks also stuck by his story, and indeed he has been leading an unrelenting defense of the ossuary ever since. But from the moment the wind shifted, Hershel and I were in the minority. Everyone else melted away. Golan was roughed up by the Tel Aviv police and then taken into custody for interrogation. He was eventually charged with fraud and forgery. How did all this happen, and why?

The "how" is easy to explain. The ossuary had passed two electron microscope tests (one in Israel and the other in Canada). It had also passed inspection by the legendary epigrapher Professor Frank Moore Cross of Harvard. Toronto's Royal Ontario Museum had even subjected the inscription to a long-wave ultraviolet light examination, the purpose of which was to determine whether there were bits of foreign microscopic debris in the crevices of the inscription. There was nothing. In other words, the ossuary was one of the most tested archaeological artifacts in history, and it passed every test with flying ultraviolet colors.

But when the run at the ROM ended, the IAA refused to let the James ossuary proceed to Nashville, Tennessee, where various Christian groups were eager to display it. Instead, the IAA insisted that Golan return the ossuary to Israel. After Golan complied, the IAA confiscated the two-thousand-year-old bone box and subjected it to one more test – the oxygen isotope test, which involves the temperature at which water was absorbed onto surface minerals. The idea is that if the temperature is inconsistent with an ossuary's (presumably) unchanging life inside a tomb, then the inscription must be a forgery. The "theory," of course, depends on the assumption of a *sealed* tomb. The "test" was never designed to include the possibility of, say, a meter of *terra rossa* mud flowing indoors.

The naysayers at the IAA believed that the first part of the inscription, "James, son of Joseph," was authentic, but that Golan had added the words "brother of Jesus." Later, the Israeli police charged that by adding those words to the inscription, Golan intended to change a $500 ossuary into

a priceless religious artifact. The problem with the IAA's isotope test, which was conducted by a cowboy-boot-wearing
geologist from the University of Tel Aviv by the name of
Yuval Goren, is that the only part of the inscription that
passed was the last letter (the Hebrew "Ayin") in the word
"Jesus" ("Yeshua"). According to those freewheeling isotopes, if any part of the inscription was authentic, it was the
second half and the forger had to have added the first part
("James, son of Joseph"). Clearly, this was impossible. But
nobody seemed to notice. The story raced around the world:
an isotope test had revealed that the patina in the inscription was not consistent with temperatures in a burial tomb
and that the second part of the inscription (the Jesus part,
the part that had passed) was a forgery. In the public's mind,
it wasn't just that the inscription was now considered a
forgery – the box itself became suspect.

While the media frenzy was raging, I went to the Israel
Geological Survey, under whose auspices the isotope test was
conducted. I met with its director, Dr. Amos Bien. He is a
nervous man in his late fifties or early sixties, and as he fidgeted, he told me that the results of the isotope test could
mean one of two things: "Either the inscription was tam-
pered with ... or ..." His voice trailed off into silence.

"Or what?" I pressed.

"Or it was cleaned," he responded.

"But anyone can see that it was cleaned," I said. "You
don't need a special test for that. You can see it with your

naked eyes. In fact, last year Dr. Ilani and Dr. Rosenfeld were worried that little or none of the patina had survived the cleaning."

"Okay," said Dr. Bien.

"Okay what?" I asked. "The entire world thinks that the inscription is a fake because of a test conducted under your auspices, and you're telling me that all the isotope test proves is that it's been cleaned?" I could scarcely believe what I had just heard.

"I wouldn't put it that way," Dr. Bein said, and fidgeted some more. "But, yes, that's essentially correct."

After a moment of stunned silence, we had the following exchange:

SIMCHA: The IAA is telling the world that the inscription is a forgery!

DR. BIEN: That's their problem. Talk to them.

SIMCHA: According to the isotope test, if anything was forged, it's the first part of the inscription. The second part concerning Jesus was validated by the isotopes.

DR. BIEN: You could say that.

As of this writing, Oded Golan's trial is still making its Kafka-esque way through Israel's court system. Months into the trial, in 2006, Dr. Wolfgang Krumbein, a professor at Oldenburg University in Germany and one of the world's foremost experts on stone patina, declared the inscription authentic and the isotope test in error. But by that point, no one was listening. As far as the world was concerned, the James ossuary was an elaborate hoax created by a greedy forger who was looking to collect millions from religious Christian suckers.

Why did this happen? I don't know. What I do know is that the IAA had it in for the James ossuary. Over the years I have tried to understand why. Maybe it was a matter of ego. When the story broke, no one at the IAA knew anything about it. When the *New York Times* called for a comment, everyone there felt blindsided. When the ossuary went to Toronto, everyone felt stupid again. Golan had honestly described the ossuary as "a two-thousand-year-old bone box" when he applied for a travel permit for his archaeological artifact. He didn't point out, however, that it had possibly the only archaeological mention of Jesus of Nazareth on its side. I think the IAA decided to pay Golan back for making them feel foolish. I don't think they sat down and plotted to break him, but they might just as well have. The police turned his life into hell. In fact, for more than a year, while the trial was proceeding, Golan was under house arrest, forbidden even to walk to the corner store for groceries.

But maybe I'm wrong. There was another reason why the IAA couldn't stand Oded Golan. He's a collector, a big collector. From the IAA's perspective, collectors are the pimps of biblical archaeology. By buying artifacts, they create a market that encourages robbers to loot ancient tombs. According to the IAA, once a tomb has been robbed and the archaeological context disturbed, its unprovenanced artifacts have lost almost all historical value. The only way to protect antiquities is to destroy the collectors. The IAA was going to make an example of Golan, an arrogant collector who seemed to be thumbing his nose at the authorities. Besides, whether he forged the James ossuary or not, several IAA officials have confided in me that they are convinced that he is a forger. Given that the James ossuary came up through the antiquities market, from their point of view it has no historical value. So what did it matter if he forged this particular artifact? The important thing was to break him.

For my part, I don't believe that only artifacts found by archaeologists have historical value. It's better if archaeologists find artifacts, but it's actually a rare occurrence. To treat all artifacts that come up through the antiquities market as forgeries is foolish. Some of the greatest finds – the Dead Sea Scrolls, for instance – were discovered accidentally by ordinary people, who then sold the objects into the antiquities market. Furthermore, to decide that someone is a forger and then to treat all of his artifacts as forgeries was simply foolishness. But wherever there are frustrated cops who can't get the goods on someone they're sure is a criminal, lines are crossed. There was and continues to be a very cavalier attitude toward the James ossuary evidence.

As for me, I eventually became persona non grata at the

IAA. Their dislike of me culminated in actual charges being leveled against me in 2006 for allegedly entering a tomb without IAA permission and then damaging it. I was in good company: Dr. Shimon Gibson was also charged and dragged into police custody for questioning.* Eventually the charges against both of us were dropped.

In this atmosphere of intimidation, discovering ossuaries related to the Jesus family became a very unpopular enterprise, but that's exactly what I spent the better part of 2005 and 2006 doing.

And it all started with a phone call from Tabor in the spring of 2004. "Simcha," he said.

"Hi, James. What's up?"

"You'll never believe what I found out."

"What?" I asked.

"What do you think happened to the Talpiot tomb after its discovery in 1980?" Tabor asked, his voice rising excitedly.

"To the best of my knowledge," I replied, "there were three archaeologists involved: Yosef Gat, Amos Kloner, and Eliot Braun. They came to inspect the tomb, took out the ossuaries, and left the tomb to the builders. I guess the builders destroyed it when they put up the Talpiot apartments."

"That's what I thought," Tabor said. "But listen to this. I was in Jerusalem hanging out with my friend Shimon

---

* As of this writing, I am in the IAA's good books, having befriended the director through a mutual friend at the Israel Ministry of Tourism.

Gibson. You know Dr. Gibson, he's a pretty well known archaeologist."

"Yes," I said, "I've heard of him."

"Well," continued Tabor, "since we excavated the shroud tomb, he asked me about my conversation with you regarding bone fragments from the James ossuary, and I told him that your theory was that it came from Talpiot, not the shroud tomb. And guess who – back in 1980 – drew the map of the Talpiot tomb that appeared in Kloner's internal 1996 IAA report?" Tabor asked rhetorically.

"I have no idea. I do have a copy of the report, so I assume Kloner drew it," I said.

"Guess again, Simcha buddy." Tabor's accent gets heavier when he is animated. "It was Shimon! Can you believe that coincidence? Shimon was just a young man then, but already a seasoned surveyor with the IAA. So Kloner called him to survey the Talpiot tomb and sketch it."

"You're kidding," I said, dropping into a chair.

"It gets better." Tabor was practically crowing. "I told Shimon how it was too bad that the tomb had been destroyed, and Shimon said that he didn't think it had been!"

The Jesus family tomb is intact? I thought. It was all I could do just to stay focused on what Tabor was saying.

"It was wild," Tabor said. "Shimon and I went to Talpiot. Shimon had a hard time getting his bearings because, of course, the neighborhood looked totally different twenty-six years ago. But there's a gas station there, and he kind of figured out the general area of the tomb by using the gas station as a marker. So we started ringing doorbells. Can you imagine? One guy speaking English with an American accent, another speaking Hebrew with a British accent, ringing your doorbell and asking if you had a tomb in your basement?"

I laughed out loud. My head was spinning.

At this point, I had to ask Tabor to phone me back on my cell. My wife and kids were ready to go to a birthday party and swim at my mom's apartment building. Tabor obliged, and I listened to the rest of his report as I was loading kids into the van. The kids were fighting, swimsuits were being packed, and as the seat belts were snapped closed, Tabor continued: "So after we rang a bunch of doorbells, one guy says: 'I don't have a tomb in my house, but the family next door have one in theirs.'" Tabor laughed out loud. I screamed for the kids to be quiet, and my wife gave me the "you can't expect kids to stop being kids when you bring your work home" look.

Tabor continued: "So we go next door. They're a nice Sephardic family. At first they're a bit shocked, obviously, but they're very gracious, and they let us in. Served us, you know, Israeli-style: tea and cookies. Then they took us to their patio and – you're ready for this?" Tabor asked.

"I'm ready," I said.

"There are two *nefesh* pipes sticking out of their patio floor!"

A nefesh pipe is a soul pipe, or spirit shaft. Rabbinic authorities insist on them when a building is erected over a tomb. The pipes have two purposes: first, to allow free access between a tomb and the outside world for the souls that once inhabited the cave; and second, to provide access to a space that builders create between the roof of a tomb and the floor of the apartment above it.

The latter involves matters of ritual purity, as understood in Jewish law. The whole issue of ritual purity is a central part of life in Judaism. Some modern people confuse ritual impurity with a primitive notion of "dirty." Jewish feminists, for example, are up in arms over the fact that Orthodox Judaism treats women as ritually impure during their menstrual cycles during which time observant Jews refrain from physical contact. The feminists see this as the result of patriarchy in traditional Judaism. But they really miss the point. Men after ejaculation are also ritually impure. The body of a loved one is ritually impure after death. The idea has nothing to do with clean and unclean. It has everything to do with life and its absence.

According to Judaism, life is holy. Where life or the potential for life exists, a state of holiness also exists. When life or the potential for life departs, it leaves behind an absence, a kind of holy vacuum. Think of an amusement park or a circus after everyone has gone home. It's not just an empty place, but an emptiness that craves the life that until recently inhabited the space. That's how Judaism sees ritual impurity. Since a fertile woman possesses the potential for life, the menstrual period indicates that the potential is now absent, until the cycle begins again. Similarly, when a soul departs from a body, it leaves behind it an absence that creates a state of ritual impurity. By the same token, a tomb that still has bodies in it is ritually impure.

Practically speaking, none of this affects anyone today, except Cohens and perhaps Katzes. Among modern Jews, people with the names Cohen or Katz are descendants of biblical priests. "Cohen" in Hebrew means "priest," and "Katz" means "holy priest." Jewish priests are not allowed to come into contact with ritual impurity even today. So, according to Jewish religious law, anyone named Cohen shouldn't live in an apartment building where there is a tomb under someone's patio. It kind of ritually invalidates the entire building. Unless – and here's where rabbinic law provides the antidote – you create a kind of air cushion between the building and the tomb, that is, you don't build your patio *on top* of the tomb – instead you build a floor on top of the tomb, leave some space, then build another floor.

I now knew enough about tombs to understand what Tabor was saying: two *nefesh* pipes sticking out of the patio could mean one thing and one thing only: there was a tomb under that Sephardic family's apartment. The Jesus family tomb had not been destroyed. In fact, there was at least one pipe leading into it. I also knew immediately that I could introduce robo-cameras through the pipe and into the tomb.

If we were in the right place, we could bust through the patio floor and enter the Jesus family tomb.

I'm a filmmaker, a journalist, and a student of history. In 2004 every fiber in my body was telling me that I was on the verge of the biggest archaeological story ever – the discovery, not just of an inscription pertaining to Jesus, but of the tomb of Jesus and practically his entire family, including Mary his mother, Joseph his brother (or possibly even his father), Matthew, and Mary Magdalene. But there were a lot of questions still to be answered. Why was the Joseph ossuary inscribed "Yosa," a kind of ancient "Joey"? In fact, since Joseph (the father) disappeared from the Gospel narrative when Jesus was a boy, one would have thought, as the majority of scholars do think, that he died in Nazareth. If the Talpiot tomb was the Jesus family tomb, how could the elder Joseph have ended up in Jerusalem? Also, what was the meaning of the second Mary's inscription, "Mariamne also known as Mara"? Who was the Matthew in the tomb? Was he the writer of the Gospel that bears his name? There was a great deal of work ahead of us, and at the end of the day, I realized that it might turn out that the Talpiot tomb had nothing in the world to do with history's most famous family.

One night in the spring, after everyone had gone to bed, I sat alone in my study. On my desk I had the bible of tomb investigations in the Jerusalem area: *A Catalogue of Jewish Ossuaries* (1994) by L. Y. Rahmani. I also had Professor Tal Ilan's definitive study of Jewish inscriptions from ancient times, *Lexicon of Jewish Names in Late Antiquity: Palestine* 330 B.C.E. – 200 C.E. (2002). And of course, I had Amos Kloner's 1996 report on the Talpiot tomb. I borrowed my kids' Crayola marker and watercolor pad and flipped past their drawings to a nice blank page. On the top I wrote, "WHAT WE KNOW" in big, bold letters and underlined the heading. Underneath, I wrote the following:

1. 1980. Bulldozer reveals tomb in Talpiot, Jerusalem. IAA called in. Archaeologists arrive; Gat, Kloner, Braun, and young Gibson. They map the tomb and remove the ossuaries to the IAA warehouse, where they catalog them.

2. Tomb has weird facade. A kind of Masonic-looking symbol on it, an upside-down chevron with a circle in the middle.

3. Another weird feature: under the silt there were three skulls that had been carefully placed – almost like guardians – at the entrances to three of the burial niches.

4. The tomb was broken into in ancient times. The usual artifacts, such as small oil lamps, glass perfume bottles, and clay jugs, were missing.

5. Contents of tomb are in Rahmani's catalog. Ossuaries never left the hands of the IAA, so there are no issues concerning provenance or forgery. Four ossuaries don't have inscriptions. Six do.

6. The ossuaries are identified as follows:

a. "Jesus, son of Joseph." Hard to read but, in the end, easily decipherable. Can it be that it's hard to read for a reason? If this is Jesus's bone box, were his followers protecting it from possible enemies? Also, this is the plainest of the ten ossuaries. Ossuaries do not get plainer than this. There is no ornamentation whatsoever. Is the modesty of the ossuary consistent with what we know of Jesus? Was this Jesus buried in haste? Both?

b. "Yosa," "Jos'e," or "Joseph." Can this be the Joseph who is mentioned on the Jesus ossuary? Is this the father? Rahmani thinks so, and he notes it in his description.

c. "Maria," or "Mary." Odd inscription. Hebrew letters. Latin version of Hebrew name. The Virgin Mary's name has always come down to us as "Maria." Exactly the way it appears on the ossuary. Rahmani thinks she may have been the wife of the Joseph buried in the tomb.

d. "Mariamne also known as Mara." Greek inscription. According to prominent academics, such as professors François Bovon and Karen King of Harvard, this is Mary Magdalene's real name. The professors don't seem to know this ossuary exists. If she is Mary Magdalene, what's she doing in Jesus's "family" tomb? Were they married?!

e. "Matia," or "Matthew." Clearly, a New Testament

name. Could this be the Gospel writer? Was he related to Jesus?

f. "Judah, son of Jesus." The most explosive ossuary in the tomb. In some ways, more explosive than Jesus. If "Mariamne" was Jesus's wife, is this their son? It's the smallest ossuary in the tomb. "Judah" died as a kid? But the Gospels never mention a son? Could "Judah" be the enigmatic "Beloved Disciple" mentioned in the Gospel of John?

At the bottom of the page, I now wrote in big block letters: "NEXT STEP?"

Normally when I have a story I want to investigate, I write up a "treatment," which is a fancy film term for "proposal." I also attach a budget and production schedule to my treatment and try to get some broadcasters involved. But this seemed a problematic course of action for this story. First, there was the problem of leaks. I could take a story as big as this to a U.S. network, but they owed me no loyalty. They could steal the idea and put it on a newsmagazine program such as *60 Minutes* or *20/20* before it was properly investigated. That way they would turn the tomb into an old story before I could get started. On the other hand, I could always go to my contacts at the Discovery Channel, the people who had funded the James ossuary documentary. But given the controversy surrounding the James ossuary, they might have become ossuary-shy. Also, they were in the midst of internal changes, and this proposal might get lost in their shuffles. I didn't like my options. The trick was to get someone on board without leaking the revelations. So I decided that before I approached broadcasters, I had to get more ownership of the story. I needed to secure exclusive access to *something* – if not the ossuaries in the warehouse of the IAA, at least the tomb under the patio that Tabor found.

During most of 2005 I was shooting my archaeology series *The Naked Archaeologist* in Israel. This turned out to be very handy because I got to meet Shimon Gibson, who, along with James Tabor, had just announced to the world the discovery of what they thought was the "John the Baptist cave," a place for ritual immersion, or baptism, which had been active in the first century. The cave also had later Byzantine drawings on its walls that seemed to depict the story of John the Baptist, Jesus's cousin on his mother's side. Just as Jesus was starting his ministry, John was beheaded as a troublemaker by Herod the Great. According to the Gospels, it was John who baptized Jesus, not the other way around. It's clear from several ancient sources, including the Gospels, that in his day John was, so to speak, bigger than Jesus. John is regarded by Christian tradition as an Elijah-type figure – the one who precedes the Messiah in order to announce his imminent arrival.

Shimon Gibson is a native of the United Kingdom. When he was a youngster, his mother moved him and his twin brother to the Negev Desert in southern Israel. There, while wandering among the dunes, the young Gibson developed a love for archaeology.

I asked Shimon to be an exclusive consultant to our upcoming documentary on the Talpiot tomb, and he agreed.

"That doesn't mean I'll go along with everything you say," he said.

"I don't expect you to," I responded.

"For starters," Gibson said, "let me tell you this: the New Testament names on the Talpiot ossuaries are the most common Jewish names of first-century Israel. Statistically speaking, finding a Jesus, Mary, Judah, and so on, in the same tomb is totally meaningless. Still want me as a consultant?" He grinned.

"Are you a statistician?" I asked.

"No," Gibson answered.

"So how do you know this cluster is statistically meaningless?"

He seemed stumped. Then a broad smile spread across his face. "The second Mary, Simcha. The second Mary ruins the cluster."

I pushed a nondisclosure agreement across the table to him. "Ah," he said with a sly grin, "you have a secret."

"I do indeed."

After he signed, and with cameras rolling, I revealed to him the latest in New Testament scholarship concerning Mary Magdalene. "According to the biggies in the field,

Mary Magdalene's real name was 'Mariamne,' the exact name we find in the Talpiot tomb buried next to Jesus."

Gibson looked stunned. "Who are these 'biggies'?" he asked, sounding quite skeptical.

"François Bovon of Harvard, for one," I said more triumphantly than I should have.

"I know Bovon. He's as credible as they come. Does he know about the tomb?"

"No," I said. "I don't think so. That's the reason for the nondisclosure."

The same revelation took place in more or less the same way in a bar in Toronto with James Tabor. As tattooed hipsters played pool in the background, I revealed to Tabor the "Mariamne" connection. He nearly fell off his stool. No exaggeration. He then insisted on poring over every article that connected "Mariamne" with "Mary Magdalene."

"It'll come down to the statistics," I said.

"Well," said Tabor, "before we go there, I'm about to make your case stronger."

Now I was the one in danger of falling off a stool. "What do you mean?" I asked.

"You know how one of the ossuaries in the Talpiot tomb says 'Yosa,' which is a diminutive of 'Yosef,' or 'Joseph'?" he asked.

"Yes. Rahmani says that this Yosa is the same Joseph mentioned on the 'Jesus, son of Joseph' ossuary," I said.

"Sure. Because he assumes that since there is a 'Jesus, son

of Joseph' and a 'Joey' in the same tomb, the two inscriptions must be referring to the same Joseph," Tabor answered.

"But it makes sense," I said.

"On a superficial level," Tabor replied, and then pointed out the reference to "Yosa" in Tal Ilan's *Lexicon*. "Out of all the names inscribed on ossuaries, the 'Yosa' in the Talpiot tomb is the only 'Yosa' ever found!" he said, his eyes burrowing into mine.

"'Yosy' is a common diminutive of 'Yosef,' even today," I protested.

"That's right," Tabor said, "but not 'Yosa.' That's unheard of today, and very rare even in ancient times. Guess where we know that name from," he challenged.

"I have no idea," I conceded.

"In the Gospel of Mark," Tabor whispered as he leaned forward. "'Yosa' or Jose in English, *Joses* in Greek – is explicitly mentioned as one of Jesus's four brothers."

4

Charlie: On Probability, Possibility, and the "Jesus Equation"

In 70 C.E., *when Titus's soldiers departed Jerusalem, they hoped that they'd left behind a dead province filled with dead people. Titus, the man who would soon be emperor, believed he had put an end to the rebellious Jews and religious reformists for at least the rest of his lifetime, and perhaps for all time. Behind him, in the subterranean night, ten ossuaries lay facing the vanished Jewish Temple, as if waiting for rediscovery, or rebirth, or both. And on one of them, these words seemed poised to endure forever: "Jesus, son of Joseph."*

I met Simcha for the first time in October 2004. Simcha is next of kin to obsessively driven, and he is thoroughly polymathic. This much was obvious from the start.

After the sun had set on Toronto and after our conversations had spanned Egypt, the universe, and everything between Thera, Crete, and the Book of Exodus, Simcha told me that he had found something very strange – "something wonderful, in fact."

On that October evening, fewer than a half-dozen people on the entire planet had seen all of the archaeological puzzle pieces and understood the secret Simcha was about to reveal. Even those who excavated IAA 80/500–509 still had no real knowledge of what they had uncovered.

"Well, here's the deal," Simcha announced. "I'm going to need someone who has no particular religious ax to grind; someone I can trust to follow wherever the evidence leads. I need a lone wolf on this project, someone who will question virtually everything."

"*What* have you guys *found?*"

Simcha grinned and placed a document on the table. Its title page said simply this: "Confidentiality Agreement."

"What on earth have you found?" I asked again.

"Well," said Simcha, "let me ask you something first. Do you think it's possible that Mary Magdalene and Jesus of Nazareth could be buried together, in the same tomb?"

"That's impossible."

"Right answer. Now, do you want me to bring you into it, or not?"

He did not have to ask a second time.

Simcha was quick to point out, on the day he brought me into the story, that the chief difference between the controversial James ossuary and the similarly inscribed ossuaries from IAA 80/500–509 was that the latter had an undisputed provenance. They were mapped *in situ* (while still in their tomb); they were excavated, photographed, and cataloged by a team of archaeologists. By comparison, the James ossuary had merely materialized on the Jerusalem antiquities market, about 1980, with no documented past at all.

"The James ossuary was interesting," said Simcha, "but it was nothing at all like this tomb. The simple reality is that the Talpiot tomb was explored and documented by *archaeologists* – by a group of archaeologists who in fact did not want to discover this combination of names and who cataloged them and dutifully stored them for safekeeping. This simple reality removes all possibility that the objects or their discoverers are part of an attention-grabbing hoax."

If anything, the long silence of Kloner, Braun, and Gibson indicated the opposite of a hoax, the exact opposite of trying to attract attention to oneself. By every indication, the archaeologists had hoped their discovery would gather dust in a warehouse until they were retired and they themselves were finally dust. By then, the controversy would belong to another generation. By then, it would be someone else's problem.

In the meantime, Simcha had received copies of the archaeologists' reports and begun studying the ossuaries. He revealed to me that, while at least two of the three surviving archaeologists had believed for more than twenty years that their tomb was built over, the tomb was not destroyed but was awaiting rediscovery, somewhere beneath a so-called soul pipe.

Working from a hunch that the second Mary of IAA 80/500–509 might be connected to Magdalene, Simcha's team conducted a search of the name Mariamne; that search led, in a single stroke, to the work of François Bovon, a New Testament scholar at Harvard University.

"And do you know what we found?" Simcha asked me, after I had signed the confidentiality agreement.

He handed me a folder containing copies of an ancient manuscript, penned in Greek, along with Professor Bovon's translation. The first page was headed by the words "Acts of Philip." In this text, Mary Magdalene was an apostle who preached and baptized and performed healing miracles. This Mary was very, very different from the Magdalene of Church doctrine, and not a "fallen woman" at all.

"Did you notice the Greek version of her name?" Simcha asked.

"According to the apostle Philip, who identifies himself as Mary's brother, she is not known as Magdalene, the 'woman from Magdala.' Rather, she is known by her given name, by the same word inscribed on the side of IAA 80/500: Mariamne."

"And tell me this: just what are the odds of this?" said Simcha. The archaeologists involved in the 1980 discovery in Israel do not know about the Mariamne connection or the Acts of Philip or about the latest research concerning ancient texts of the New Testament period. Conversely, and just as amazingly, none of the leading experts on ancient Christian and Gnostic scripture knows about the tomb or about the ossuaries in the IAA warehouse."

While the Bovon-Mariamne connection was compelling, it was far from conclusive. The proof of this cluster of biblical names would be revealed in the numbers. How unusual was it, really? I needed to compare "Mariamne" and the other names, statistically, against the number of times these names appeared on other ossuary inscriptions.

But while I was thinking statistics, Simcha revealed that there was the possibility of DNA. The normal practice of the Israel Antiquities Authority was to collect the bones from recovered ossuaries and turn them over to religious authorities for reburial. However, some sort of mud, or mineralized sediment, had collected as a thin hard layer on the bottoms of several ossuaries from IAA 80/500–509. Little splinters of bone were trapped in the mineral beds, and now bone fragments from two ossuaries had been sent to a lab in

Canada. The lab had reported to Simcha earlier in the week that it looked as if DNA was extractable from the remains.

"And who are we talking about?" I asked.

"Jesus and Mariamne" came the reply.

The DNA of "Jesus, son of Joseph"? It seemed to me that Alice's fall down the rabbit hole was a paragon of predictability by comparison to the Talpiot tomb. In moments such as this, the normal reflex was to try reining in the chaos and return a measure of order to the universe.

"Wait a minute," I said. "If the numbers, after I run through them, do suggest that this is the final resting place of Jesus and his family, isn't the ossuary of the risen Christ supposed to be empty?"

"What do you think? *Should* his ossuary be empty?" asked Simcha.

"Well," I said, "maybe. Maybe not. People who believe in a physical Resurrection would not be affected by the discovery of a Jesus bone box. In the Gnostic Gospels, Jesus appears before the apostles as a sort of holy ghost – here again, gone again. And he continues manifesting in this way for almost two years after the Crucifixion. In the four Gospels, Jesus only sometimes has a physical form – as when Doubting Thomas Didymos touches the five wounds only minutes after Jesus enters the room, spiritlike, through shut doors (see John 20:26–29). The author of Luke wrote almost apologetically, acknowledging at the start that all of this sounds strange but that this is how it appears to have happened. Read your Luke and John and you'll see what I mean. These people believed in a Resurrection that at times seemed to have been more or less physical, and at other times seemed entirely spiritual.

"In any event, even a physical Resurrection doesn't depend on the fact that the first tomb was empty. It depends on Jesus's appearances among the disciples. A Christian believer can believe that Jesus was removed from the first tomb, traditionally identified with the tomb under the Holy Sepulchre in Jerusalem, and laid in a second tomb. With respect to his Ascension to heaven, the New Testament also does not tell us that its chroniclers believed that Jesus, when he ascended, needed to take his entire body with him. So if you believe in a physical Ascension, the ossuary is a problem. But if you believe in a spiritual one, it becomes an object of veneration."

Lacking a time machine, science can reveal nothing about what the disciples really witnessed or believed with regard to the Resurrection. But the statistical evidence, the clues written in the chemistry of the tomb's crystalline patina, and the results of the DNA tests were waiting to reveal whether this was the genuine article.

The Gospel according to Matthew tells us that as Jesus hung dead on the cross, the evening of the Sabbath, heralding the traditional day of rest, was almost upon the city. A wealthy and influential disciple named Joseph of Arimathea went to the Roman prefect, Pilate, and received permission to remove Jesus's body from the cross and to bury him before sunset, in accordance with Jewish law. With the Sabbath about to arrive, and with burials prohibited during the Sabbath, there was no time to do more than wrap Jesus in a shroud of cloth. Joseph of Arimathea laid the body temporarily in "his own new tomb, which he had hewn out in the rock: and he rolled a great stone to the door of the sepulchre, and departed" (Matthew 27:57–60).

Independent of the New Testament, the Roman-Jewish historian Josephus, writing in approximately 80 C.E., reported that "the Jews used to take so much care of the burial of men, that they took down those who were condemned and crucified, and buried them before the going down of the sun." (*The Jewish War,* 4:5, 2).

If all had gone according to contemporary custom, the body would have been relocated after the Sabbath and moved to Jesus's family tomb. The bones and the shroud of Jesus would have been collected from a shelf in the tomb about a year after the Crucifixion and burial. From there, they would have been placed in an ossuary and slid into a niche for a final resting place.

But as Matthew 27:61–66 tells us, all did not go according to custom. And there was Mary Magdalene, and the other Mary, sitting [that Friday evening] over and against the sepulchre. Now the next day, that followed the day of the preparation, the chief priests and Pharisees came together unto Pilate, saying, 'Sir, we remember what that deceiver said, while he was yet alive – *After three days I will rise again.* Command therefore that the sepulchre be made sure until the third day, lest his disciples come by night, and steal him away, and say unto the people, *He is risen from the dead:* so the last error shall be worse than the first. Pilate said unto them, 'Ye have a watch: Go your way, make it as sure as you can.' So they went and made the sepulchre sure, sealing the stone, and setting a watch.

It is interesting that Matthew records a contemporary tradition that shows how the authorities worried that Jesus's body would be taken by his disciples. They had gone underground, so to speak, and were not to be seen during the Crucifixion. But it was expected that they would now come and move the body. It is not odd that the authorities would have set "a watch" to secure the body of a man they perceived as a revolutionary leader, the "King of the Jews"; it is odd, however, that they would have secured the tomb by "sealing the stone." Tombs were sealed at the time of burial so as to prevent the body from being dragged away by animals. This mistake in the text is a clue that the writer of Matthew was not familiar with the mechanics of secondary burial. He probably added this scene as a way to refute a rumor that Jesus's body was taken by his disciples.

There is another clue in the text as to what might have happened that "next day," the day of the Sabbath. Obviously, "the chief priests and Pharisees" hadn't posted a guard yet. The tomb was accessible. They had assumed that Jesus's disciples would not move the body on the Sabbath since among Pharisees that would have been regarded as a desecration of the holy day. They assumed that the disciples would wait until sunset – that is, until after the end of the Sabbath – and "come by night." They may have assumed wrong. Several times in the Gospels, Jesus's disciples appear to be more lenient with regard to Sabbath law than the Pharisees and Jesus himself (see Matthew 12:1–21 for one example). It's entirely possible – using the Gospels' own timeline – that the disciples came "by day," *during* the Sabbath. If they did, they could have easily moved the body. In fact, by being positioned to act, they could have waited until sunset in the tomb and then moved the body immediately *after* sunset, but *before* the guard had been posted. So it's entirely possible that Jesus's body ended up in a family tomb. If there was such a tomb, what would it look like to modern archaeologists?

December 14, 2004
To Father Mervyn Fernando, Subhodi Institute, Sri Lanka

Dear Fr. Fernando:
An interesting question has come up in discussion,

and I would seriously like your thoughts on this, even if it is only hypothetical. What if archaeologists actually found, say, the bones and DNA of Jesus? Would a discovery such as this necessarily contradict what Christians believe about the Resurrection story?

See you later,

Your friend, Charlie P.

Dear Charles:

Your query is very interesting, though hypothetical. The Gospels which relate to the life of Jesus were probably composed between a.d. 75 and 110. Among the earliest New Testament writings are some of the letters of St. Paul. The "classical locus" about the Resurrection of the body is in St. Paul's first letter to the Corinthians, end of chapter 15, verse 35 onwards. What he says there would apply to the Resurrection of Christ, too. That is, the risen body of Christ (as understood by the apostle Paul) is a spiritual one, not the material/physical one he had in his lifetime. That physical body would have perished, and if any parts of it (bones) are recovered/identified, it would in no way affect the reality of his Resurrection. Warm and heartfelt greetings for a joyful Christmas and a New Year full of divine blessings.

– Mervyn

It would all come down to statistics, I figured. After the story came out, after the requisite howls of derision, rewriting of history and retraction of statements, the facts of the Talpiot tomb would stand. They were simply too clear cut. And then, it would come down to statistics. "What are the odds," people would ask, "that the Talpiot tomb really belongs to Jesus of Nazareth, and not some other Jesus?"

So by New Year's Day 2005, I had a list of names from scores of ossuaries discovered in the Jerusalem hills, along with commentary from epigraphers so experienced at reading inscriptions that they could sometimes identify the same handwriting on ossuaries unearthed kilometers apart. It was time to do a preliminary statistical analysis. Israeli archaeologists had dismissed the Talpiot cluster without even contacting a statistician. I have training in statistics, so I gave it a go.

I sat on my favorite bench in Central Park. Young people on rollerblades were whizzing by, and chess players were deep in thought surrounded by clusters of onlookers. I took an unused chess table and put two notepads on it. One yellow, one white. On the yellow pad I wrote: "Preliminary Underlying Assumptions." The white pad was for the math.

The math of IAA 80/500–509, a.k.a. the Talpiot tomb, was a matter of seeing if one could "prove" that the Talpiot tomb was the tomb of Jesus of Nazareth by taking the most conservative statistical approach possible. I started, naturally, by going straight after the "Jesus" inscription. How would that name stand up against a couple of hundred inscriptions on other ossuaries? How common was "Jesus, son of Joseph"?

According to scholars such as L. Y. Rahmani, Tal Ilan, and Rachael Hachlili, Jesus and Joseph were common names in first-century Jerusalem; for example, among the 233 inscribed ossuaries cataloged by the IAA, the name Joseph appeared 14 percent of the time and Jesus appeared 9 percent. It is estimated that, at most, during the entire period of ossuary use in Jerusalem the male population was 80,000. Out of these, 7,200 would have been called Jesus and 11,200 would have been called Joseph. Multiplying the percentages against each other (.09 × .14 × 80,000), we get 1,008 men who would have been called Jesus, son of Joseph during the century of ossuary use. In other words, approximately one in 79 males was called Jesus, son of Joseph. On my white pad, I wrote: "1 out of 79."

But how many of those 1,008 men living right before, during, and after the time of Jesus of Nazareth were buried with a Maria or a Judah or a Matthew?

From this point onward, the "Jesus equation" was simply a matter of factoring the probability of each name in the tomb cluster, one after the other, and multiplying them against each other.

Nearly one-quarter of all the women known from ossuaries of the time were named Mary or some close variation thereof. But ossuary 80/505 told a different statistical story.

This "Mary" was a Latinized version of the Hebrew name. As it turns out, James Tabor and Shimon Gibson would later find a very similar inscription in their "Tomb of the Shroud," but in 1980 the Mary of IAA 80/505 was quite rare, written in Hebrew letters as "Maria."

A similar first-century inscription, "Maria," was known from the ruins of Pompeii's "House of the Christian Inscription." So it might have been adopted as the Christian version of "Miriam" because that was how Jesus's mother was known. As it also turned out, Mary of Nazareth, in the Acts of Philip and in other surviving apocryphal books, was differentiated from Mary Magdalene by the name Maria.

Professor Tal Ilan records 8 Marias on 193 ossuaries. Therefore, approximately one out of 24 females was called Maria. So I wrote "1 out of 24" on my white pad.

"Judah, son of Jesus" had never been specifically mentioned in either noncanonical or canonical versions of the New Testament. And though the Jesus of the Gospels had both a beloved brother and a trusted disciple named Judah, I decided to attach no mathematical significance to *this* ossuary. Any value would have lowered the probability and therefore helped our case. So, taking a conservative approach, I neutralized this ossuary completely.

Next came the "Mary" known as "Mariamne," inscribed in Greek on ossuary number 80/500. The name was actually written "Mariamn-u," that is "... of Mariamne" with a decorative flare, or tail, at the end. The "nu" was a diminutive of the more familiar "Mariamne," which itself was a Greek version of Miriam – in English, Mary.

The second part of the inscription "Mara" was a Greek rendering of an Aramaic word meaning "Lord" or "Master."

The complete inscription could be read as "*of* Mariamne, also called Lord/Master."

The title on the ossuary seemed perfectly consistent with the Mariamne described in the Acts of Philip as the sister of Philip. There she is described as an apostle or "master." She is also explicitly equated with the woman the Gospels call Mary Magdalene.

Professor James Tabor pointed out that the same grammatical structure on a handful of ossuaries from other sites revealed that the introductory "of" referred to the ossuary itself, and that the inscription could therefore be read as: "(This is the ossuary) of Mariamne, also known as the Master."

This inscription, and it fits with what we know of Mary Magdalene, presents us with a unique situation: there is simply no other ossuary inscription like it. Since it was a one of a kind, out of 193 inscribed ossuaries with women's names, one could say that only one in 193 women could have been called "Mariamne also known as Mara." On my pad I wrote "1 out of 193."

At this point, I multiplied 1 over 79 by 1 over 24 by 1 over 193; what I got was 365,928. Meaning, based on a preliminary calculation, it was possible to say that the number of men likely to be called "Jesus, son of Joseph," to be found in a tomb with a Latinized "Maria," and to be associated in that *same* tomb with a Greek-inscribed "Mariamne also known as Master" accounted for *one* out of about 365,928. Put in a different way, since – at most – only 80,000 males lived in Jerusalem during the time period of ossuary use, it would take about four Jerusalems to produce another Jesus with this combination of names on the ossuary.

One thing was already certain: even though "Jesus," "Joseph," and "Mary" were common names in first-century Jerusalem, the *cluster* of those names now appeared very uncommon. Step by sequential step, the numbers were saying that this combination of names should *not* have occurred by chance even once during the entire lifetime of Jerusalem's ossuary culture. More and more, with each new entry in the "Jesus equation," Simcha's belief that the Jesus family tomb had been discovered was evolving, before my very eyes, from a preliminary hypothesis into a viable theory. This was the result from only four ossuaries, and there were two ossuaries yet to come.

The next ossuary was "Jos'e." The Gospel of Mark (6:3) makes specific mention that Jesus had brothers and sisters, and names the brothers: "Is not this the carpenter, the son of

Mary, the brother of James and Jos'e, and of Judah, and Simon? And are not his sisters here with us?" In the Gospel of Mark, Jesus's brother Joseph is known by his nickname, "Jos'e," just as the name appears on ossuary number 80/504.

In his approach to the "Jos'e" inscription, Amos Kloner, trying to propose alternative explanations and acting from legitimate scientific skepticism, had argued that, though "Jos'e" was an uncommon inscription, it was a contraction of "Joseph," the second-most-common name during the Second Temple period.

There was, however, another way of interpreting the "Jos'e" inscription. The nickname was unique. It did not appear on any other known ossuary, and it was mirrored in the New Testament. Factoring the inscription at almost one in 519 male ossuaries recorded by Professor Tal Ilan, and multiplying 365,928 by 519, we get almost 190 million.

But on a gut level, that seemed too much. So I decided to agree with Kloner and to treat the "Jos'e" inscription as just another "Joseph" in the tomb. I was going with 14 percent of males being called Joseph, that is, one out of every seven. If we multiply 365,928 by 7, we get one in just over 2.5 million.

"Checkmate," said the old man sitting next to me.

And then there was Matthew.

Some names, such as Jonah and Daniel, would have led us

to question the entire assemblage because they did not appear in either Joseph's or Mary's family tree as provided in the Gospels. Assuming that the genealogy in Luke 3 describes that of Mary, the mother of Jesus, as many scholars believe, "Matthew" was a common name in her family. It is, as James Tabor has argued, a priestly name, and Mary, by her relationship with Elizabeth, mother of John the Baptist, had a priestly connection. Also, Mary's grandfather was called Matthew, so it is entirely possible that, for example, a first cousin called Matthew, after the grandfather, might be buried in the family tomb. Furthermore, in the Acts of the Apostles (1:23–26), there is an interesting incident where Jesus's disciples vote on who will replace Judas Iscariot. A Matthew is elected. If this Matthew was a member of the family, that would explain his sudden elevation to the status of disciple. In any event, the "Matthew" inscription on the ossuary in the Talpiot tomb did not explicitly match any known family member. Statistically, it didn't *invalidate* anything, but neither did it *validate* anything. I discounted it.

Now I turned my attention to a number of symbols that seemed to accompany the inscriptions. Among the nine limestone boxes that had been authenticated and cataloged, there existed symbols and letters of seemingly chilling improbability. On 80/503, an odd mark preceded the words "Jesus, son of Joseph." Nearly two millennia ago, someone had scratched a large *cross*-mark into the limestone, attaching its base precisely to the bottom of the first stroke of the word "Jesus." The cross stood taller than the name and was tilted to the right side of the inscription (that is, at the beginning of the right-to-left Hebrew writing), at an angle eerily suggestive of medieval church imagery showing Jesus carrying his own instrument of torture and humiliation. The depth and width of the mark were identical to the strokes of each letter in the inscription, suggesting that the cross and the words were etched with the same stylus, by the same hand, and at the same time – with the cross etched only seconds ahead of the name.

In his 1996 report, Amos Kloner had dismissed the cross-mark as an engraving made either by a stonemason or by the person who had collected the bones for the Jesus ossuary. Such incisions were believed to have aided masons and family members in matching the proper lids to the proper ossuaries in the proper orientations. A small "V" or an "X" on the left side of an ossuary, matching the same small incision on the left side of a lid, would have been consistent with the many examples of matching "mason's marks" known from other ossuaries. However, mason's marks did not typically occur as *part* of someone's name, nor were they typically inscribed *larger* than the name itself; they also typically had a matching mark on the lid.

In this case, the most glaring anomaly of all (if the cross was to be explained away as a mason's mark) was that instead of being matched by a large cross (or a cross of any kind) on the lid of the "Jesus" ossuary, there was, on the lid, a "V," or chevron, and a deeply incised, six-spoked star (with one of its spokes diverging into a barely discernible "V"). Whatever the cross, the star, and the "V" meant, they had no precedent in the realm of mason's marks.

The ossuary of "Matthew" also bore strange symbols. On the vessel's inner surface, someone had inscribed what appeared to be hastily scrawled letters of the Hebrew alphabet: a lower-case "Mem" (the letter m), a lower-case "Tav" (t), and a lower-case "Hey" (a). The symbols remained, for the moment, "illegible." But they could be read as "Matya," – Matthew. Perhaps this was a mason's note to himself prior to adding the more formal inscription outside.

Mariamne's ossuary displayed two side-by-side Vs (with no matching mason's marks on the lid).

Ossuary 80/506 had no name. Only a solitary symbol spoke clearly: a cross-mark dominated one whole side and was larger than a mason's mark had any right to be. In his report, Kloner had dismissed IAA 80/506 thus: "The rear panel bears another large mason's mark."

Amos Kloner would remain forever reluctant to consider viewing the cross-marks or the chevrons or the Hebrew "Taws" as anything more significant than a collection of mason's autographs. The cross, especially, would be a point of contention, against which he would argue the widespread textbook dogma that the symbol of the cross never came into use as a Christian symbol until Constantine's time, about 312 C.E.

In order to merit so many decades of repetition as to become a self-perpetuating "fact," one would have expected that the 312 C.E. dividing line – "if you see the symbol of a fish, it's *before* Constantine; if it's a cross, it came *after* Constantine" – would be based on volumes of data actually pinpointing, in time, a couple of hundred cross and fish symbols found in archaeological sites.

Surprisingly, any careful backtracking to its origin quickly revealed that the Constantine dividing line had been around since about (or slightly before) the nineteenth century and appeared to have been based on no data at all; it was a self-fulfilling prophecy, a tautology. Indeed, the symbols – the fish and the cross – had become key diagnostic features in dating an archaeological site. Put simply: fish means you're digging down before 312 C.E.; cross means after.

In the manner of all tautologies, such dogma had made many explorers victims of a curious logic: if you found a cross inscribed on an artifact, this meant that the artifact was inscribed *after* 314 C.E.; if you could prove that the artifact (as in the case of the Jesus ossuary) dated from, say, about 70 C.E., then the inscription was surely anything but a cross.

The fact is that the early Jesus movement would not have adopted an instrument of torture as a religious symbol. As the Dominican father Jerome Murphy-O'Connor, New Testament professor at Jerusalem's École Biblique, once stated, "For early Christians to walk around with crosses around their necks would have been like people today wearing little electric chairs around their necks." But this doesn't mean the early followers of Jesus didn't use crosslike symbols that did not represent the Roman cross. In other words, the early Jesus movement may very well have used a crosslike sign as a religious symbol, but it would not have represented the instrument of torture on which Jesus was nailed. Crosslike symbols probably predated Constantine's cross and only later became transformed into the symbol of the cross we know today.

In January 2005, the "Jesus" ossuary and its "cross" cried out for a reality check: archaeological glimpses into the earliest decades of Christianity revealed that a multitude of sects were already using symbols of the cross by the time Vesuvius buried Pompeii, some forty years after Jesus and the Crucifixion. In Egypt about 80 C.E., people who worshiped Isis and Osiris, Seth and Jesus, and who called themselves Gnostics were prefacing the chapters of their Gospels – chapters that already spoke of Jesus's Crucifixion and Resurrection – with hand-painted crucifixes that had been merged with the ancient Egyptian symbol for "life," the "ankh." Thus, west of Jerusalem, on the Nile, more than two centuries *before* Constantine, a Christian-like sect had hybridized the ankh and the cross.

In Pompeii's lesser-known sister city, Herculaneum, the Vesuvian ash cloud of 79 C.E. had cocooned a mansion all the way up through its second floor, with every strip of wood not merely fossilized but preserved intact and without decay for two millennia. On the upper floor of this "House of Justa," a small room, or "chapel," had been painted plain white – the only room in the estate that was not decorated with elaborate frescoes. On one side of the room, a perfectly preserved wooden shrine resembled the ornate pagan shrines found in neighboring homes, except that this shrine, like the room itself, was small and plain – and its base had been designed to allow one person to kneel. On top of the wooden "altar," at eye level to the kneeling person (presumably the leader of the congregation), lay a simple bowl. And above the eye level of the kneeling worshiper, a wooden cross had been affixed with nails to the wall.

If, by about 80 C.E., crosses or crosslike symbols could appear at two points across the Mediterranean – in Egypt and in Italy – then why not also in Israel's Tomb of Ten Ossuaries?

There really was no reasonable argument against people in Jerusalem, if they followed Jesus's brother James and believed in Jesus as a Prophet or Messiah, using the symbol of the cross as early as 70 C.E.

Insofar as the statistics of IAA 80/500–509 were concerned, however, I decided not to incorporate *any* of these marks into the "Jesus equation." One reason for this was that there existed no reliable means of assigning actual number-values to symbols that had not yet been cross-referenced in a census of other ossuaries – especially if some of those other "cross-marks" and "chevrons" had matching symbols on ossuary lids and might indeed represent some sort of mason's marking system.

Professor Camille Fuchs, a professor of statistics at Tel Aviv University, said that in evaluating ossuary inscriptions of this kind, we have to remember that only a small *elite* could afford family crypts and that inscribed ossuaries represented *literate* people, who themselves were a fraction of the Jerusalem population at the time. Had I lowered the population of Jerusalem during the period of ossuary use by limiting our investigation to well-to-do literate people, the numbers would have played too strongly in our favor. I decided to ignore both wealth and literacy.

At this point in my statistical analysis, my probability factor held at one in 2.5 million. Meaning, the odds were 2.5 million to one in favor of the Talpiot tomb being the tomb of Jesus of Nazareth.

*   *   *

In 130 C.E., *the emperor Hadrian, grieving over the death of his young lover Antinous, noticed a new star flaring suddenly brighter than the rest. He named the dying sun Antinous, believing it somehow embodied the young man's soul. The name would scarcely outlive Hadrian's dream to build an everlasting "Temple of Jupiter" upon the rubble atop Jerusalem's Temple Mount. Hadrian's dream, predictably, ignited a second Jewish revolt, just as people, some six decades after the first revolt and the burning of Jerusalem, thought it was finally safe to return to the city.*

By 180 C.E., when Jerusalem was once again being rebuilt and the Crab Star glowed as red as blood, the early Church father Irenaeus of Lyon wrote condemnations against the Gospel of Judas, the Dialogue of the Savior, and the Gospel of Mary Magdalene. Many changes had occurred among the followers of Jesus. Having begun their ministry, apparently, as a Jewish reformist movement never intending to start a new religion, they had split, by Irenaeus's time, into Judeo-Christian, Gnostic, and Gentile Roman/Greek sects every bit as antagonistic toward one another as Irish Catholics and Protestants of some still remote future.

Meanwhile, the ten ossuaries continued their journey toward a distant, troubled generation, with all of their secrets intact and unchanging.

5

Charlie: Beyond the Book of Numbers

So far, the secret itself was still safe. But mounting an expedition to locate and film the tomb and to pursue all the inevitable laboratory work would require bringing production executives and scientific specialists into the confidentiality agreement. With each new signature, a new element of uncertainty would enter the project: all that was necessary for the story to break in the news and mushroom out of control before we had all the science or had checked and triple-checked the evidence was for just one person to break under the burden of what he or she knew and start dropping hints about knowing where the tomb of Mary Magdalene and Jesus of Nazareth – and their son too – might be found. No one had yet leaked any actual details about what had been found or what was being learned. But beyond those few who were pledged to confidentiality, there was an expanding circle of people with need-to-know status who were handling assigned fractions of the project without knowing what the collective whole meant. The parts they were handling were hints in their own right, and these were, by necessity, intelligent and competent people. Sooner or later, the veil of secrecy was bound to fray.

For the time being, Simcha's people had given the expedition an appropriate but misleading title: "Project Egypt." The desks in their offices were covered with Coptic-to-English translations of Gnostic texts, the majority of them from Nag Hammadi, Egypt. Project Egypt seemed as good a title as any for hiding a secret in open view.

"So here's the deal," said Simcha. "We've got many months of work ahead of us, and we've got to bring several new people into it – "

"And each person you bring in is a potential risk," I said.

"Exactly. So the question of the hour is: who do we trust?"

I did not have to think about it for very long. "During my life," I told Simcha, "I've met thousands of people. I trust six. One of those six happens to be James Cameron."

Polymaths.

Somehow, they always seem to find one another.

Not many people knew, in 2004, that the landing system for a Mars probe had been designed by *Terminator* creator James Cameron, or that the filmmaker was a co-designer of the Europa space probe, or that he had led some of history's most fascinating deep-ocean scientific expeditions, or that he could hold his own in multiple scientific fields simultaneously.

If you have ever wondered where the polymathic artist-scientist-explorers of our time are hiding – the Da Vincis of our time – they're not painting canvases and chapel walls. They're pushing forward the frontiers of a newer medium, painting pictures that move and sing, sometimes in high-definition 3-D. It seemed logical to the point of crashingly obvious that after the tremendous economic success of his 1997 film *Titanic*, James Cameron, freed at last to do whatever he wished, turned more and more of his attention to engineering and science, to exploration, and to filming documentaries about scientific adventure. The path he chose seems obvious now – as obvious as most of history's surprises are when viewed with 20/20 hindsight.

Simcha Jacobovici was another of those twenty-first-century, camera-wielding polymaths, another seeker who was drawn to documentary filmmaking, partly because it sometimes allows people a life devoted almost entirely to learning. It should have surprised no one, therefore, with regard to the Tomb of Ten Ossuaries, that Simcha was the first to zero in on a few unconnected dots unrecognized by the specialists.

But we didn't contact Cameron right away. Throughout February 2005, the chatter and speculation about something unusual in "Egypt" began intensifying throughout the journalistic community. Simcha received notice from some big-time television producers that they knew he was on to something big, and they seemed to be offering a "no expense spared" sponsorship if he would join forces with them to the exclusion of all others.

The project was beginning to unravel fast, Simcha judged. Before the tomb could even be located, he feared the cat was going to get out of the bag. If this happened, one could only guess at what mistaken or even divisive interpretations could be broadcast to the world in the rush to be first with the news, or what damage might be done before IAA 80/500–509 could be properly studied and protected.

The worry about leaks was like a thousand paper cuts, and now people were beginning to sprinkle salt onto the wounds. As a filmmaker, Simcha had involved a broadcaster whom he trusted. He was hoping that the search for the tomb and the science that would follow would be financed by the making of a documentary film. But for one reason or another, the broadcaster was now hesitating to green-light the project.

"Does your offer to introduce me to James Cameron still stand?" Simcha asked. "And can he keep a secret?"

"I'll bet my reputation on it."

March 8, 2005
Dear Jim:

I'm attaching my preliminary report ... Sorry I could not tell you anything about it when we met in January; but you'll understand after you've read the details ... I've been working on this for a while – at first as devil's advocate trying to explain away the assemblage of ossuaries and artifacts as a statistical anomaly. As you'll see, the probability of the assemblage is one chance in about 2 million. The Mount Athos Codex (the Acts of Philip) which I shall send separately, after the Non-Disclosure Agreement, parallels the burial cluster I have identified for the tomb – which pushes the probability curve to even more incredible levels. This was all found in situ, in its true archaeological context, and excavated by archaeologists. So, what we're dealing with is, as usual, serious and thoroughly tangible forensic archaeology.
See you later.
– Charlie P.

March 8, 2005
Simcha:

This is the ultimate archaeology story, if it can be verified. And of course the ramifications throughout the world will be profound. I'd love to work with you on this. I can't promise that I will do it as of this

moment, I'd need to know a lot more, but I can
promise you absolute secrecy ... You should send me
your non-disclosure agreement, so we can meet (you,
Charlie, myself) and discuss this further.
   Thanks,
   – Jim

On March 21, 2005, Simcha, Jim, and I met at Jim's sprawling Malibu home to discuss the project for the first time. Within seconds we all felt comfortable with each other and, in deference to Simcha, over kosher vegetarian food we got down to business.

"The thing that disturbs me about this story," said Jim, "is how people seem to have just looked away, and looked away. Yes – I can understand that they were missing a vital piece of information: the 'Mariamne' name, spelled that way in Greek ... but how could everybody ignore this compelling cluster of names?"

Anyone could hear the frustration in Jim's words. The scientists who first entered the Talpiot tomb were an enigma to him, having behaved as if they truly lacked scientific curiosity. Either that, he guessed, or they had been afraid of something.

"You have to get into the Israeli mind-set. The names on the ossuaries, as far as Israeli archaeologists are concerned, are typical first-century Jewish names," Simcha replied. "So they weren't about to touch a politically and religiously sensitive issue for the sake of some very common Jewish names. But they would have taken notice if they knew about the connection between 'Mariamne' and 'Magdalene.'"

"I understand that Mariamne is a key piece of the puzzle," Jim said. "But someone should have noticed. Look at Charlie's statistical analysis of the number of people alive at that time in Jerusalem."

"It's a very narrow window," Simcha confirmed. "Maximum of a hundred years."

"Yes. And throughout that span, a maximum of seventy to eighty thousand people," I said.

"Ending in 70 C.E.," Simcha added.

"Not a very big window at all," Jim agreed. "So, even though Jesus and Joseph may be common names, each showing up on maybe one out of every ten or twenty ossuaries, it's like saying, 'Pick a number between one and ten.' Those are common numbers. But a four-digit combination lock, with each wheel ranging from zero to nine, has a ten-thousand-to-one probability. That's why combination locks work. How could they not have seen it?"

"They're not statisticians," Simcha said. "And they didn't turn to statisticians. It's called *chutzpah*."

"I don't know about that," Jim continued. "Even setting aside the Mary Magdalene piece, it still seems like there was a very small number of families that could have owned this tomb. Maybe it's a handful. But even if you had a one-in-five chance that it was the Jesus family, why would you just let the tomb be plowed over – which is essentially what the IAA believed had been done? Destroyed! And why would you just let the ossuaries be filed away in silence? I'm concerned that there's an agenda."

"And here's *another* oddity," I put in. "Do you realize how obscure Kloner's 1996 report really is? A tomb of this size, with its unusual ornamentation over the entrance, should have been published in one of the field's more widely read journals."

"Weird," said Jim. "They never published an academic report."

"You must understand," I explained, "that Kloner's 1996 report was probably read by only a few dozen people – maximum. An internal IAA report would have, by its very nature, blended undetectably into the background of more than a thousand similar ossuary catalogs. So if you never saw the IAA's internal report, or if you happened not to be an avid reader of ossuary catalogs …"

"You wouldn't have known that this tomb exists," said Jim.

"And *that*," said Simcha, "is why Professor Bovon at Harvard never knew! When I met him, he was writing a paper about Mary Magdalene and mentioned, almost in passing, that her name was really 'Mariamne.' He had documented every instance in which 'Mariamne,' or 'Mariamn-u,' or some other variation on the name was mentioned. The only thing Bovon never mentioned was the Mariamne ossuary. He still doesn't know about it. He's not an archaeologist."

"The pieces have to be put together," Jim said slowly. "And the only ones sitting at the nexus of all this information right now ..."

"Right now about half of us are sitting at this table," said Simcha.

"What about the 'Judah, son of Jesus' ossuary? What's he doing there?" Jim injected.

"After they killed fathers, they went after their kids," Simcha said. "The Romans didn't mess about. They called Jesus 'King of the Jews.' They mocked his royal lineage. Any surviving son would have been a target. He had to be hidden. That's why we haven't heard of him."

"Personally, Jim, I think he's the 'Beloved Disciple,'" I said.

"Or is he Judah, the brother of Jesus mentioned in Mark? Or, are they all one and the same – 'Beloved Disciple,' 'brother,' 'Son,'" I said, looking at Jim and Simcha. "Look at the history of Roman slaughter. The children of a contender were doomed – and yet, siblings were sometimes allowed to survive. When they killed Caligula, they also killed his infant child, but his sisters were spared, and his uncle Claudius even survived to become emperor. So, within Jesus's inner circle, they knew that the Romans would kill the Prophet's child, while a little brother might be granted at least a fighting chance."

"So what you're saying is that Judah, the 'little brother' of Jesus might actually have been the child of Jesus all along," said Jim. "And the key to his survival was for the disciples to say he was really someone else's child."

"It's not impossible," I said. "Remember, even in the Bible it states that Abraham said his wife Sarah was really his sister in order to save himself. Also, according to Eusebius, around fifty years after the Crucifixion, the emperor Domitian hauls two of Judah's grandsons before him because the Romans still feel threatened by the descendants of Jesus."

"It sounds like madness when you first hear it," Jim thought aloud, "but there's a certain logic to it. The existence of this child of 80/501, this child Judah, would have been concealed – probably even from most of the disciples – when Jesus was still alive. Concealed, probably, by Jesus's directive."

At this point, Simcha revealed something new. "There were ten ossuaries in the tomb. Ten were cataloged. Six had inscriptions. Four did not. But Tabor and Gibson checked the old records and guess what?" Simcha said.

"What?" Jim and I both asked.

"There are only nine ossuaries in the IAA warehouse. One's gone missing."

"Which one?" we asked.

"80/509, a 'plain' ossuary," Simcha answered. "But it's the only one not photographed and its measurements are rounded out."

"What do you make of this missing ossuary?" Jim asked.

"I figure it went missing somewhere between Talpiot and the IAA headquarters at the Rockefeller Museum," Simcha said. "What must have happened was that somebody took an ossuary. And the next day Gat and the others had to start explaining why they counted and measured ten and why they brought only nine into the warehouse. So number 509 ends up being written down as broken or damaged, with rounded measurements – 60 by 26 by 30 centimeters – with no photo, and with a notation that it was 'plain,' lacking visible inscriptions."

"And that was that. Nobody questions it. Nobody thinks about it. Nobody cares?" I said.

"Why is this missing ossuary important?" Jim asked.

"Because I think it's the James ossuary," Simcha answered.

"I thought that was a forgery," Jim said.

"Everyone thinks so. Because that's how the story's been spun," Simcha said. "But I think it's the real deal. Besides, nobody argues that the ossuary is fake, and nobody argues that the first part, 'James, son of Joseph,' is anything but authentic. Everyone's arguing about the second part of the inscription: 'brother of Jesus.' Let's say it could be demonstrated that the missing ossuary is the James ossuary ..."

"Adding James to the cluster would send the statistics into the stratosphere," I said. "There'd be no question that this is the Jesus family tomb."

Nothing was going to keep them from passing through the doors into *this* lost world. None of them in the room that day in California was going to pass this cup away. The Tomb of Ten Ossuaries was a mystery beyond imagining, emerging as if by sheer accident, into their own time. Like a message in a bottle, the cluster of ossuary inscriptions had sailed a gulf of two millennia, bringing its odd mixture of archaeology and the sacred, of DNA and patina, of Jesus and Magdalene. It drew the three of them toward a family about whom the world had received, until now, only biblical accounts and vague historical mentions, and one member of that family – "Judah, son of Jesus" – was a person about whom history had known nothing at all.

As they made preparations to examine the tomb, the artifacts, the scriptures, and the apocrypha, they also knew that they would come closer and closer to that most famous of families. Their own lives would become haunted and occasionally deeply troubled by the past, by the scientific and the sacred, by the profound and the profane. Once you begin to reconstruct a vanished people or a family and bring them alive in imagination, you create, after a fashion, ghosts in the mind's eye.

April 5, 2005
Dear Charlie:

The documentary film is a go. Within days of Jim

joining the team we were able to get broadcaster support from the Discovery Channel, C-4 in the U.K., and Vision TV in Canada. The quest for the tomb can truly begin.

Best,

Simcha

*   *   *

Below Jerusalem, still sleeping within the earth, bones in the Tomb of Ten Ossuaries continued to bathe in mineral vapor. By 312 C.E., when Constantine ceased fighting against Christians and decided to join them instead, the bones had already acquired substantial membranes, or patinas, of calcium, silicon, and trace metals. Sometimes – as in the case of the ossuary that would one day be called IAA 80/506 – much of an inscription or decoration eventually suffers evaporation and is rendered indecipherable (save for, in the case of 80/506, the large cross-mark on one side). In other places, a patina grows, layer upon layer, almost like the layers of a pearl (albeit even more slowly). The mineral patina, as it accretes onto the surfaces of teeth and brow ridges, forms an occasionally preservative and self-sealing shell, an additional layer of shelter against the outside world. One of the defining characteristics of a tomb's patina is that, like the organic gemstone amber, if it grows thick enough, it might preserve traces of marrow and dried blood, including DNA, the molecular software in which every human being is uniquely written.

6

A Mary Named Mariamne

The pinnacles of Mount Athos rise out of the Aegean Sea like the watchtowers of a lost city, guarding the northeastern shore of Greece.

During the autumn squall season, processions of monks and pilgrims climb the stone towers, whose summits are often completely hidden by low-hanging cloud banks. On terraces and cliffs, mist-shrouded gardens are filled with all manner of fruit-bearing trees. And whenever the winds shift and the clouds disperse, the highest of Athos's twenty cliff-top monasteries attain stunning views of the Aegean Islands, spreading westward in long chains toward the volcanic remnants of Thera.

The Acts of Philip is an apocryphal New Testament text left out of the official canon. In the second century, "apocryphal" meant either "secret" or "rejected." The Acts of Philip was widely quoted by early Christian writers but was eventually lost save for a few fragments. In 1976 scholars François Bovon and Bertrand Bouvier were permitted to examine the contents of the library at the Xenophontos Monastery on Mount Athos. There, miraculously preserved, they discovered an almost complete fourteenth-century copy of the Acts of Philip transcribed from texts compiled perhaps a thousand years earlier.

In June 2000, Bovon and Bouvier published the first complete translation – into French – of the Mount Athos version of the Acts of Philip, with its identification of Mary Magdalene as "Mariamne," the sister of the apostle Philip. The Acts of Philip provides us with a much more complete version of Mary Magdalene than the Gospels.

In 2006 Simcha met Professor Bovon at the Harvard School of Divinity where Bovon teaches. "This is how the story unfolds," Bovon explained. "In the Acts of Philip, you have two parts. In the first part, Philip is sent on his way by the risen Jesus, but he is weak and full of anger, and afraid to go alone. And in the second part, his sister, Mariamne, is with him, and also the apostle Bartholomew."

"'And it came to pass,' the eighth chapter, ninety-fourth verse of the Acts of Philip begins, 'that when the Savior divided the apostles and each went forward according to his lot, it fell to Philip to go to the country of the Greeks.'

"Upon hearing this, Philip burst into tears. 'And he thought it hard,' this dangerous assignment, and he weakened his resolve, whereupon Jesus turned to Philip's sister, to strengthen and to guide him: 'I know, thou chosen among women [that your brother is vexed]; but go with him, and encourage him, for I know that he is a wrathful and rash man, and if we let him go alone he will bring many retributions upon men [in punishments wrought by heavenly and corruptible power]. But lo, I will send Bartholomew and John to suffer hardship in the same city, because of the great wickedness [among] them that dwell there ... And do thou – change thy woman's aspect – and go with Philip.' And to Philip, [Jesus] said, 'Why art thou fearful? For I am always with thee.'

"When you follow the early chapters of this journey," said Bovon, "the scribes have the Lord saying to Mary, 'You are a woman, but you have the [inner, spiritual] strength of a man, and you must comfort and give council to your brother.'

"And she is a strong figure, Simcha – identical to the picture of Magdalene we receive from another ancient text, the Gnostic Gospel of Thomas. According to these scribes, Jesus seemed to empower women. This must have been revolutionary in his time – this idea that a woman could be the priestly and spiritual equal of the male. As a matter of fact, this sister of the apostle Philip, when we first meet her, is already very strong and faithful and close to the Lord, whereas Philip begins in much the opposite direction."

"Now," asked Simcha, "does it specifically say that Mariamne is his sister?"

"Yes," Bovon said quickly. "It is explicit that she's not his sister in only a spiritual sense; she is clearly a sister in the family of Philip. And it's also made clear that this Mary cannot be confused with the mother of Jesus, because Mary the Virgin is mentioned separately in this same text, in a context that is completely different from the sister Mary, who journeys with Philip.

"What's just as explicit, throughout the Acts of Philip, is that Philip's sister carries even the title 'Apostle.' Whenever the text describes these three apostles, traveling from city to city, it gives their names in the same sequence: Philip, Mariamne, and Bartholomew. So she's considered an apostle, which means 'to be sent,' and she was sent, just like the two other apostles. There was no difference."

"*This* Mary Magdalene," Bovon told Simcha, "this Mary from the Acts of Philip, is clearly the equal of the other apostles – and, as depicted, is even more enlightened than Philip.

"Another interesting aspect is that this Mary emerges completely formed as a leading church figure – with no mention of her previous life, aside from being Philip's sister. But the overriding message is that she's seen positively as a Christian missionary. And it's very interesting to me that she does everything Philip and Bartholomew do as male missionaries.

She preaches. She performs baptisms and healings. She calls down miracles."

In Acts of Philip 8:95, when the risen Jesus appears before Mariamne, he speaks of the miraculous powers given to the apostles and expresses concern that when the pagans rise up against Philip, he may turn abusive and wrathful with those same powers, not yet having risen to Jesus's message, as in Luke 6:35–36, to be kind and merciful to the thankless and even to those who would do evil. Thus, Mariamne – Jesus's "chosen among women" – is to go with Philip wherever he goes.

"And do thou," Jesus says, as a final instruction to Mariamne, "change thy woman's aspect."

At least one scholar has translated this instruction to mean simply, "And, Mariamne, change your clothes. Don't wear that impractical summer dress on the long road to Greece."

Bovon perceives a rather more mystical meaning, buried now in a church culture lost to antiquity. He observes that a very similar message is echoed in the final verses of the Gospel of Thomas, a message that a manly or womanly body is to be viewed as amounting to nothing more than an outward husk that "clothes" the spirit; all that really matters, in the final judgment, is the "spirit" that dwells within.

If indeed the Mary of ossuary number 80/500 was the same apostle Mary that Bovon had found, then her physical and spiritual journey to her final resting place had been unusually difficult.

As recorded in the Gospel of Thomas, Simon and Peter, in sayings 22 and 114, eventually rose and spoke out against Mary Magdalene. Declaring that a woman was not worthy of spirit-life, the two men demanded that Mary be ejected from the congregation. And Jesus replied, with more than a hint of wry humor, "Behold! I shall guide her as to make her male, that she too may become a living spirit like you men – and ... male and female [are made] into a single one, so that the male will not be male and the female will not be female" (Gospel of Thomas, saying 114).

The matter of Mary Magdalene's status in the ministry and her conflict with Peter was addressed again in the Gospel of Mary Magdalene, discovered at Nag Hammadi, Egypt, in 1945. In that text, chapter 5 opens with a loss of courage among Philip and the other apostles, much as is described in the Gospel of John's post-Crucifixion passages and in the Mount Athos Acts of Philip:

"They were grieved. They wept greatly, saying, 'How shall we go to the Gentiles and preach the Gospel of the kingdom of the Son of Man? If they did not spare Him [Jesus], how will they spare us?'"

Here again it was Magdalene who spoke, and who began to strengthen the men's failing resolve: "Do not weep and do not grieve nor be irresolute, for His grace will be entirely with you and will protect you" – which, as told in the Acts of Philip (8:95), was the very same message given to the brother of Mary Magdalene: "Why art thou fearful? For I am always with thee."

Gird thy loins and stand like men, Mary continued (in Magdalene 5:1–3): "Do not weep … But rather, let us praise His greatness, for He has prepared us and made us into men."

This text also relates that a year and a half after the Crucifixion Jesus appeared again before Mary Magdalene (without manifesting himself before the rest of the apostles), and he gave her a final revelation, and an instruction.

Mary kept her dialogue with the Savior hidden. But Peter urged her to reveal what she knew, saying (in accordance with 5:5–6 of the Gospel of Mary Magdalene), "We know that the Savior loved you more than the rest of women. Tell us the words of the Savior which you remember."

When she said that the Apocalypse would not occur in their lifetime but in the distant future, she confounded and angered the apostles.

After he heard this, Peter, in Magdalene 18, lashed out. "Did [Jesus] really speak privately with a woman and not openly [with] us? Are we to turn about and all listen to her? Did he prefer her to us?"

"Then Mary wept," the Gospel reads, and she confronted Peter: "Do you think that I have thought this up myself in my heart, or that I am lying about the Savior?"

At that point, Levi rose to the Magdalene's defense and admonished Peter: "Peter, you have always been hot-tempered. Now I see you contending against the woman like the adversaries. But if the Savior made her worthy, who are you indeed to reject her? Surely, the Savior knows her very well. That is why he loved her more than the rest of us."

In the third-century Gnostic text called the Gospel of Philip, also found at Nag Hammadi, it states: "The Lord loved her [Mary Magdalene] more than all other disciples and often kissed her on her ..." (55). Here there is a hole in the text where many scholars believe the original stated "mouth."

In the second part of the Acts of Philip – in what Bovon calls "the second act" – Philip's sister, again, is anything but the wallflower of Church tradition. The miracles that had manifested during the lifetime of Jesus were now replicated, including (in Acts of Philip 1:1–4) the Lazarus-like raising of a Roman worshiper of Apollo and Ares from the dead.

Philip could not always call forth such miracles unless Mariamne helped him. When he replicated Jesus's restoration of sight to the blind, he rubbed a man's sightless eyes with saliva he had dipped from his sister's mouth.

It seems that the Acts of Philip are a window on early Christian belief, and on the meaning of the IAA 80/500–509 inscriptions.

"In this text," Bovon explained to Simcha, "Mariamne's group traveled through Syria, northward into the Greek-speaking world. And this apostle, Mariamne, is attested to in ancient Christianity as a Greek formulation for Mary

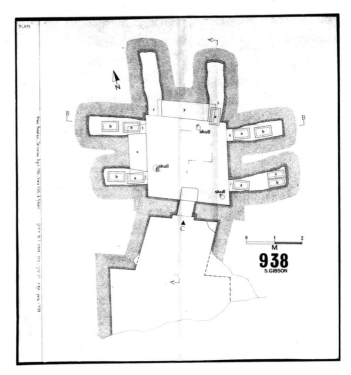

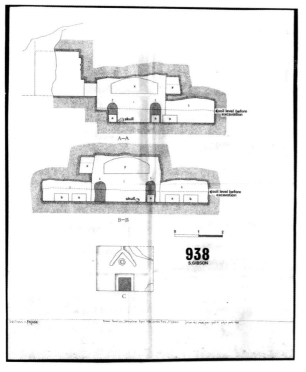

ABOVE: An overhead view of the Tomb of Ten Ossuaries mapped by Shimon Gibson in 1980. The ten ossuaries are shown in the precise positions in which they were originally found, as are the three skulls excavated by Dr. Gat.

LEFT: Shimon Gibson's side view shows the depth of *terra rosa* soil (the "rose earth") that had slowly entered the tomb. Over the course of several centuries, it had risen fully one meter.

Revealed by dynamite and a bulldozer accident, the antechamber, viewed from the tomb's courtyard, was exposed as if cut open by a mighty cleaver.

December 2005: Simcha and his team examine inscribed symbols at the end of an ossuary row in the Israel Antiquities Authority's warehouse.

Simcha and one of his co-researchers examine Ossuary Number 80/503 ("Jesus, son of Joseph") in the IAA warehouse.

The facade of the Jesus ossuary is one of the plainest on record. Appearing to have been damaged and rejected by its own stone masons, the Jesus inscription itself cuts across several deep and seemingly unintentional, older scratches.

The only decoration on the facade of 80/503, following a cross-shaped "Taw," reads, from right to left: "Yeshua [son of] Yehosef"—Jesus, son of Joseph. That the most sacred of the tomb's names was recorded on one of the most ordinary ossuaries is consistent with much of what Jesus preached, including the Gospel of Judas Thomas (saying 66), in which Jesus said, "Show me the stone which the builders have rejected. That one is [my] cornerstone."

Only three ossuaries in the tomb were decorated: The nameless 80/508, the Mariamene ossuary (shown here), and the ossuary seeming to belong to her son, Judas.

Inscribed in Greek, the Mariamene ossuary proclaims: "[This is the ossuary] of Mariamene, also known as Mara [the masculine and feminine version of Lord]."

The "Matthew" ossuary is the only one plain enough to compete with the Jesus ossuary for the title of "most ordinary"—driving home Jesus's message that the ordinary and even flawed among humans could become apostles. The surface of the Matthew ossuary (like others from the tomb) displays pitting from centuries of mineral and bacterial erosion under the influence of the *terra rosa* soil in-flows.

This is how the Tomb of Ten Ossuaries appeared on December 14, 2005. Primary burial shelves are seen beneath two arches. The walls, and every surface within the tomb, are covered with a crystalline patina of *terra rosa* mineralization.

Holy books and religious writings fill two ossuary niches to exactly the depth once reached by in-flows of "the rose earth."

After the Tomb of Ten Ossuaries was excavated, and before it was capped in concrete and steel, the religious authorities designated it a final resting place for holy texts. Simcha called this "a peaceful and fitting, and somehow even a poetic end."

Simcha and Charlie entered the central chamber of the Jesus Family Tomb on December 14, 2005. Given a choice between this discovery and the tomb of "King Tut," both agreed that they would have chosen this tomb. This tomb's treasure lay in the information preserved in its inscriptions, and in its biological remains, and in the chemistry of its patina.

Charlie searches for a clean section of tomb wall from which to obtain a patina sample. He could never have imagined a more extraordinary cave.

Simcha pauses at the antechamber symbol, before descending to the central chamber, on December 14, 2005. Fragments of holy books carpet the bottom of a 20th-century "spirit shaft." Above the shaft, a 1980 construction crew, guided by the local orthodoxy, had built a garden and planted it with roses.

After the first Crusade, the large circle and chevron symbol from the tomb's antechamber was replicated in Templar books about the Kingdom of Heaven. About AD 1500, Carucci's *Supper of Emmaus* recreated Luke 24's post-resurrection supper in a village near Jerusalem. In Florence, this Renaissance period painting appeared to capture a Crusader-period symbol's evolution from an orb in a triangle to the all-seeing eye of God.

On December 15, 2005, miniature robots, called "bots," performed a detailed reconnaissance of the second chamber. Currently, this is Israel's only pristine, unexcavated ossuary tomb.

Two ossuaries lie undisturbed in a niche of the second chamber. Bot reconnaissance revealed more inscriptions, written in Greek; but the space between the ossuary facade and the tunnel wall was too narrow to allow a clear reading.

In the rose garden, Simcha was meeting new people and making new friends.

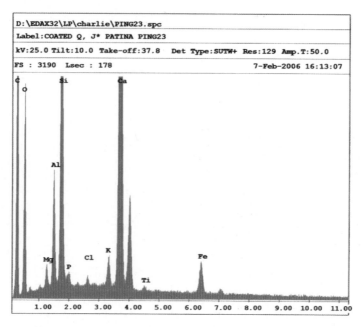

Ping 23 illustrates the typical elemental spectrum of the Talpiot Tomb's wall and ossuary patina. This particular patina sample is from the Jesus ossuary.

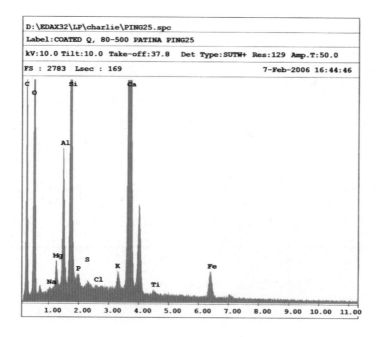

Ping 25 probed the "Mariamene" patina, verifying that it was, in all essentials, an echo of the elemental spectrum revealed everywhere else in this same tomb.

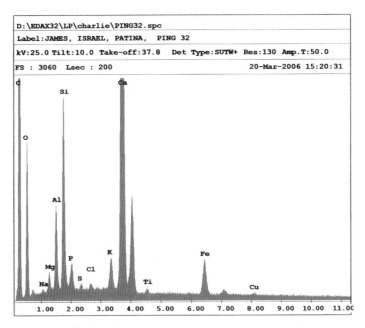

D:\EDAX32\LP\charlie\PING32.spc

Label:JAMES, ISRAEL, PATINA, PING 32

kV:25.0 Tilt:10.0 Take-off:37.8 Det Type:SUTW+ Res:130 Amp.T:50.0

FS : 3060 Lsec : 200   20-Mar-2006 15:20:31

Ping 32 probed the elemental spectrum (or patina fingerprint) of the James ossuary. Its patina turned out to be an echo (or match) to the Jesus Family Tomb, suggesting that the controversial and un-provenanced ossuary could indeed be the missing tenth ossuary.

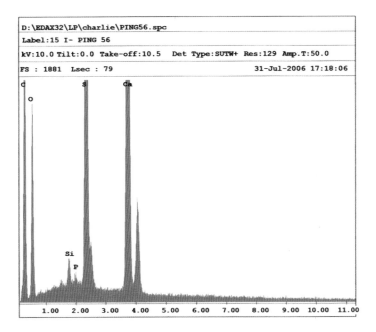

D:\EDAX32\LP\charlie\PING56.spc

Label:15 I- PING 56

kV:10.0 Tilt:0.0 Take-off:10.5 Det Type:SUTW+ Res:129 Amp.T:50.0

FS : 1881 Lsec : 79   31-Jul-2006 17:18:06

Ping 56 is an average, representative patina fingerprint from another ossuary tomb. There are no iron, titanium, or potassium peaks typical of *terra rosa* soil. Other differences were also immediately apparent.

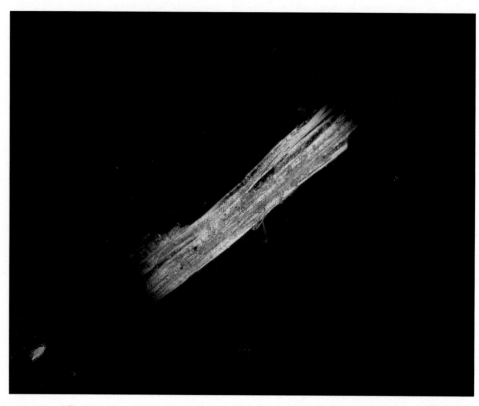

A fiber bundle extracted from the center of a mineral concretion in the Jesus ossuary turned out to be made from the plainest of materials, appearing to represent a burlaplike fabric made from pulped straw.

Magdalene – and here, in the original Greek, in these Acts of Philip, we have, of course, been reading this very same name.

"To be clear," said Bovon, "in the Acts of Philip the first Mary – Magdalene – is called Mariamne. The second Mary is also mentioned, but only once, in a speech about the birth of Jesus. And she is called – "

"Maria," Simcha finished for him.

"*Maria*," Bovon repeated.

"And Mary Magdalene – "

"Is clearly Mariamne," said Bovon. "So there is no confusion here between the two persons."

Jerusalem, in those days, was an international crossroads of trade under Rome – a condition reflected in the Talpiot tomb cluster, whose names were written in Aramaic, Greek, Hebrew, and Hebrew-inscribed Latin. The tomb appeared to be communicating that Jerusalem in this period was not only bilingual but probably trilingual. The epigrapher Frank Moore Cross had already found the inscription assemblage most remarkable, even in a trilingual city. Something unusual had been recorded in this assemblage. Among the three generations represented in the Tomb of Ten Ossuaries, one would normally have expected (as one normally saw in other tombs) that if these were children burying their parents, they would be using the same language for each burial – unless, the epigrapher guessed, these people traveled widely and came back to Jerusalem with nicknames and names of endearment from foreign lands.

As yet, Bovon did not know about IAA 80/500–509 and its unusual assemblage of names. Even so – and it was impossible for Simcha to conceal his excitement – Bovon's conclusions about Mariamne were converging on Talpiot.

"The New Testament's Mary Magdalene," Bovon continued, "began as a wealthy sponsor of the Jesus ministry, originating from his neighborhood near the Sea of Galilee. Now, archaeologists can tell you that this region was very much bilingual. Sepphoris, not very far from Nazareth, was a major Roman-dominated, Greek-speaking city. So I would expect that Mary Magdalene spoke Greek in addition to Hebrew and Aramaic. She should have been bilingual, I would say."

"Yes!" said Simcha. "*So close* to Sepphoris! It would make perfect sense that she would be with Greek-speaking people and that her name – "

Simcha cut the rest of his sentence short.

"Did you know, Simcha, that to this very day the Greek Orthodox Church celebrates Mary Magdalene – whom thay call Mariamne – every twenty-second of July?"*

"No," Simcha answered. "I did not know this."

Then he asked a question of his own. "Now, professor – St. Philip, you say, is associated with leading Greek-speaking followers of Jesus. And Mariamne is associated with Philip. I'm just wondering: if some archaeologists were

---

* To the Greek Orthodoxy, the July 22 celebration reveres "Saint Mary Magdalene, the Holy Myrrh-Bearer and Equal-to-the-Apostles."

eventually to discover the tomb of Mary Magdalene, would you expect her name to be inscribed in Greek?"

Bovon looked at him quizzically, as if awaiting either the punch line of a joke or a revelation of some sort.

"You see," Simcha began, "until you mentioned all of this, I might have anticipated that, if Mary Magdalene's ossuary existed at all, it would be inscribed in Hebrew or Aramaic."

"Not necessarily," said Bovon.

"Where would we expect her to be buried?" Simcha asked.

"At the end of the martyrdom story of Philip, Bartholomew and Mariamne do not die with him as martyrs, but instead details are given about their destinies. Bartholomew is supposed to go to Asia Minor, and Mariamne to the Jordan Valley – not very far from her home. Now, I don't know if this text is supported by any other evidence. It seems a strange piece of information: to say where she is supposed to die. It's contradictory of other traditions."

"So, she goes back to the River Jordan," Simcha said.

"Homeward. Yes."

"Somewhere in – ?"

"In Israel. This, again, is somewhat different from the predominant tradition – which has her settling somewhere in the south of France. Yet, at the end of the Acts of Philip, Mariamne goes home to Israel, and that's where she would die and be buried. This is the earliest tradition."

"Then we would need archaeological evidence, or – "

Bovon cut in: "Even archaeology will probably not prove

anything ..." He trailed off suddenly into thought, then raised an eyebrow and gave Simcha a suspicious glare.

"We might find her tomb," said Simcha.

"You hope so."

"I do. I do hope so."

Simcha's smile was gone now.

"*Have* you found something?" the professor asked. "That's the reason you're here, isn't it?"

The Acts of Philip provided very important information to be weighed against the Talpiot tomb. First, it provided a name for the mother of Jesus: Maria, and one for Mary Magdalene: Mariamne; second, it provided a status for Mariamne – she was an apostle, a teacher, or, to use the Aramaic, a "Mara"; third, she moved in Greek circles; and fourth, her bones were buried in Israel.

*   *   *

All these years, the Tomb of Ten Ossuaries slept. As the sixth century opened, whenever Persia and Byzantium's Holy Roman Empire were not fighting "the barbarians of the north," or each other, they would try to attack, and to claim, the Holy City. Later, Emperor Heraclius's Christian soldiers captured Jerusalem about 610 C.E. Then while Heraclius was attempting to suppress an Arab rebellion in Syria, an unusual letter was sent to his imperial outpost at Bostra, south of Damascus. The letter required translation from a strange desert language. As desert scribes recorded it, the message –

which called upon the emperor "to acknowledge the one true God" – was answered with what might be called the silence of contemptuous indifference. The messenger was simply told to "be gone." As it turned out, the letter was penned by an Arab leader the Christians had chased into the eastern desert, by someone who still followed the Prophet Jesus but had himself emerged as a prophet. The man called himself Muhammed the Prophet of God.

In 638 C.E., Jerusalem was captured by the caliph Omar, and seventeen years later Muhammed's followers routed the last remnants of the Byzantine fleet.

Another century came and went. And another. And another. Everything in the world was changed, and changing, and yet, except for a slowly deepening patina, everything in the Tomb of Ten Ossuaries remained the same.

7

The Twin

Why would Philip's sister be buried in Jesus's tomb? Was she his wife? And why would there be an ossuary next to them that has inscribed on it the name Judah, son of Jesus? Was he their son? In none of the Gospels, be they canonical or apocryphal, is Mary Magdalene – Mariamne – described as being married to Jesus. Nor is a child of Jesus ever mentioned. And yet, logically, if Jesus had a wife and son, either they would not have been spoken of at all, or they would have been spoken of in code.

Jesus, his family, and his followers were all acutely aware that they were living in a Roman society and that Romans killed all heirs to a contender for kingship in territories they controlled, while often allowing siblings to survive.

Even in Rome, within Jesus's lifetime, during the emperor Tiberius's struggle to place himself on the Roman throne, the three most favored grandchildren of his predecessor, the emperor Augustus, were killed, along with their father Agrippa (Augustus's son-in-law). Julia (Augustus's daughter and Agrippa's wife) was banished to a remote island for what turned out to be a sentence of death. After Tiberius became emperor, Agrippa's daughter, Agrippina, was arrested and beaten to death. Another heir of Augustus's, Germanicus the Younger, adopted by the emperor specifically as an inheritor of the throne, died, like Augustus himself, under mysterious circumstances. Yet while one sibling died, the other, Claudius, was spared. Claudius survived because he was never adopted by Augustus and was never perceived by Tiberius as a candidate for emperor.

During the Passover season, about 30 C.E., "when they heard that Jesus was coming to Jerusalem," wrote the chronicler of John 12:12–13, a great multitude of people "took branches of palm trees, and went forth to meet him, and cried, 'Hosanna! Blessed is the *King of Israel* that cometh in the name of the Lord.'" The local governor must have felt particularly vulnerable during that Passover season, for the winds of rebellion were gathering strength at home and abroad. In Rome, a man named Aelius Sejanus, commander of the Praetorian guard, tried to grab the throne. Tiberius eliminated Sejanus, his wife, his lover, and his two preadolescent children. However, a *sibling* – Sejanus's sister – was allowed to live.

The message was simple and direct: *if we kill the father, we will look next for the wife and children.*

All the years leading up to and following Jesus's arrival in Jerusalem, the message would be constantly reinforced: if they killed the Messiah – the King of Israel – then the wife and child of the Messiah were also in jeopardy. But a mere sibling might have a good chance at survival, especially if he kept a low profile. It was as simple as that.

As was their policy, the Romans could be counted on, in revolution-prone Jerusalem, to view the bloodline of any claimant to the Davidic throne as a real and lingering danger. According to the Gospels, the Roman prefect Pilate wrote, on the placard above the royal pretender's head, "Jesus of Nazareth the King of the Jews." They fixed a crown of thorns on his head, placed a reed for a staff in his hand, and clothed him in purple – all in apparent mockery (John 19:2, Matthew 27:29). The brothers of Jesus, and the apostles, surely knew what the Romans would do next. By all accounts, Romans were very good at hunting down sons, daughters, and wives.

So a wife of Jesus, if she existed, might be code-worded as the "companion," or "beloved" friend, of Jesus. And little Judah, though he might already have been around for ten years or thirteen years on the day of Crucifixion, would have been known – even to most of the apostles – not as "Judah, son of Jesus," but as someone else's child, perhaps a younger brother of Jesus.

Given Roman policy, if there did indeed exist a "Judah, son of Jesus," then the surviving members of the Jesus movement would not have been inclined to shout out his name in the marketplace. Instead, a code was bound to arise: "Have you seen Jesus's 'brother'?" Or, "Have you seen the little 'twin' today?"

But if the ancient texts spoke in codes, is it still possible to decipher them?

The Gospel of Mark (6:3) states in no uncertain terms that Jesus had a family and that it included, at the very least, siblings: "Is not this the carpenter, the son of Mary, the brother of James, and Jos'e, and of Judas, and Simon?"

In Christian tradition, "Judah" the brother of Jesus comes down to us as St. Jude, one of the Apostles. Another Apostle comes down to us as Judas Thomas Didymos.

The connection between "Judas" – or Judah – and "Thomas" occurred often in antiquity. For example, the Gnostic Gospel of Thomas opens with these words: "These are the secret sayings which the living Jesus spoke and which *Didymos Judas Thomas* wrote down."

Who is this mysterious "Didymos Judas Thomas"?

"Didymos" was a word, not a name. Quite literally, and simply, it was the Greek word for "twin."

As for "Thomas," no such name has ever existed in Hebrew. This too is a word and not a name. Thomas – "Te-om" in Hebrew – has always meant "twin."

151

The power in the meaning of these two words – one Greek, the other Hebrew – is revealed when we return to the first sentence of the Gospel of Thomas. Here, the chronicler proclaims that these "secret" teachings of Jesus were written by Didymos Judas Thomas, which translates as "Twin Judah Twin."

The name *strongly* suggests that Judas (the brother) and Thomas were indeed one and the same person. In the Gospel of Thomas (saying 11), Jesus says to Thomas, "On the day when you were one, you became *two*." That seems to be exactly what happened to Judas. He became both Judas and Thomas: "Twin Judas Twin."

This strange code would be impossible to break were it not for an ossuary in Talpiot inscribed "Judah, son of Jesus." Can it be that the son became the "twin" – perhaps an ancient code for "junior" – in order to protect him from the Roman authorities? Can it be that Jesus's son has been hiding – touchingly, like a child – in plain sight all along?

In Mark (12:1–12), Jesus tells the parable of a good man who lets his vineyard to husbandmen (farmers). After a time, the landlord sends his servant to collect a portion of the fruit as payment. The servant is attacked, beaten, and sent away empty-handed. The landlord sends another and then another, each suffering worse abuse than the one before, and the last being killed. Finally, the landlord sends his "well-beloved son" and heir, confident that the husbandmen will not harm him, but they kill him as well.

The Gospel of Thomas seems to preserve a version of this same parable in which the son and heir is murdered by the husbandmen while the servants are merely abused. This version hints at a deeper and more immediate meaning for a son of Jesus, if such existed:

Jesus said, "There was a good man who owned a vineyard. He leased it to tenant farmers so that they might work it and he might collect the produce from them. He sent his servant so that the tenants might give him the produce of the vineyard. They seized his servant and beat him, all but killing him. The servant went back and told his master. The master said, 'Perhaps they did not recognize him.' He sent another servant. The tenants beat this one as well. Then the owner sent his son and said, 'Perhaps they will show respect for my son.' Because the tenants knew that it was he who was heir to the vineyard, they seized him and killed him. Let he who has ears, listen." (Gospel of Thomas, Saying 65)

Perhaps Jesus is talking in theological terms. Perhaps, as many have interpreted, the parable is describing his own death. Yet, in what appears to be a more ancient form, the parable of the vineyard could have a more direct and simple meaning. It could be referring to the fate that would have awaited any surviving son sent into the world by Jesus, an interpretation bolstered by the fact that the chronicler of the parable is none other than Didymos Judas Thomas ("Twin Judas Twin").

In Saying 13, Judas Thomas writes of secrets kept between him and Jesus and concealed forever from the apostles, who ask him, "What did Jesus reveal to you?"

And Didymos Judas Thomas replies, "If I tell you one of the things which he told me, you will pick up stones and throw them at me; a fire will come out of the stones and will burn you up."

*   *   *

Eight hundred years *had passed, and yet the tomb remained pristine. No one had yet entered and arranged three human skulls on the floor of the central chamber. The chambers of the tomb were still relatively clean, save for a thin film of silica glitter and apatite crystals and a light dusting of eroded chalk-stone. During all these vanished years, the floor and walls had been left to the dominion of cave mites and tiny beetles. On occasion, a juvenile centipede was able to squeeze through a seam between the antechamber wall and the seal stone. The entire cave ecology was probably capable of sustaining a few of these animals to adulthood – just barely. Save for the etchings of a handful of malnourished centipedes, the Tomb of Ten Ossuaries was as silent as the deserts of space. But silence was only a respite. It could not last forever. Nothing lasts forever.*

8

Charlie: The "Jesus Equation" Revisited

Within a small circle of scientists, explorers, and scholars, an obscure tomb in a far-flung corner of the Jerusalem hills had captured the imagination like no other scientific subject. In 1980, the question of the "Jesus, son of Joseph" inscription was answered with a quick and easy dismissal: all of the names were common.

What was ignored all those years ago was that the names – taken individually – were not the issue. Rather, what should have been examined was the entire *cluster* of names, which was indeed uncommon.

As seen earlier, I had applied a very conservative statistical test to the Talpiot cluster, arriving at a lower limit of about one chance in 2.5 million that this tomb could belong to anyone but Jesus of Nazareth and his family. Accordingly, about 2.5 million males would have had to live in Jerusalem – some thirty-one times the city's male population – before a family unrelated to Jesus of Nazareth could produce this cluster of names just once by sheer chance.

Simcha sought a second opinion from Professor Andrey Feuerverger of the University of Toronto, one of North America's leading statisticians. Like me, Feuerverger constructed his equation conservatively. Like me, he assigned no value to the "Judah, son of Jesus" inscription and counted the unusual "Jos'e" as just another Joseph. In the end, Feuerverger's version of the equation was standing in the same statistical ballpark as mine, sort of: one in 2.4 million instead of one in 2.5 million.

He then emphasized: "One of the things that turns out to be most interesting about this tomb," Feuerverger reported to Simcha, "is that, if you focus on the names individually, you can easily come away with the impression that there is nothing the least bit unusual about this particular cluster.

"However, Simcha, your team was correct to point out that the proper way to analyze this is to look at all of the names in unison.

"And what happens when you do this," the statistician confirmed, "is that even if the individual probability of each particular name is not terribly small, when they are factored all together, they start to build a picture in which the overall tomb assemblage is a very rare event."

"It really is a possibility," Feuerverger said, "that this particular site is in fact the tomb of the New Testament family. It is a possibility that I think now needs to be taken seriously."

Feuerverger was especially impressed (on a mathematical level) with the "Mariamne-Mara" inscription. "That," he said, "is an extremely unusual one – with a Magdalene connection from the Acts of Philip, a connection that appears to convey that she belongs in this tomb."

Feuerverger then started working on a paper on the Talpiot tomb for publication in a statistics journal. Before submitting it for peer review, however, given the explosive nature of his findings, he submitted it informally to some colleagues who told him that his reasoning and his numbers appeared to be correct, but they cautioned him that publishing statistics about anything related to a Jesus family tomb might turn out to be very controversial indeed.

At this point, it occurred to Feuerverger that, no matter how conservative his approach to the "Jesus equation" had been, somebody, somewhere, would argue for a more conservative strategy. So he decided to rethink the equation.

Suddenly, he called Simcha and announced, "I've got it. I'm not going to go simply with the probabilities of the names on these ossuaries all turning up together and treating them as if they all occur in a vacuum."

"Are you going super-conservative on us?" Simcha asked.

"I'm just trying to be accurate," the mathematician explained.

"So here is what I am going to do. I'm going to factor, against this cluster of names and against the present probability results, what I will call a *surprise factor.*"

What this meant was that Feuerverger was going to give a power to the names of Jesus's family members who were *not* in the tomb. Their power was to *diminish* the mathematical force of the names that *were* in the tomb.

"Here's how the surprise factor works," Feuerverger began. "Simcha, I know you went 'Wow!' when you read 'Mariamne' and when you learned that this might be Mary Magdalene. I know you believe that the name 'Jos'e,' as a brother of Jesus, is very significant. That's the wow! factor, or what I call a *surprise* factor. But you can't have it both ways. Given that 'Simon' was also a brother, you would have said 'Wow!' to a 'Simon' as well – you would have argued that a 'Simon' inscription in the tomb *increases* the likelihood that this is the Jesus family tomb, so his *absence* should *decrease* the likelihood.

"I'm *raising* the probability restrictions," Feuerverger explained. "I'm going to factor in all the 'missing' brothers, if you will, as a way of diminishing the likelihood that this is the Jesus family tomb."

Since "cousin Matthew" had been declared statistically neutral, Feuerverger decided not to assign a surprise value to missing apostles or cousins.

The absence of an ossuary belonging to Joseph, the father of Jesus, was another matter to be considered. By all accounts, Joseph seems to have died away from Jerusalem – before Jesus began his ministry – and probably should not have been in the Talpiot tomb.

While it was true that a "Joseph, father of Jesus" inscription (even though Simcha could explain its absence) would have possessed a huge "wow!" factor, Feuerverger was not certain that a "negative Joseph value" needed to be assigned. In this instance, the evidence dictated that a "Joseph, *father of Jesus*" was represented by the inscription that read "Jesus, *son* of Joseph." By this same standard, if the "Jesus" ossuary had included "Jesus, son of Joseph, brother of James," this would have had a positive value, not a negative value, even if a "James" ossuary happened not to be present in the tomb.

Building the "Jesus equation" from the tomb cluster and factoring the probabilities of individual names had been a relatively simple and straightforward procedure. Diminishing the significance of the names on the ossuaries promised to be just as simple and straightforward.

Feuerverger's first challenge, the missing Simon, was short-lived. "Simon," like "Matthew," was among the most common names on first-century ossuaries; it was so common, in fact, that in a tomb of ten ossuaries, with five of them presumably male, the chances of finding a Simon (one out of every four men) was a mathematical certainty – no "wow!" factor, statistically speaking. The absence of a "Simon" ossuary was therefore equal to its presence: the name "Simon" was an interesting but neutral name, whether or not it happened to be present, and had no numerical value at all.

The lack of a "James, brother of Jesus" inscription was different, and powerful. The name "James" (or Jacob), in accordance with both Rahmani's and Ilan's numbers, occurred on only 2 percent of ossuaries, or one out of fifty. The lack of a "James" impacted negatively on the equation.

The absence of "Judah, brother of Jesus" in the Talpiot tomb also had a power to diminish. The name Judah occurred on ossuaries with a frequency of 10 percent, or one out of ten. His absence now mattered.

By the end, Feuerverger accounted for all this by dividing the 2.4 million by a factor of four to allow for "unintended bias" in the historical sources. At that point, the "probability factor" went down to 600,000 to one in favor of the tomb from the previous 2.4 million to one. He now further divided the 600,000 by 1,000, i.e., the maximum number of tombs that might have once existed in Jerusalem, dating to the first century.

When he did all that, he got to a "P factor" (probability factor) of 600 to one in favor of the tomb belonging to the family of Jesus of Nazareth.*

"Is this disappointing?" Feuerverger asked Simcha.

---

* As of this writing, Feuerverger's paper has been submitted to a leading American statistical journal and is being peer-reviewed.

"I don't mind," Simcha said. "It's a good result, because this means that even when we factor in ossuaries that are simply not there and tombs that have not been found and may not exist ... at the end of the day, if I were a betting man and you let me be the house, and you could assure me that each time a player spun my wheel the odds were 600 to one in my favor, I would not hesitate to play."

But then Simcha asked Feuerverger, "What if it should turn out, somehow, that 'James, the brother of Jesus' also belonged in this tomb?"

"You mean, the so-called James ossuary?"

"Yes. What if it turned out to be more than just 'so-called'?"

Andrey Feuerverger slowly let out a loud whistle. "If the evidence were to point in that direction," he said, "the numbers, I think, would climb to at least one chance in 30,000. If this name could be factored into the 'Jesus equation,' then it would be what we call an absolute statistical slam-dunk."

"But remember," he said, "even without James, a P factor of one in 600 means that if you had a drug that you claimed cured cancer and it failed to cure only one in 600 patients, you would be looking at a Nobel Prize."

* * *

West of Jerusalem, *the last vestiges of Egypt's book-copying industry had been plowed out of existence. The Library of*

Alexandria – attacked by Christians, by Muslims, and then by Christians again – had been ashes since the early eighth century. Yet by 900 C.E., in Cordoba, Spain, and in Jerusalem, Islamic and Jewish scholars were founding libraries and reintroducing a system of pipes, cisterns, and irrigation channels. In the hills above and around the tomb, the two Semitic tribes worked together, reintroducing street lighting, alchemy, and terraced farming. A new mathematics was dethroning the clumsy Roman numerals and replacing them with Arabic numerals and had also developed algebra and the first equations of chemistry and the physical sciences. New metallic alloys, dyes, and optical glass truly did seem to be pointing the way toward an emergence from the Dark Ages, but this was not to be. For the Talpiot tomb, the long sleep of civilization meant that its own sleep would continue for at least a little while longer. Without an age of expanding knowledge and industry, the tomb remained beyond the reach of scientific revelation. Discovery and understanding belonged to another time.

9

The Jesus Standard

There will always be those for whom the idea of connecting people in the New Testament with bones in ossuaries is a nonstarter.

There was (and still is) among scholars a strong resistance to the possibility of finding any archaeological artifact that can be directly linked to the Gospel accounts of Jesus and his family.

And yet – and this may come as a surprise to most readers – scholars are happy to connect ossuaries with leading characters from the Gospels as long as they are not related to Jesus or his family. For example, ten years after the Talpiot tomb was found, a bulldozer revealed the name Caiaphas in a tomb near Jerusalem's Peace Forest. An announcement then went out – from the scholarly community – that the family tomb of the Temple high priest who persecuted Jesus had been found. The story made headline news internationally.

The tomb that the bulldozers uncovered was about half as large as the Talpiot tomb and had no antechamber. Among the artifacts inside were ceramic oil lamps and a small bottle made from fine Roman glass bearing remnants of an oily perfume. The most exceptional finds were two ossuaries bearing the name Caiaphas. The more decorative of the two – indeed, among the most decorated of all known ossuaries, with its pentacles of carved, flowerlike rosettes framed by palm branches – was inscribed with the name Yehosef bar Qafa', or Joseph, son of Caiaphas, identified as the high priest in the Gospels (Luke 3:2, John 11:49) whose full name is provided by Josephus (*Antiquities of the Jews*, 18:2).

Statistically speaking, the "Joseph" part of the Caiaphas inscription is one of the most popular male names of the Jerusalem region during the Second Temple period. Among inscriptions of male names, "Joseph" appeared with a frequency of about 14 percent, while "Caiaphas" was rare (less than one appearance in 200, or roughly 0.5 percent). Using these percentages as a guide (.14 × .005), one out of every 1,400 men in Jerusalem could be expected to be named Joseph, son of Caiaphas.

Interestingly, scholars have never done the math on this ossuary. They just assumed – rightly, as it turns out – that the ossuary must have belonged to the infamous Caiaphas of the New Testament. Today, the Joseph, son of Caiaphas ossuary is on permanent display in the Israel Museum. It is described as the box that once held the mortal remains of the high priest.

Without the statistics, why are scholars so sure they have the right Caiaphas? David Mevorach, the curator responsible for the Hellenistic and Roman periods in the Israel Museum, states that two things lead him to this conclusion. The Caiaphas name is "rare," and the ossuary is very "elaborate," suggesting a high priest.

But the Caiaphas ossuary is not the only one that scholars have linked to the New Testament. Incredibly, using the same soft standards, scholars agree that the ossuary of *another* leading figure of the Gospels has *also* been found.

At Jerusalem's Fifth Station of the Cross there is a chapel dedicated to Simon of Cyrene, the man who, according to the Gospels, helped Jesus carry his cross en route to the Crucifixion. The Gospel of Mark (15:21) identifies Simon and his two sons by their names and place of origin: "And they compell[ed] one Simon of Cyrene ... the father of Alexander and Rufus, to bear his cross." It seems that Simon had come on pilgrimage for the Passover festival from Cyrene (in modern-day Libya) to Jerusalem, where he had his fateful encounter with Jesus. Unbeknownst to the tens of thousands of pilgrims who come to the Fifth Station on the Via Dolorosa to pray in the Chapel of Simon of Cyrene, his ossuary has been found. Today it sits under a table in a ware-house at the Hebrew University in Jerusalem.

The story of the Simon ossuary began in 1941, when Israel still existed under British rule and the bombing of Pearl Harbor was about to bring America into the Second World War. The tomb of Simon's family was discovered in the Kidron Valley east of Jerusalem by Professor Eleazar Sukenik.

The Simon family tomb was simple and single-chambered. On its floor, there were eleven ossuaries with twelve inscriptions and fifteen names. In addition to a cluster of names that were common in Cyrene, one of them had the famous "Simon" inscribed on its side. On the lid of this same ossuary the name "Cyrene" appeared.

According to Biblical Archaeology Society analyst Tom Powers, with all else that was happening in the world in 1941, it must have been very easy for the "Simon of Cyrene" inscription to escape public and even scientific attention. So the ossuary lay neglected and then was finally forgotten until 2003, when Powers published an article on it in *Biblical Archaeology Review* ("Treasures in the Storeroom: Family Tomb of Simon of Cyrene," July–August 2003). Today scholars are in basic agreement that this ossuary belongs to the important New Testament figure who by all accounts became one of the early followers of the Jesus movement. Again, how can they be so sure? After all, the name Simon is the most popular of all names used by Jews in the first century C.E.

"When we consider how uncommon the name Alexander was," said Powers, "the facts *do* fit. The names on the ossuaries point to a family that originated in Cyrenaicea, and one inscription bears the name Alexander, who is identified as the son of Simon – in the same relationship as described in the Gospels."

Powers's case is compelling.

In 2006, at our request, James Tabor examined the ossuary at the Hebrew University in Jerusalem. He confirmed that the place name Cyrene was inscribed on the lid – and on one side, inscribed in Greek, he read these words: "Alexander (son) of Simon." On the other side, written in green chalk, one name, Simon, appeared above the other, Alexander, suggesting to Tabor that the bones of both father and son had been buried in the same ossuary.

But how well does "Simon" stand up against the math? Well, though Simon is a common name, Alexander – as Powers points out – is quite rare, and the link to Cyrene is rarer still. Nonetheless, if we were to subject the Simon of Cyrene ossuary to Feuerverger's "surprise factor," Simon would suffer, because though his son Alexander is attested in the inscriptions, his other son, Rufus, who is mentioned in the Gospels, is notable by his absence.

In any event, even after subjecting the inscription to Feuerverger's standards, there is still a 200-to-one probability in favor of the Simon of Cyrene ossuary. Though the numbers are not as compelling as the Jesus family tomb, scholars have accepted the Simon of Cyrene ossuary as the genuine article. After all, Simon is not Jesus. He just helped him with his cross.

*   *   *

In 1054 C.E., on the fourth day of July, the last dying shriek from the Crab Star, lying in state already six thousand years, reached earth. The Crab Nova, as it rose above Jerusalem's eastern horizon, grew bright enough to cast afternoon and late-evening shadows, and for almost two weeks it seemed as though the sun had gained a sister. After more than a year, it faded away.

Of course, none of the Crab's false daylight (or daylight of any sort) reached the tomb, but some small measure of the star's actual dust – including the nuclei of new and peculiar atoms accelerated to light-speed by the nova – passed through the chalk-stone and the bones and continued onward into the earth's crust. Some of the lighter, more ghostly parts of the Crab passed clear through the earth itself, while behind them, atoms of calcium and silicon occasionally halted and captured in chalk and in bone a tangible nucleus of stardust, so that the ossuaries of a man named Jesus, a woman named Mary, and a son named Judah preserved the very substance of a flaring and dying star – which, centuries before, in 70 C.E., must have heralded (as described by Josephus) the burning of Jerusalem. Accordingly, this same star also heralded a thousand Messiahs who would rise against Rome and end on the cross, including an infant named Jesus.

In 1099 C.E., a Crusader army – a rough beast of an army whose hour had come round at last – took Bethlehem, then traveled on toward Jerusalem. On the outskirts of the city, the Crusaders fought among themselves over which group of conquerors would control shares of any gold or jewels found behind the gates. Then, according to Church historians, after a brief episode of bloodletting among its own ranks, the army breached Jerusalem's walls and moved in.

By this time, the Gospels, in their final written form, were already more than seven hundred years old, but most of the northern invaders could neither read nor write. Church scribes recorded that it soon became impossible for men to ride on horseback without being splashed by the blood in the streets. Within Jerusalem's walls, Muslims, Jews, and Greeks by the thousands – wounded defenders, young scholars, women with infants crying in their arms – were rounded up, shepherded into mosques and synagogues, barricaded inside, and burned alive. On the night the Crusaders arrived, another layer of carbonized ash began fouling the air and seeping slowly into the ground, helped along by spillage from vandalized aqueducts. The conquerors rejoiced that Christianity had at last returned to the Holy City. *In the Tomb of Ten Ossuaries, the descending ash carried the promise of more potent acids arriving with the next rains, the promise of more dissolved sand and rock in the groundwater, the promise of a thicker, more protective patina over teeth and tibiae, and over the inscription "Jesus, son of Joseph."*

10

Whence Came the Nazarenes

Long before the Crusaders arrived, someone had carved terraced farms above and around the tomb, creating a hillside quilt-work of braided troughs filled to their brims with carefully gathered and leveled earth. Known as the *terra rossa,* this rare agricultural soil was laced with titanium and iron. In the glare of sunrise, and again at sunset, the "rose earth" reflected brilliant reds, painting the hills in a rosy glow.

Somewhere near the twelfth century, somewhere near this time of Crusaders and Templars, the Tomb of Ten Ossuaries was breached by what would eventually become known as the entry of the "*terra rossa* people." They were neither local Jews nor local Muslims, for they followed the customs of neither.

The intruders opened the seal of the fifth ossuary niche, removed the northernmost ossuary, studied it, and pushed it gently back into place but with one end still protruding. All the ossuaries survived without any signs of being damaged or looted.

In the center of the tomb, the *terrarossa* people left a calling card, of sorts. Three skulls were placed in the chamber in an odd and clearly ceremonial configuration.

Then, by a strange swerve of history, the tomb came to be sealed a second time and was either forgotten or kept secret, once again disappearing into history.

*   *   *

Looking out his office window on Santa Monica Boulevard, Jim Cameron is confronted daily by the Santa Monica Masonic Temple, whose second floor is adorned by a draftman's divider in the shape of a chevron, enclosing a letter "G" in the shape of a circle. The symbol looks for all the world like the chevron and circle on the facade of the Talpiot tomb.

"We've got to address the similarity," Jim told Simcha one day. "I mean, anyone with a U.S. dollar bill in his pocket will notice it – and many of them will know that this symbol has been associated with Christian heresies. We can't just ignore it."

No one involved in the investigation really wanted to see history imitating art, like something out of a Ron Howard/ Dan Brown script. "But what if," Jim Cameron proposed, "what if, for all his twists and turns of plot, Dan Brown just happened to get some of it right?"

"Okay," Simcha said, "Let's play "Da Vinci Code" for a moment. And let's base our speculations as far as possible on facts. To begin with, instead of Leonardo, let's look at Pontormo, his lesser-known student."

Ever since the success of Brown's runaway bestseller *The Da Vinci Code*, Leonardo's painting of *The Last Supper* had attracted a lot of attention. And yet, in terms of a "code," by far the more interesting and relevant painting – one with unmistakable symbols in it – is the painting by his student Jacopo Carucci da Pontormo, called *Supper at Emmaus*. "It's also a 'supper,' but as far as we're concerned a 'better' supper, because it comes *after* the Crucifixion," Simcha said.

Pontormo's painting re-created the post-Resurrection supper at the village of Emmaus, about seven miles from Jerusalem or "about threescore furlongs," as recorded in the Gospel according to Luke.

In the Luke account, two of those who had witnessed the empty tomb were walking toward Emmaus, discussing what had happened, when "Jesus himself drew near, and went with them." Somehow, the men didn't recognize him when he asked why they appeared so sad.

One of them then said to Jesus, "Art thou only a stranger in Jerusalem, and hast thou not known the things which are come to pass there in these days? ... [Things] concerning

Jesus of Nazareth, [who] was a Prophet mighty in deed and word before God and all the people."

Jesus then walked with them, speaking about scripture and prophecy, still unrecognized, even as they invited him to stay at Emmaus for dinner. "And it came to pass, as he sat at meat with them, he took bread, blessed it, and broke [the bread], and gave it to them."

And then, after appearing to be a tangible being who broke bread and who ate, Jesus made himself suddenly recognizable: "And their eyes were opened, and they knew him; and he vanished out of their sight" (Luke 24:13–31).

This is the supper that became the subject of Pontormo's painting. Jesus is the central figure, naturally. He is breaking bread, just as in the Gospel of Luke, naturally. He is the only figure with a halo over his head, naturally.

What's *unnatural* is the glowing shape above Jesus's head – a triangle, with an all-seeing eye in its center. If Pontormo knew something about a Jesus family tomb and the symbol on its facade, how did this knowledge travel from Jerusalem to Florence, across fifteen centuries, to become encoded in Pontormo's painting?

"I have a theory," said Simcha. "I can't quite prove it yet, but we're just playing the "Da Vinci Code," after all."

Jim seemed amused. "Let's hear it," he said.

"I think the original followers of Jesus, variously called Ebionites, Nazarenes, and Judeo-Christians, didn't just 'disappear' at the time of Constantine and the rise of the

Gentile church. I think they hung around for a *long* time, despite the fact that Eusebius called them a heresy in the fourth century. So what does that tell us?" Simcha looked at us expectantly.

"They went underground," I said.

The "Ebionites" still existed in small groups when Bishop Eusebius finished penning Constantine's *Church History* 325 C.E. He regarded them as "a trap" for the first Christians, arising from a heresy that involved seeing Jesus as "a plain and ordinary man" (book 3:27). For all his great miracles and prophecies, the Ebionites believed that Jesus lived a thoroughly human existence and was born, like a normal human being, "of intercourse between Joseph and Mary" (book 5:8). Eusebius was further offended by the fact that the Ebionites, while acknowledging the Resurrection and following Jesus's teachings, insisted on observance of the Jewish Law, or Torah.

"They observed the Sabbath and the whole Jewish ceremonial," Eusebius objected, "but on the Lord's Days they celebrated the rites like ours in commemoration of the Savior's Resurrection. Because of these practices, then, they have been dubbed *Ebionites,* a name indicating the poverty of their intelligence, since the name means 'poor' in Hebrew." In other words, in the vernacular of the day, Eusebius called the Jewish followers of Jesus a bunch of idiots.

Yet this much is certain: Jesus and the two Marys, and all of the original apostles, and Jesus's earliest followers in

Jerusalem (including Simon of Cyrene), were Jews. James and the others who established the first Jerusalem church were establishing what, in the first instance, was a Jewish movement.

When they weren't called "Ebionites," the early followers of Jesus were called "Nazarenes." Whatever the origin of this name – perhaps because Jesus was from Nazareth, or a "Nazarite" (a kind of biblical ascetic) or because it refers to a "Netzer," that is, a branch of King David's family – the earliest Jesus ministry seems to have been called "Nazarene." In Matthew (2:23), the term is applied to Jesus himself – "that it might be fulfilled which was spoken by the prophets; he shall be called a Nazarene." The ministry of the Nazarenes was referenced about the year 57 C.E., when Paul was brought to trial before Felix of Caesarea. Tertullus, Paul's prosecutor, says: "We have found this man a pestilent fellow, and a mover of sedition among all the Jews throughout the world, and a ringleader of the *sect of the Nazarenes*" (italics ours).

In his reply, Paul accepts the name without hesitation – and then he proudly and even defiantly defines this Nazarene heresy in the following words: "This I confess unto thee, that after *the way* – which they call heresy – so worship I the God of my fathers, believing in all things which are written in the law [of the Hebrew Scriptures] and in the prophets" (Acts 24:5, 14).

"Nazarene," in the time of James, "brother of the Lord,"

176

appeared to define the earliest Jewish followers of the Messiah-rabbi from Nazareth – including men like Paul. When Paul and Barnabas went to Jerusalem to debate the inclusion of Gentiles into the church – without the Jewish requirement of circumcision – the final decision was rendered by James: "Wherefore my sentence is, that we should trouble not them, which from the Gentiles are turned to God; but that we write unto them, that they abstain from the pollutions of idols, and from fornication, and from [eating] animals that [are] strangled, and from blood" (Acts 15:19–20). In other words, as long as Jerusalem stood, it was the Nazarenes/Ebionites who called the theological shots in the Jewish Jesus movement, and they seemed indistinguishable from the general Jewish population.

Indeed, the Roman writers Tacitus and Gaius Suetonius, in their chronicles of the emperor Claudius's reign, were never quite able to distinguish the early Judeo-Christians from Jews generally. "The founder of [the] sect, [was] a certain Chrestus [Christ]," Tacitus wrote. "[They were] held in check for only a time, [but] the wicked superstition broke out once again, not only in Judea, the birthplace of the malady, but even here in the city [of Rome] itself" (*Annals*, xv.44). According to Suetonius (in *Life of Claudius*): "Because the Jews at Rome caused continuous disturbances at the instigation of Chrestus, [Claudius] expelled them from the city."

Although they are said to have disappeared after the

destruction of Jerusalem, we have historical clues that the Jewish Christians were still around long after. Besides Eusebius, we have the interesting tradition surrounding the finding of the "True Cross." According to Christian tradition, Helena, the mother of the emperor Constantine, came to Jerusalem to locate historical sites associated with Jesus. To find the site of the Crucifixion, Helena gathered the local "rabbis." Clearly, these could not have been mainstream Jews since they would not have carefully preserved traditions surrounding a man they considered a false Messiah. Just as clearly, the people Helena gathered must have been Judeo-Christians.

In the story, Helena acknowledges that the "rabbis" have "secret knowledge" related to the historical sites of Jesus's ministry. Through torture, she forces one Judeo-Christian by the name of Judas – who would later become both a bishop and a Christian martyr – to divulge the secret location of the Crucifixion.

"What if Helena didn't ask all the right questions?" Simcha asked. "If there was a Jesus family tomb, and she never thought to ask about it, the Judeo-Christians would never have volunteered the information. What if, seven hundred years after Helena, the scene was replayed? This time the Judeo-Christians gave up the heretical secret – namely, that the body of Jesus was entombed in Jerusalem."

"So the Judeo-Christians are still around in the eleventh century," Jim said. "And they are about to be put to the sword by the Templars. At that moment, they reveal who they are and they lead the Templars to the tomb. Somehow, they convince the knights of the historicity of their site and, in essence, convert the Templars to their heresy. It's a good story. But hard to prove!"

The fact is that on the antechamber wall of the tomb that enclosed the ossuaries of Jos'e, Judah, Maria, Mariamne, and Jesus, someone had carved a chevron with a circle in its middle.

Today a similar symbol, represented as a complete pyramid (or triangle) enclosing the all-seeing eye of God, can be found in churches and Masonic temples around the world – from modern stained-glass windows in the Church of the Annunciation in Nazareth, to ancient paintings in the Monastery of the Cross in Jerusalem, to carvings on the tower of the Aachen Cathedral in Germany, to the Masonic Temple across from Jim's office in L.A. And yet, no one knows what this symbol really means.

About the time that Simcha and his crew were searching for the tomb under a patio in Talpiot, James Tabor was making a closer study of the Simon of Cyrene ossuary, looking at the names Simon and Alexander written in faded green chalk, under multi-angled lighting.

Suddenly, serendipitously and at just the right angle, the shifting lights shadowed something no one had noticed before. The incision was crude and apparently quite ancient;

it seemed to have been etched with barely more attention to detail than the graceful swirl beneath the "Mariamne" of 80/500, or the cross etched into the nameless 80/506. Yet there was no doubt in Tabor's mind what the incision was supposed to convey: it was a chevron framing a circular gouge (modern or ancient?) to produce an inverted "V" enclosing a dark circle.

There was no sign of a second "V" on the lid. It did not seem merely coincidental to Tabor that a first-century mark similar to the symbol above Talpiot tomb's entrance should appear on the ossuary that bore the name of the same Simon, father of Alexander, who was believed to have become, along with his family, an early follower of Jesus.

Could it be, Tabor wondered, that the chevron, like the symbol of the fish, was yet another early symbol of Jesus's first followers? In the turbulent, anti-Christian times of Nero through Vespasian, could this have been a *secret* Judeo-Christian symbol?

"I've heard it said," Charlie now observed, "that the circle in the chevron on the Talpiot facade is nothing more than a poorly executed rosette, and rosettes have been found by the hundreds on first-century Jerusalem ossuaries. We have to be ready for this."

"First of all," said Simcha, "there's nothing 'poorly executed' about the facade on the Talpiot tomb. But what, after all, is a 'rosette'? The fact is, scholars don't know."

"Many historian types say it signifies nothing more than

a simple, easily executed decoration. Hardly possible. people did not – and do not – choose symbols for their graves simply because they are easily carved. So, what was its meaning?

"Today the Star of David refers to Israel, but two thousand years ago, most Jewish symbols referred to God and His Temple – not to Israel itself. So what was the symbol for Israel? Well – why *not* the ubiquitous rosette? I'm not pulling this idea out of nowhere. In the Song of Songs (2:1–2), Israel refers to herself as 'the rose of Sharon,' and God refers to Israel as a flower 'among thorns.' It's explicit. In the Song of Songs, it meant Israel among the nations true to God. On an ossuary – and especially in Roman times – it probably referred to the hope of a 'true Israel' among the thorns.

"As for the triangle," Simcha continued, "there exist many examples of this as an abbreviation for the front of the Temple in Jerusalem. On the principle that symbols get simpler, on the oldest ossuaries the triangle was supported by columns, but later, some artists dropped the columns and kept the triangle. After 70 C.E. and the end of the ossuary tradition, the triangle appears in many synagogues. But what's unique about the large triangle in our tomb's antechamber is that it's unfinished. It's just a chevron. Shimon Gibson believes this means something, but he does not know what. Here's what I think: clearly, if a complete triangle symbolizes the Temple, the unfinished triangle symbolizes the Temple that was (as Jesus predicted) destined to fall and which was yet to be rebuilt." The Third Temple. The Temple of messianic times, of the "End of Days."

Viewed in this manner, the chevron and circle symbolized, during the last years before the tomb was sealed and the Temple fell, a hoped-for Resurrection for both the Temple and Israel.

"Okay. That may explain the symbol on the façade, but it still doesn't explain how it made it into Pontormo's painting," Jim said. The fact is that the chevron and the circle suddenly showed up throughout Europe, as if by spontaneous generation, *after* the First Crusade. One of the earliest examples – perhaps *the* earliest example – involved a medieval Christian monk named Lambert from St. Omar of France, who had painted what he called *The Heavenly Jerusalem*. Suggestively, the book for which the painting had been commissioned was intended to preserve elements of Crusader theology. Lambert's painting of *The Heavenly Jerusalem* was dominated by circles within chevrons – the same symbol that is carved above the portal of the Talpiot tomb.

Lambert was not alone. The symbol appeared to take on a life of its own and was most often associated with heretical groups such as the Templars and later the Freemasons. It's in this historical context that the symbol appears in *Supper at Emmaus,* suggesting that the secret of Jesus's Ascension was still alive at the time of Da Vinci and Pontormo. But who might have discovered the secrets of the tomb in the eleventh century? Well, it is a fact that the tomb had been entered, perhaps at the time of the Crusades, by people who not only discovered the tomb's secret, but *understood* it.

They had broken in a long time ago. A meter-deep layer of gradually accumulating "rose earth" said so. Whoever breached the seal did not vandalize the tomb interior – and if they removed anything at all, then their looting appeared to have been restricted only to oil lamps, perfume bottles, drinking cups, and other utensils typically found in the antechambers of similarly designed tombs.

If the missing artifacts had in fact been removed by the intruders – then why? In other tombs, such items were fashioned from ordinary baked clay and stone. They were of no value. Unless, perhaps, someone believed the artifacts were connected to Jesus?

Well, the intruders, whoever they were, appeared to be more interested in leaving something behind than in taking anything away. They brought three skulls into the central chamber and carefully placed them on the floor.

According to Luke (23:33), *three* men were crucified on the hill of Golgotha, which is identified in Matthew (27:33) as the "place of a skull." An honor guard of three skulls on the floor could have symbolized the real Golgotha.

"Speculation," said Jim.

"Yes, but the skulls on the floor are part of the facts of the case," I said.

"Well, let's review the facts." Jim said. "It *is* a fact that the Templar knights were in Jerusalem during the entire century of the First Crusade. It is also one of the mysteries of history how they accumulated a lot of power and wealth in very little time. Many have speculated that they had something on the church. Eventually they became too successful – too many kings and bishops owed them money. During the near-total extermination of the Templars, the church leveled so many accusations against the knights that separating fact from rumor and fabrication is an intractable problem."

But among the more interesting accusations were assertions that the knights worshiped a human skull. Also that this skull was allegedly connected with the family of Jesus (usually, it was said to belong to John the Baptist). It was also said that the Templars performed a secret ceremony in which an initiate was obliged to walk a triangle and a circle around a skull and crossbones and that they had gained their wealth through the discovery of sacred Jerusalem relics, which bound them together and, for a time, gave them some manner of secret power over the Vatican.

What if the accusers had gotten some of it right? What if the Templars, who were involved in the general slaughter of Jews and Muslims during the Crusades, did come across a small group of Ebionites – a surviving branch of the early Jesus movement?

Stranger events were already on record. In Iraq, a group calling themselves "Mandeans" have survived into the twenty-first century. They appear to be members of an ancient sect that follow the teachings of John the Baptist and reject Jesus. If the Mandeans could survive in Iraq into the present day, why couldn't the Judeo-Christians survive in Jerusalem until the eleventh century?

Considering the slaughter recorded by their own scribes – a "victory" in which the streets between the synagogues and the mosques flowed red like open veins – it was possible to imagine the knights preparing to put one small sect of captive Jews to the sword. It was also possible to imagine that, like "Judas" before Helena in the fourth century, in what they believed to be the last seconds of their lives, they began crying out the name of Jesus. In this manner, the Templars could have rediscovered the Nazarenes or Ebionites, centuries after they had been officially "stamped out." Their curiosity aroused, perhaps the conquerors spared the lives of some of these Judeo-Christians – who then (either by cooperation or by torture) shared their ancient secrets with the Templars.

Was it possible, then, that this led to the strange intrusion into the tomb attested to by the archaeology? An encounter between Templars and Nazarenes would explain much. Was it possible that the tomb became, briefly, a shrine in Templar rituals? The three skulls seem to suggest as much. Was it possible that the Judeo-Christians shared with the Templars secret scriptures, convincing them to join the Judeo-Christian heresy? The Church certainly thought of the Templars as heretics who denied Jesus's divinity. Was it possible that

Templar leaders were interred in the tomb – accounting for the skulls discovered there? What better way to honor one's leaders than to bury them in the real "tomb of Christ"? And was it possible that the Templars removed one or more skulls from the ossuaries themselves? This certainly would explain the bizarre charges against them.

Perhaps the Templars also took the symbol on the facade back to Europe, accounting for the introduction of the pyramid and the "all-seeing eye"; did they know that Jesus had not *bodily* ascended to heaven? Did the Church believe that the Templars were in possession of the skull of Jesus of Nazareth?

Few documents have survived to describe what actually happened to the Knights Templar. But one of the few pieces of documented, contemporary writing on the subject relates to the Church's absolution of four Knights accused under the Inquisition. It is called "The Chinon Parchment" (named after a castle in France where the interrogations took place). It is dated August 17–20, 1308, and was released from the Vatican Secret Archives only in 2002.

Up to the time of the Chinon document's release, stories of the Templars' being brought down by accusations ranging from skull worship through witchcraft and black masses were largely the substance of undocumented legend. No one really knew what the charges had been. In this document, however, it is clear that the accused *were* charged with idol worship, spitting on the cross, and attending secret ceremonies involving a head, or a skull, or an idol made from a human head.

On Friday, October 13, 1307, King Philip IV of France, with the cooperation of Pope Clement V, moved quickly and effectively to destroy the Templars. That morning, the arrests and inquisitions began, and by nightfall as many as two thousand Knights Templar were either imprisoned or dead.

Some Templars were widely reported as having fled to territories outside French and Vatican control. In fact, the Templars' small fleet of Mediterranean ships disappeared into legend. The outlawed ships flew a flag emblazoned with a symbol first seen on Templar gravestones: the skull and crossbones. Even the name of the flag was Templar in origin – "Jolly Roger," derived from *jolie rouge,* the name given by French Templars to the red flags flown by their thirteenth-century warships.

During the twentieth century, archaeologists excavating Templar graves noticed that the knights' legs had been removed, and the femurs crossed within the casket, under the skulls, in imitation of the skull and crossbones figures carved onto Templar gravestones. Where does this symbol come from, and does it support a connection between the Talpiot tomb and the Templars?

Jerusalem ossuaries vary in length according to the length of the longest bones in the human body, the femurs. Even today, when archaeologists open an ossuary, what they are usually faced with is a skull – which went in last – and crossed femurs beneath. The smaller bones – usually reduced to dust – are below. For the Templars to arrange the bones in their graves in this manner meant that the bodies had been exhumed *after* a primary burial. They obviously went to a lot of trouble to position their dead in this way. It seems that the Talpiot tomb may finally explain all of the Templars' long-lost secrets.

Also, if Simcha is right and the symbol on the facade is related to the promise of Jesus – as a Jewish Messiah – to build a Third Temple at the "end of times," then even the "Templar" name may be related to the Talpiot tomb. For years people suspected that the Knights Templar derived their name from some archaeological discovery they made on the Temple Mount in Jerusalem. But is it possible that their name was derived from their conversion – so to speak – to a surviving Judeo-Christian heresy centered on the Talpiot tomb and related to the expectation that Jesus would rebuild God's Holy Temple?

"Pretty wild," Jim said.

"Not as wild as what we're going to do next," Simcha laughed.

11

Simcha:
The Rediscovery

Mahane Yehuda in Jerusalem is a microcosm of Israel itself: a marketplace made up of Jews and Arabs, rabbis and priests, religious and secular. The air is rich with the smell of lamb shawarma broiling on open pits and fresh falafel being deep-fried. Vegetables, fruits, oils, and chickens squawking in their cages – you can find anything in Mahane Yehuda. My favorite stall belongs to a Yemenite healer who diagnoses his clients while they stand under a macramé tent and he blows smoke up their noses. Depending on what he thinks you suffer from, he prescribes one of his amazing organic juices as a cure. Guava juice, pomegranate juice, citron juice, and all kinds of other exotic drinks are ingested at his place as a way to get rid of indigestion, lower cholesterol, and delay ejaculation.

In this sea of humanity, I met Yossi, the eldest son of David, owner of the apartment built over the Talpiot tomb. David was nervous dealing with a foreign television crew. He couldn't understand our interest in the tomb. But because he believes that the tomb always brings good things to him, he was open to dealing with us. Back in 1980 he was able to get his apartment/condo for a song because people didn't want to live above a burial tomb. "I don't mind," he said to me. His wife of thirty years chimed in, "We always get good energy from the tomb." But David was uncomfortable with television and with stories related to Jesus. His is an Orthodox Turkish Jewish family, and the last thing in the world he wanted was to look out his window and see a line-up of American evangelical Christians waiting to kneel in veneration on his patio. "Speak to Yossi," he said. "Whatever Yossi says."

Yossi runs the family vegetable business in Mahane Yehuda. Although he grew up in an Orthodox Jewish home, he became even more observant after he finished his military service. Yossi never went to university, but he's very well educated. He has an intense curiosity about all sorts of things, especially religion and history. He's also a former commando in the Israel Defense Forces.

"What's under the patio?" he asked me when we met.

"I'm not a hundred percent sure," I said, "but I think it's connected to Jesus." The conversation might have ended right there, but Yossi was intrigued by me: Israeli-born, I

grew up in Canada; I'm fluent in Hebrew, but missing everyday words; and I'm an Orthodox Jew who grew up in a secular home and is better versed in Marxism than rabbinics.

"What's your interest in Jesus?" he asked.

"Aren't you interested?" I answered.

He sized me up and started laughing. "You think he's
buried under the patio in my parents' apartment?" he asked
incredulously.

"Maybe at one time," I said, "but all the ossuaries were
removed in 1980."

"So why bother?" Yossi asked.

"I think the tomb may still hold some secrets. It has never been properly excavated," I replied. "Besides, if it *was* the
burial tomb of Jesus, it has tremendous historical value."

"How will Christians take this?" he asked.

"I don't know," I said. "If someone thinks of Jesus as completely not human – which is actually *not* a position of Christian faith – he'll be upset that Jesus's tomb may have been
found. On the other hand, the Gospels say that Jesus's first
burial was in a temporary tomb and that he disappeared
from it. At least one of the Gospels records another story. In
the Gospel according to Matthew (28:13–15), there was a
rumor, which Matthew calls a lie, circulating in Jerusalem
that Jesus's disciples took their master's body, ostensibly to
rebury him in a permanent tomb. For Christians, what
'proves' the Resurrection is not that the first tomb was empty, but that people encountered Jesus after the Crucifixion.

So whoever believes in a Resurrection from the first tomb should have no problem believing in one from the second tomb."

"How do you know this stuff?" he asked.

"Well, I talked to priests and ministers," I said. "I asked them how they would react if Jesus's body was discovered. One said that it would shake up his faith. The others said that it wouldn't matter. I then made the hypothetical argument about a Resurrection from a second tomb, and they were intrigued and kind of relieved. They had never thought about it. The whole idea of a Jesus family tomb isn't on the Christian theological radar.

"But there is a bit of a possible theological wrinkle," I added, looking at Yossi's intense face. "For Christians, as far as I understand, the next step after the Resurrection was the Ascension. That's where Jesus goes up to heaven to be reunited with his 'Heavenly Father.'"

"So?" Yossi prodded me.

"So ... if a Christian believes in a physical Ascension, meaning that Jesus took his body with him to heaven, the idea of a Jesus tomb will be disturbing. On the other hand, there is no theological agreement about that among Christians. Many believe in a *physical* Resurrection but a *spiritual* Ascension, and a Jesus family tomb will not contradict, or confirm, that particular belief."

"And Jews, will we be upset?" he asked.

"I don't see why," I answered. "Jews obviously don't

believe in Jesus's divinity or Messiahship, but we do believe that he existed as a historical figure. The Talmud confirms this, and Josephus, in at least one line referring to Jesus's brother, also confirms this. So he existed. If he existed, from a Jewish point of view, there is no reason that there shouldn't be a family tomb somewhere. And it actually makes sense that Jesus's family would choose the area of modern Talpiot for a family burial cave. After all, geographically, Talpiot is about halfway between Jesus's traditional family home in Bethlehem and Jerusalem, which is the seat of power for any family claiming descent from King David. Remember, Jesus claimed royal descent on both his mother's and his father's side."

"But will the Jewish community be upset with this discovery?" Yossi insisted.

"When Gentile Christianity began to worship Jesus as a god, Jews pretty much wiped Jesus off our historical memory," I replied. "Maybe that was necessary once, but not today. There is no reason that we should bury part of our history in this manner. Rabbi Akiva believed Simon bar Kochba, the Jewish revolutionary of the second century, to be Messiah. In the end, he was wrong. But does that mean that we wipe Rabbi Akiva, our greatest rabbi, from our memory?"

"Heaven forbid," Yossi said.

"Does that mean we wipe Simon bar Kochba out of our collective conscience?" I asked.

"But we would have, you're saying, if anyone had started worshiping him," Yossi replied.

"That's right," I replied. "If this family tomb turns out to be what we think it is, both Jews and Christians can rediscover the historical Jesus, each from their own perspective. Everyone will deal with the information in his or her own way. But in answer to your question, I don't think this archaeological discovery should upset Jews. In any event, the tomb exists. We're not making it up, and people should be able to handle the truth. You can't do archaeology, or report on archaeology, while worrying about who's going to be upset about the facts. You just have to present the facts, and people interested in the truth will just have to deal with them. And they always do," I concluded.

After a long silence, Yossi asked, "And how do you intend to get into the tomb?"

"By introducing robo-cameras into the nefesh pipes, confirming that we're in the right place, cutting a hole in your parents' bedroom wall, and entering the cave," I answered. Yossi laughed so hard that I had to laugh with him. But I really didn't know what was so funny since that was exactly what I intended to do.

After Yossi agreed, in principle, to cooperate, I explained to him that I wanted several things. First of all, I wanted to sign an exclusivity agreement with the family. No matter how famous this tomb might become, I wanted it understood that I had exclusive television access to it. Second, I asked him to relocate his family to a hotel while we were investigating the tomb. We agreed on a price for the inconvenience. Yossi was honest and fair. "It'll be hard for my father to leave his home, even for a few days," he said. "His home is his castle. He's not one of those guys who likes traveling and moving about. But I'll arrange it."

Yossi now presented me with his conditions: "First, our family is not mentioned in the film," he said. "Second, you keep me posted on what's beneath our house. And third, we get prior rabbinic approval for this endeavor." The last condition scared me. In Israel, religion is also politics. As previously mentioned, the rabbinic authorities and the archaeological community are not the best of friends. Archaeologists are often targets of stones at tomb sites because religious folk see them as desecrators of ancient tombs – people who show no respect for the dead. For their part, the archaeologists see the rabbis as primitives whose medieval notions stand in the way of scholarship and progress. Yossi wanted me to go with him to B'nai Brak, a bastion of religious conservatism in Israel. He wanted me to meet with the legendary (or infamous, depending on your view) Rabbi Schmidl, the main rabbinic thorn in the archaeological community's side.

"Let's compromise," I said. "Let me peer down the pipes without rabbinic permission, and then, if there really is a tomb there, I'll meet with Rabbi Schmidl before we go into it." We had a deal. We then sealed it with a "Memorandum of Understanding" written on the back of a paper placemat taken from a hummus restaurant nearby. All I had to do now was find the tomb and convince Rabbi Schmidl to let me do what no archaeologist in Israel was allowed to do: officially enter an ancient burial cave.

A few weeks after I closed my deal with Yossi, I returned to Israel with my crew. My co-producer, Felix Golubev, is originally from St. Petersburg, formerly Leningrad in the Soviet Union. Felix is of medium height and in his forties. He speaks with a heavy Russian accent and suffers from what I've diagnosed as "repetition compulsion" – the need to ask you the same thing twenty times, followed by "You're sure?" Felix is also one of the best and most meticulous documentary producers on the planet. We've been working together for years.

In 1996 Felix and I went searching for the so-called Lost Tribes of Israel. The result of our labor was the feature documentary *Quest for the Lost Tribes,* which aired around the world. At one point in our journey we were on the Pakistani side of the Khyber Pass, and to cover more ground I decided to split our team in two. I took my part of the crew north, and Felix took a camera and the camera assistant south to Queta, which after 9/11 would become internationally infamous as the headquarters of Al Qaeda. At the time, we knew that there were some bad people around, but we didn't realize how bad, or where exactly they congregated. We were looking for the Tribes, after all, so the bad guys weren't uppermost in our minds.

Felix was not thinking about Al Qaeda, but he was concerned that he might run into the Taliban, the radical Islamic militia that had been created by Pakistani intelligence and that ruled Afghanistan at the time. "If I run into the Taliban in Queta, what do I do?" he asked me. Without missing a beat, I broke into my own version of the Harry Belafonte classic "Banana Boat Song (Day-O)."

"Sing this to them," I crowed: "Come, Mister Taliban, Taliban banana, daylight coming and me got to go home."

A few days later, on the Afghan border, just outside Queta, a truck full of armed Taliban pulled Felix's car aside. They didn't speak English, and Felix doesn't speak Pashtu, the language of Afghanistan. So he started singing, "Day-o … me say day, me say day-o … daylight come and me wan' go home … come, Mister Taliban, Taliban banana … daylight come and me wan' go home." The Taliban fighters grooved to this new anthem, and as he drove through the most dangerous territory on earth, Felix had an armed escort for the rest of his journey. From time to time, they all broke into the "Banana Boat Song."

For the tomb shoot, Felix recruited Itay Heled, an Israeli who was living with his wife and kids in Toronto. Itay is a very serious person. He's so serious that he looks quite tough. And yet this former paratrooper is a softy who likes to write children's books and, unlike most Israelis, always asks for permission. Itay worked for decades in the Israeli film industry, so he knows everyone. Whenever we needed something, like a builder who could take a tomb apart, one of Itay's family members or friends would show up and get the job done.

Bill Tarrant is an expert in robotic cameras. Normally, we couldn't have afforded Bill or his cameras, but he's Jewish and hadn't been to Israel in years. He loved the idea of returning on an adventure and using his cameras to track down Jesus's tomb.

This was my core team. Of course, we always had a cameraman, soundman, and assistant with us. But Felix, Itay, and I would work long after everyone went to sleep and get up long before they got up. There were always a million things to do: track down municipal plans to make sure that if we burst into the tomb, we wouldn't bring the building down; meet with the condo unit association and buy their cooperation; meet with the Israel Antiquities Authority and gain access to the Talpiot ossuaries – it never ended. There was always a crisis. Yossi's father got homesick, the residents got angry, the IAA got suspicious, and so on.

There were many things that could have gone wrong. First, it turned out that the condo association believed that Yossi's patio technically belonged to the building, so any benefits that Yossi's family were getting had to be shared equally. Yossi felt that the condo association were a bunch of nosy neighbors who should stick to their own business and not butt into matters that didn't concern them. At the end of the day we managed to satisfy Yossi's family and the neighbors. As for the nefesh pipes, which supposedly led to the tomb, I couldn't be sure that they actually led anywhere. Builders often humored rabbis by installing pipes that led nowhere. That way the rabbis would be happy because they wouldn't know better, and the builders would be happy because they could get on with their work. Going into the shoot, I really didn't know if the pipes in Yossi's apartment were bogus or authentic. Later, one archaeologist suggested that the builders might have filled the entire tomb with cement so as to get rid of the cavity. If that was the case, we were out of business.

Pouring over various IAA reports, we also learned for the first time about the second tomb that had been unearthed twenty meters to the north of the Jesus tomb. The "second tomb," as we called it, had never been excavated. As with the first tomb, the IAA had been called in. And as with the first tomb, Dr. Amos Kloner had arrived on the scene. But as mentioned, that's when he made a big mistake. According to the builders, when Kloner got there he stepped regally into the tomb. He then picked up an infant's ossuary and unceremoniously dumped its contents to lighten his load. As he carried the little ossuary out of the tomb, hundreds of yeshiva "buchers" (rabbinical students) who were watching Kloner from a nearby academy descended on the site.

Kloner ran for his life, and the students formed a protective circle around the tomb, not letting anyone else disturb its occupants. The stand-off was finally broken when the

IAA, the builders, and the students reached a compromise. The tomb would be resealed and left undisturbed and unexcavated. The builders would then build around it.

What bothered me going into the patio shoot was that I could not locate the second tomb twenty meters north of the patio. It wasn't for lack of trying. We fanned out all over the area, rang doorbells, and crawled into thorny bushes. But we found no pipes and saw no hint of a tomb anywhere to the north of Yossi's apartment.

So with all these questions in mind, there we were on June 25, 2005, sitting on the patio, waiting for Bill to drop his cameras down the six-inch pipes. The first pipe led nowhere. There were two possible reasons: either, as we feared, these were dummy pipes installed by the builders to fool the rabbis, or pipe number one led to a "purification space" meant to create a separation for ritual purposes between the building and the death chamber. We now tried the second pipe. This was no bogus pipe. At thirteen feet, we hit an impediment. Again, there were two possible reasons: either the entire tomb cavity was filled with earth and cement, or debris had made its way into the pipe and blocked it.

We tried everything. We even tried using our $100,000 camera as a battering ram to dislodge the blockage. Nothing worked. Then Bill came up with a great idea: "Let's call a plumber. He'll know how to dislodge things." At first, it seemed odd to break into what might arguably be the greatest archaeological find of all time with the help of a plumber, but when I couldn't come up with a better plan, we called one.

Plumbers being busy, we had to wait for over twenty-four hours. In the meantime, we called Dr. Uri Basson, an expert in sonar imaging. It turned out that sonar-imaging guys are less busy than plumbers. Cheaper too. Basson arrived within a couple of hours, pulled a contraption that looked like a vacuum cleaner with a computer attached to it out of his trunk, and started to work. His job was to confirm that there was a tomb under the patio and that it hadn't been filled in or destroyed. Basson methodically ran his vacuum cleaner up and down the patio. After about two hours, he declared that there was indeed a giant cavity underneath.

Thursday, September 15, 2005
From Simcha Jacobovici to James Cameron
Report from day 1 on location in Jerusalem:

Hi Jim.
We got the family out of the apartment, put them up in a hotel, and have full run of their premises.
Because the patio is in a courtyard and can be seen by numerous other apartments, we built (using the pretext of an upcoming wedding) an awning over the patio – so, we have total freedom of movement and no one can see what we're doing. It felt like a set-up for a bank heist.

Because of a combination of human error and faulty transformers, we managed to burn out the robo-bot cam controls on our second dry run. New robo-cam control being flown in from Germany.

We did manage to put probes down the two "soul" pipes on the patio. The second probe went some 20 feet (about 6 meters) down the pipe. The pictures are pretty dramatic but there is debris blocking the pipe. Tomorrow, hopefully, we will push through. Our probes cannot push through by themselves, into the tomb. We're going to bring in a plumber, to unblock the path for the bots.

Archaeologist Shimon Gibson knows we're in town. He's totally cooperative. But he doesn't want to know anything more at the moment other than the fact that we're doing reconnaissance.

Good night,

– Simcha

The next morning Itay managed to secure the services of the best plumber in west Jerusalem. Teddy had everything: knowledge, a plumber's butt crack, and a gun strapped to his waist. He also knew how to unblock pipes. After half an hour of fiddling with a special metal wire called a "snake," he broke through the debris and unblocked the nefesh pipe. We were back in business.

As we watched on a monitor, Bill now lowered the robo-cam into the pipe. We had built a sort of awning over the patio so as to keep busybody neighbors away. The shade also made the picture sharper. The camera went down five … ten … fifteen feet. Nothing. But the tomb was deep. Very deep below the patio. After twenty feet, we suddenly saw the edge of the pipe. I can't describe what that felt like. The pipe that was supposed to provide access for the souls of the departed was now providing us with access to another world. I couldn't get over it. The tomb under the patio, like all Jerusalem tombs involved in secondary burial, was not *hundreds* of years old but *thousands* of years old. Like Alice stepping through the looking-glass, we were stepping through time. I suppose explorers in outer space or deep below the oceans must feel something like this – suddenly breaking through one reality and entering another. On the monitor, I could see the edge of the pipe and the cavity beyond. I could barely stop myself from jumping out of my skin. Then we were in.

The camera's focus and light adjusted as the robot hung suspended in the cavity below the patio. I was looking for the chevron, the upside-down "V" or "Y" with the circle in the middle. It seemed to make sense. If they were trying to give free access to souls, the pipe could only have been placed outside the tomb, next to the entrance. It couldn't have been placed on the sides or the back of the tomb. As we stared at the images, I was dumbstruck. I saw a gable, and I looked for a chevron. But then I saw kokhim (burial niches) – *what are these doing* outside *the tomb?* I asked myself. Then I saw ossuaries. We weren't *outside* the tomb – our camera was *inside* the tomb. We were recording what no one else had ever recorded – a first-century Jerusalem tomb, a tomb from the time of Jesus, in pristine condition. It was breathtaking to explore, manipulating the robot by remote control. Everyone was ecstatic until I turned to my jubilant friends and said, "I have good news and bad news."

"What possible bad news?" Felix asked. "I mean, we have it, we actually located the tomb!"

"The good news," I said, "is that we are inside this tomb, not outside of it, as we had expected. Also ... we have the only footage ever shot of an unexcavated Jerusalem tomb from Jesus's time."

"So what's the bad news?" Itay asked.

"The bad news is that our tomb – the tomb where the Jesus, Maria, and other ossuaries came from – should be empty. The ossuaries, after all, are at the IAA. We're in the wrong tomb."

The initial jubilation was now followed by stunned silence. "So what the hell is underneath this patio?" Felix asked.

"I have no idea," I muttered, torn between deep disappointment and the excitement of discovering something new.

"Don't you get it?" said Itay. "We're in the second tomb. We thought the second tomb was north of this one, but actually the tomb we're interested in is to the south."

"He's right," I said. "The reason we didn't find a tomb twenty meters to the north is because this is that tomb. Our tomb must be twenty meters to the south of here."

Felix flipped through his research binder. "The IAA report states that the second tomb was found when the builders drove a sona tube through the ceiling. Our nefesh pipe must be going through that pillar and emerging inside the tomb. Look here," he continued excitedly. "According to Kloner, they didn't excavate the second tomb because the ceiling was unstable and they were worried it would collapse."

"At the time, Kloner may have been blowing smoke," I said. "He didn't want to mention the baby ossuary or the yeshiva students."

"According to the internal IAA report," Felix continued, "there are at least three Greek inscriptions on the ossuaries below our patio, but Kloner couldn't decipher them in the haste."

My head was spinning. We were in the *wrong* tomb. But we were *inside* whatever tomb we had located. There were inscriptions, but none of them were deciphered. What if they were related somehow to our story? What if there were apostles or other family members buried here? After all, families were buried in clusters. Some of the ossuaries were very ornate and very well carved. The people buried here were important. Then there was the "face." "Do you see it?" asked Felix. We all saw it, but no one wanted to mention it. On one of the ossuaries, the one on whose side was an elaborately carved rosette, the patina seemed to suggest the face of a bearded man, staring straight at us.

"It's the patina," I said. "It's like cloud gazing. You'll always find a pattern that looks like something."

"Yeah, but I wasn't looking, and neither were you. Patina or no patina, it creeps me out," Felix said. "Of course, there are rational explanations," he continued, "but the fact is that we all see it, and we are all seeing the same bearded man."

"It's just a pattern in the patina," I said, half believing my own words.

We spent a good half-hour exploring the tomb with our robo-cam. Kloner's twenty-six-year-old map of the tomb had been quickly drawn and, as a result, was fundamentally wrong. It was missing kokhim, for example. We phoned Kloner and let him know what we had. He was very excited and promised not to divulge anything to anyone if we agreed to show him our footage. Later, we screened the tapes for him on the balcony of the Begin Center, overlooking the Old City of Jerusalem. There's a great restaurant there called White Nights. Between courses, Kloner watched the footage on a small monitor. His face beamed with delight at seeing the first-ever moving images of an unexcavated first-century Jerusalem tomb.

Of course, there were lots of important questions to be answered with respect to the second tomb, but we had to put these aside for the moment. Four buildings, a garden, and a parking lot surrounded the tomb we had entered with our cameras. Somewhere in there was the tomb we had set out to uncover, the one we were calling the Jesus family tomb. We now spent half the night with Basson and his sonar vacuum cleaner trying to locate a cavity under the ground in ever-widening circles from the patio tomb. We found nothing. We climbed into every sewer and stuck robo-cams into every opening in the garden south of the patio. I was hoping the tomb was not under the parking lot. If it was there, we would never be able to access it. It would just be a cement-filled cavity by now.

The guys wanted to go back to the hotel, while I was determined to find the tomb that very night. But as I was jumping from garden to garden, I must have gotten too close to a window because I was suddenly confronted by a knife-wielding husband convinced that I was a Peeping Tom staring at his wife. As he waved a steak knife at me, I tried to convince him that the only bones I was interested in had spent thousands of years in the ground. I guess he must have figured that the story was too wild to be a lie because he put the knife away, muttering something about what he would do to me with that knife if I ever came by his window again. I decided it was time to go to sleep, and we decamped to the hotel. The search for the Jesus family tomb would have to wait.

Friday, September 16, 2005
From Simcha Jacobovici to Jim C. and Charlie P.
and James T.

Hi all. A quick update from the front lines of tomb hunting. As it turns out, there are two tombs in our area, within fifty meters of each other. They may be related.

We got our robo-cams inside. I can't overstress how important this tomb is. By agreement with the religious authorities, Israeli archaeologists are not allowed to excavate tombs. They can only engage in "salvage" archaeology after a tomb has been broken into by looters or revealed by construction accidents. As a result, no one – I repeat no one – has ever filmed a first-century tomb in Israel, in near pristine condition. Ossuaries in situ … in a Jerusalem tomb dating back to the time of Jesus. But it's not our tomb.

Ah, yes – did I mention that in the process of the above, we got our bot stuck inside the tomb and that we are still trying to retrieve it?

Finally, today, we did some ground-penetrating radar tests in the parks and walkways downhill, and we think we have located the general area of the second tomb. The tomb. Sunday morning, we're investigating it.

Will keep you posted.

Best, Simcha

The next day we were back at the Talpiot apartments. Since

we were no longer protected by the awning on the patio but running around in full view of the residents, with Basson leading the way pushing the sonar equipment, we became the talk of the block. In Israel everyone feels a sense of ownership, so I had to explain our presence to about twenty different people in the span of a few hours. I kind of danced around the questions, joking that I was looking for Jesus's tomb. When I was lucky, that claim sent the busybodies chuckling on their way; when I wasn't, they stuck around for a while wanting to know what we were *really* looking for.

In the meantime, Itay had tracked down one of the building's foremen, the engineer Efraim Shochat. Shochat was now retired. He said that, unlike most builders, because he was a religious Jew, he always respected the dead and made sure that the tombs his bulldozers uncovered weren't destroyed. He also ensured that his workers never dumped bones unceremoniously into the garbage.

Shochat remembered both tombs. We told him that we had located one of them under a patio. He laughed, recalling that they couldn't avoid that location for the patio since all the building's pillars had already gone up before they drove through the second tomb's ceiling. "The first tomb is free and clear of buildings," he said. "We built away from it."

"Can it be under the parking lot?" I asked.

"No," he said, "the parking lot has a cistern under it … a place for water storage in ancient days. It's huge," he continued. "The way I found it was because we kept pouring cement there and it kept disappearing. I thought someone was making off with the cement, so I investigated. It turned out that the cement was flowing into this huge underground cave or cistern, much bigger than a tomb. We finally filled it up," he laughed.

"Did you pour cement into the first tomb?" I asked, catching my breath.

"Oh, no. The tomb you're looking for is probably under one of the terraces that we constructed to deal with the slope," Shochat answered, to my relief.

Shochat had to go to the street below the apartments to get his bearings. "You have to remember that things looked a little different then," he said, "and I was much younger." As we made our way to the street, he would stop next to the buildings and point out the craftsmanship. "A lot of builders skimped on the quality, pocketed the money, and screwed the eventual tenants. Not me," he said with pride. "Look at these stairs, look at these joints, look at the entrance floors. Real marble." For my part, while I respectfully acknowledged the workmanship, I did my best to get Shochat to the street below. The day was dragging on. Basson hadn't found anything. Soon people would be coming home from work, and I would be faced with a tsunami of questions.

Shochat oriented himself between two buildings and pointed straight up. "There," he said, pointing to the first level up the hill. "It should be there."

I ran up the stairs to where Shochat was pointing, but nothing immediately jumped to my eye. There was a pretty big cement slab, five feet by five feet, in the garden, but Shochat didn't think that amounted to anything. For his part, Basson couldn't get a reading under the cement slab. "There's probably metal there," he said. At this point, Shochat was speculating that the tomb must be across the little garden where the cement slab lay, behind the earth that was used to terrace the hill. "If the tomb's there," said Sarael, Itay's cousin, the builder who was now on hand anticipating a possible breakthrough, "then you've got trouble."

"Why?" I asked.

"Well, you can't just bulldoze your way into the terrace. You need reinforcements, or things will start coming down," he laughed. "It can be done, but it's a complicated job. Not like breaking through a bedroom wall into a tomb, as in the original plan."

Basson was now driving his sonar vacuum sideways along the terrace, I was climbing from one terrace to another, and Shochat was waving his arms like a half-mad conductor, getting us to move from here to there. Sarael was having a great time. Itay was embarrassed, and the neighbors started gathering around – little kids back from school, elderly people with no place to go, Russian immigrants, some Syrians, and even one or two Romanians. The carnival atmosphere in the landscaped area between the buildings culminated with the arrival of a blind woman, who put her hand on the slab of cement and announced: "The tomb is here. Underneath. What you're looking for is here."

I made my way from the upper terrace to her. "How can you be so sure?" I asked.

"I've been living here from the beginning," she said. "The archaeologists had left the tomb open. And the kids used to go in and out when they played. I think people must have been scared that a kid would get hurt, and they built this slab on top. But it's there. No question about it."

"What do we do?" Felix asked.

"Sarael," I said, "drill a quarter-inch hole straight into the cement. Bill, stick one of your little cameras in there and let's see if she's right." Sarael got Anwar, one of the two workmen with him, to start drilling.

"This is an archaeological site," Itay said. "We may need IAA approval to go in. Besides, we're on private property. This isn't Yossi's patio. We have no deals with anyone allowing us to go in. You can't just start smashing up private property."

"One thing at a time," I said. "According to Israel's antiquities law, you only need IAA approval if you want to step onto an active site, or a site that the IAA closed. There's plenty of empty tombs and caves in various national parks. Tourists walk in and out of them every day."

"But this isn't an open site," Itay objected.

"It is as far as the IAA is concerned," I said. "You heard the lady. It was covered by tenants, not the IAA. If anything, the tenants might get into trouble for closing what should be an open site. By opening it, we may be helping them out," I answered.

"You should have been a lawyer," Felix laughed. "But what if they don't want our help and regard this as their private property?" he asked.

At that moment, Bill called out, "Come here, Simcha." I ran over to the cement slab. Bill was sitting on it with a kind of plastic tarp over his head to block out the sun. I crawled under the plastic and looked at his tiny monitor. It took a few seconds for my eyes to adjust, but what I finally saw were some rusting iron steps leading to ...*something*. I couldn't really tell, but it looked promising. I threw the tarp off my head. Bill pulled out the camera, and Anwar proceeded to seal the tiny hole. I went to the blind woman. "Whose garden is this?" I asked.

"It's not clear," she answered. "It falls, as you can see, between these buildings. I'm on the board of the condo association of that building there." She pointed to the farthest of the three. "We have to renovate this area," she said. "Look at the steps."

"They lasted a long time," Shochat said, suddenly coming to life.

"Yes," said the blind woman, "but there are changes that have to be made, and it is not clear who this garden belongs to. In fact, the municipality says that it belongs to the city."

"Who do you think it belongs to?" I asked.

"Our building," she said, smiling.

"I agree with you," I said. "Please, can I test your theory that the tomb we're looking for is under the cement slab?"

"Sure," she answered.

"I have your permission?" I asked.

"Absolutely," she said laughing.

"Fellas," I said, turning to my people, "get ready to roll cameras. Sarael, remove the stone slab."

As everyone kicked into action, Amir, the Israeli sound-man, leaned over to Itay and whispered, "We're all going to jail."

"I heard that," I said. Then I added, "For your information, according to the law, if a tomb is left open by the IAA, it does not require IAA approval to enter it, and according to this lady here, the garden belongs to her building, and as a full-fledged member of the condo association, she's given us permission to enter it. We're in no position to get involved in inter-condo squabbles. We needed permission. We got permission. We're not trespassing. Dr. Basson," I muttered, "stay close."

As Anwar started blasting at the cement with hammers, Felix leaned over and whispered to me, "You're right. If the cops come, it's always good to have at least one guy with the title of 'Doctor' at the scene."

It didn't take long to smash the cement along the edge of what turned out to be a cement-covered iron plate. The plate wouldn't budge, however. We then noticed that the iron

railing surrounding the little garden was welded to the plate
in a couple of places. Out came the electric saw, and pretty
soon the plate was free of the railing. Sarael, Anwar, and the
other workmen were now trying to push a huge stone to create an opening for us so that we could look down into the hole
below. Everyone joined in. "Felix," I said, "we're rolling a big
stone, possibly from the mouth of the Jesus family tomb."

"I get it," he said, and kept pushing.

Suddenly the cement-covered plate gave way and slid a
few feet into the garden. I looked into the cavity below and
immediately felt a lump in my throat. About twelve feet
down was the tomb entrance. Carved right above it was the
chevron and the circle.

I grabbed a flashlight and climbed down the iron steps I
had seen on the robo-cam. Suddenly I came face to face with
the object of my quest. I think I kind of hugged the facade –
the enigmatic symbol that had guarded the tomb for two
thousand years. I looked down. The entrance was practically covered in debris, so I had to slide on my back into the
tomb. It was pitch-black, and the air was musty. No oxygen
had entered the burial cave for almost thirty years. I found
it hard to breathe, and I started coughing. A gust of air blew
in from above, and I tried to catch my breath. In the light of
my flashlight, dust particles were now propelled into the air.
I thought I was seeing things, but it seemed to me that there
were Hebrew letters swirling in the beam of light, a kind of
metaphysical, kabbalistic dance of letters.

By now, Felix and John, the cameraman, had also climbed into the tomb. Paul, the assistant, was working the lights from the entrance. We looked around. There was no question that we were in the right place. Six kokhim, laid out exactly as in Gibson's map. There were also two carved benches that, if we were right, once held the bodies of the Jesus family as their flesh decomposed and the bones were readied for burial. Over one bench there seemed to be an inscription, but I couldn't really tell. There was a kind of reddish earth over everything. Also, I suddenly realized that we were awfully close to the ceiling, sitting on mounds of something. *What's in here?* I thought. On closer inspection, the kokhim looked full of ... bodies.

"What are those?" Felix whispered.

"I don't know," I whispered back. And then I saw a pair of *tefillin* in the beam of my flashlight.

Tefillin (phylacteries) are leather boxes that traditional Jews strap to their left arm and forehead when they pray in the morning. The boxes contain bits of scripture. We do this in fulfillment of the biblical injunction to bind the law "to your mind and to your heart." In the Book of Exodus, the tefillin are called "Totaphot," probably originally an Egyptian word. The oldest examples were found on Masada near the Dead Sea, dating back to the fall of the last bastion of Jewish resistance to Rome, about forty years after the Crucifixion. "Felix, there are *tefillin* in here," I said.

"Ancient?" he asked.

"Modern," I replied.

"What are they doing here?" he asked. I looked around, and then it struck me. "This is a *genizah*," I said.

According to Jewish law, once they've been damaged, you can't throw out holy texts such as prayer books or Bibles. They have to be buried like human beings. A burial chamber for holy texts is called a *genizah* in Hebrew. Rabbinic academies have trouble disposing of all their damaged texts. Back in 1980, when they realized that the IAA had left an empty burial chamber behind, with the help of local residents who were afraid their kids would get hurt playing in the tomb, rabbis must have turned the ancient burial chamber into a *genizah* and then sealed it. The Hebrew letters I saw floating through the air were the remnants of damaged holy texts, and the "bodies" in the kokhim were canvas bags full of decomposing sacred writings.

It was then, crawling over the piles of modern texts falling apart at the touch of my fingers, that I realized that I had somehow latched on to a damaged Book of Jonah. It was one of the texts buried twenty-six years earlier by the local rabbinic academy in their newly formed *genizah*. The irony, which was not lost on me, was that Jesus, who spoke in parables and codes, told his disciples that the only "sign" that he would pass on to them regarding his mission on earth was "the sign of the prophet Jonah." Christian theologians have always interpreted this to mean that just as Jonah spent three days in the belly of the whale, Jesus was predicting that he would spend three days in the belly of the tomb before he was resurrected. I had studied this passage in Luke because I believe Jesus was following in the footsteps of Jonah when he sailed to the mysterious "land of the Gadarenes." It was on this fateful trip to the land of the Gadarenes that Jesus, according to the Gospels, quelled the tempest, and it was in the necropolis of Gadara that he exorcised demons from two men and transferred the demons into a herd of swine (Matthew 8:24–27; Mark 4:35–41; Luke 8:22–25). It was a code. Strangely enough, I had been working on that code, parallel with the search for the tomb. Now I found myself crawling in the dark over half a dozen books of Jonah, in the belly of what was arguably Jesus's death chamber.

We called Shimon Gibson and asked him if he could immediately come to Talpiot. "It's not under the patio" was all I said. As we were filming and waiting for Gibson to return to the tomb he had helped excavate so long ago, all hell broke loose above the tomb. Tenants from a nearby building called the police. I climbed up the rusty iron steps and found myself face-to-face with an angry mob trying to disconnect our electricity. "What the hell are you doing?" one shouted.

"Filming," I answered. "And you better not touch any of my equipment," I added.

"Are you threatening me?" Mr. Cable Disconnecting Guy (CDG) asked. "I've called the police. I'm going to lay charges of trespassing and damaging private property," he said as he fumbled with the electrical wires leading to the lights we now had in the tomb.

"Unless you want to add assault to the charges, I suggest you lay off our cables," I said. The blood rushed to my face, and I grabbed the cables from his hands.

There was now a classic Middle East showdown between the tenants and the crew. Though the tenants backed down and decided to wait for the police, they still shouted at me, "Who gave you permission?"

"Shoshana," I replied, pointing to the blind woman.

"She has no authority," they shouted.

"That's not my problem," I said as the police arrived on the scene. At the same time, tenants from Shoshana's building arrived to support us. The cops were amused. They even called for mounted reinforcements. They had shown up for what had seemed like a normal inter-condo dispute gone bad and discovered an ancient tomb, a television crew, and several dozen tenants about to come to blows over who owned what piece of property.

"Let's start at the beginning," the officer in charge said in officer-speak. "Who called the police?"

"I did," said CDG, the irate tenant whom I had threatened with bodily harm if he didn't leave my wires alone. CDG then proceeded to explain that I was the source of all the trouble because I was trespassing and damaging his private property.

"Who are you?" The cop now turned to me.

"I represent several foreign broadcasters," I said, "and I work with this scientist," I continued, pulling poor Basson into the center of the action.

"Never forget. It's good to have a doctor around," Felix whispered to Itay.

There was about an hour's worth of screaming from all sides. Finally, the cop said that if CDG wanted to press charges, that was his prerogative, but doing so would involve a long drawn-out affair in court. CDG's resolve weakened momentarily. "Look here," I said, seizing the moment. "Suicide bombers are prowling around Jerusalem, and we're screaming at each other for no good reason. How about we do this: I ask for your retroactive permission. You say yes, but you put a price on it; say, we have to pay for a little children's swing set right here beside the tomb. We finish our filming, we seal the tomb as good as new, and everybody's happy." CDG was thinking hard on this when his son arrived. His son was a friend of Basson's, and he prevailed on his dad to accept. Pretty soon, we were all friends. Refreshments were being served, cops were watching the filming, we had signed an exclusive deal for access to the tomb, and the kids were celebrating their new swing set.

Unaware of what had happened, Gibson arrived at the scene. "Shimon," I said, "look. We found the tomb." Gibson looked below and was visibly moved. Not only was this history, but it involved a bit of personal history for him, as he had mapped the tomb when he was just starting out in archaeology.

"I want to interview you in there," I said.

Gibson hesitated. "I work in the country," he said. "I need IAA permission."

"It was an open tomb," I replied.

"True enough. And technically, you're right. But I work here, so if you want me in there, I have to call and get permission." Gibson called. The IAA said that there was no problem, and we climbed into the tomb together. Gibson relived his experiences in the tomb and then left.

After Gibson left, we continued to shoot and explore. We didn't know when we would get another chance. The sun set, and the neighbors all went inside. I was trying to get a good shot of what seemed to me to be an inscription when again there was a commotion up above. When I returned to the surface, I found myself face-to-face with an IAA district supervisor. "You have no permission to enter this tomb," she said. "Please close it immediately." As it turned out, there was an IAA employee living directly opposite the tomb. Every day she would see the cement slab out of her kitchen window, yet she never knew it hid an archaeological site. When she saw us, she decided to call her bosses. Whoever she spoke to didn't care about the police, the tenants, or the IAA representative who gave Gibson permission to enter the tomb. They decided to shut us down.

On the one hand, it was sad. On the other, we had finished all we had set out to do. We found not one but two possibly related tombs. We filmed them both. We explored them and mapped them, and we even returned one of the original archaeologists to the site of the discovery. But it was very late. We were tired. And we had no more fight in us. So we got our equipment out of the tomb. With sparks flying into the night, we watched the slab slide back into place. Once again it looked like a small cement square in the middle of a flower garden.

After our trucks were packed, I looked into the courtyard from the parking lot. The neighborhood was going to sleep. Behind me in the distance was the Old City of Jerusalem, straight ahead was Bethlehem, and below, under the cement slab, was arguably one of the most important discoveries ever made.

Sunday, September 18, 2005
Simcha J. to Charlie P. and Jim Cameron and James Tabor

We found it! We seized a rare opportunity, smashed open the cover, and went in. We told Shimon. He came. He asked permission from the IAA. They gave it. Then the neighbors showed up. The police showed up. Everybody showed up. Then the IAA showed up and closed us down. But filmically, we got everything we needed and more. Sorry you couldn't be there, but it was a small window of opportunity that we just had to grab while the grabbing was good. Will tell

you more later … We made peace with the residents,
and they signed a release for the tomb. As for the
IAA: They've made a de facto peace with us. I'm
exhausted. The tomb is sealed again.
  – Best, Simcha

Sunday, September 18, 2005
Charlie P. to Simcha J.

So many questions I want to ask. Failing a silt core
sample, the patina growth sequence, preserved over
almost 2,000 years, should tell much about the chem-
ical (and bacterial) history of the tomb. Again, this
sequence may be unique to each tomb. Were you able
to get a patina limestone sample from the tomb walls,
with patina in situ on the rock? A thumbnail-size
sample (or three) is all we'll ever need. Please say yes.
Hope you can get back in. I sometimes get the feeling
that the tomb would be easier to reach were it 2.5
miles under the sea. There, of course, we'd be dealing
primarily with nature's laws. I prefer nature's laws to
human law, and to unpredictable human behavior.
It's much easier to know where you stand with
nature. I hope we can get back inside. I'll only need
ten minutes. See you later.
  – Charlie P.

Monday, October 24, 2005
Simcha J. to Charlie P.

Charlie:

 We were unable to get silt core samples. None of the original silt layer survives, I'm afraid. As I mentioned, the entire tomb is a meter deep in modern prayer books and scrolls. It is being used as a genizah: under Jewish law, a burial place for damaged holy books. Poetic. But it disturbs the silt analysis ... I chipped a layer of patina off the wall, a one-cm diameter sample, into a plastic container, and I put it in my little zip-up pocket in my cargo pants – for safekeeping, you understand ... As you probably know, one's clothes don't smell very nice when brought home from damp tombs. I was exhausted and had left everything zipped in my pants when I returned home; and my wife threw them straightaway into the washing machine while I slept. So much for the patina samples. Sorry, but we'll get into the tomb again, in a few weeks. I now have an excellent relationship with the condo owners who nearly strangled me last month. We'll go in together and you'll do whatever analysis you want.

 Best,
 Simcha

12

Charlie: The Voices of Time

In 1535, Charles V, the Holy Roman Emperor, took a combined fleet of Spanish and Italian ships carrying German and Italian artillery and cavalry detachments and destroyed much of the Arab fleet in the harbor of Tunis, before moving on to blast through the gates of Tunis itself. In Jerusalem, the sultan Suleiman, hearing that Charles V had spoken openly about renewing the Crusades, commissioned the Ottoman architect Sinan Pasha to redesign and fortify the city's walls, both defensively and offensively, in accordance with the dictates of artillery- and gun-based warfare. Within the six years required for Charles V to strengthen his hold on the port of Tunis and to expand his fleet into an international coalition, the new wall and its defensive towers completely encircled Jerusalem, looking much as the gates and walls would appear to visitors in the twenty-first century. The wall itself turned out never to be needed in the war for which it had been designed. In 1541 a rapid-fire succession of winter squalls all but annihilated Charles V's fleet.

Tax records from the construction period documented 557 Greek Orthodox Christians living permanently within Jerusalem's walls, along with 216 members of the Armenian Church, 176 Coptic Egyptian Christians, 92 members of the Syrian Church, and several Franciscan monks. The Swiss pilgrim Ludwig Tschudi recorded in his journals that the Greek Orthodox Christians spoke Arabic and lived like Muslims, with the priests of the Church, like Muslim clerics, being permitted to marry and to have children.

The Jerusalem Greek Orthodox stood apart from the other Christian churches in one additional detail: they revered Mary Magdalene almost as highly as Mary, the mother of Jesus, and they celebrated St. Magdalene as "equal to the apostles."

*   *   *

Today we visited the IAA warehouse. An afternoon of silent awe, mingled with catastrophe.

The warehouse was row after row after row of dated and numbered ossuaries – more than one thousand ossuaries, stacked floor to ceiling. IAA 80/500–509's ossuaries were together in a remote corner (except for those of Judah, son of Jesus and Maria, which had been separated from the rest and removed to the Israel Museum). They were stacked on three shelves. The Matthew ossuary had been broken on one side of its rim, and I collected a sample of cast-off patina, which had preserved a clean cross-section of the limestone matrix, with its tomb patina overlaying the matrix.

It appeared that someone had scoured and vacuumed clean the entire interior of the Matthew ossuary – for there were scarcely more than a few hundred milligrams of loose organic material, or debris of any sort, in the bottom for future laboratory analysis.

The Mariamne ossuary was different. The *terra rossa* dust had become part of a layer of mineralization that settled on the ossuary interior, about a millimeter deep (thicker than a sheet of cardboard). The IAA had left the mineral layer more or less intact. Bacteria, as they accreted the minerals and fixed them in place, had formed flattened, concentric concretions, some of them resembling pancake-shaped pearls. Under a hand-held magnifier, I could see that the concretions had preserved bits of fiber (shroud?), tiny chips of what might have been bone, and what appeared to be near-microscopic and partially fossilized remnants of mostly disintegrated wood.

Next came the ossuary marked with an "X"-like cross next to the words "Jesus, son of Joseph." The layer of accretion in the bottom of the box seemed to contain far less organic debris than the Mariamne accretion bed, and less than the accretion beds of neighboring ossuaries. Nevertheless, there was evidence of the "squashed pancake" concretions – each of which was bound to contain, in its center, a little nugget of fossilized organic debris and perhaps a fleck of bone or a fragment of blood-smeared shroud. I sampled this.

I had hoped for a sample of "Jesus" patina attached to stone matrix, but unlike the Matthew and Mariamne ossuaries, there were no preexisting clean breaks in the Jesus ossuary, with matching shards lying in the bottom of the box. I couldn't just pick up a flake. The IAA attendant said that if I *really* needed to take a sample in order to reconstruct accurately the two-thousand-year chemical history of a tomb, I should do so.

But I could not do this. None of the IAA personnel knew what we knew. None of them really suspected how truly important this ossuary might be. I could not bring myself to remove the necessary tools from my bag, to chip away at a tiny cross-section of stone. Even a two-millimeter-wide sample was too much for me to cut off, even if my *not* doing so meant leaving behind an important piece of the scientific puzzle.

To even think of chipping the Jesus ossuary felt like an act of vandalism.

About two hours later, the ossuary provided a sample of its own accord, during a moment that was next of kin to having held the Holy Grail in one's hands (which, in a sense, was what number 80/503 came closest to being) and then to have seen it shattered.

Late in the afternoon, an attendant and an assistant were loading the Jesus ossuary into a semi-permanent crate lined with protective foam. The whole process was being recorded in high definition when the ossuary – arguably the most priceless of all Christian relics – snapped in two along its center and, one part of a second later, seemed to implode.

On other expeditions, I've seen camera equipment and lighting systems and deep-sea bots worth hundreds of thousands of dollars crashed and broken; I've watched A-frames on ships buckle and kick up entire decks of steel plate – and always such events brought instantaneous and seemingly unending strings of curses.

That's exactly what anyone would have expected this time, but cursing wasn't even in it. The cameras recorded long, long seconds of stunned silence, during which everyone seemed to be thinking, *Are we all seeing the same thing? Did this really just happen?* Whole wars had been fought over Jerusalem, and for nearly two thousand years this artifact – "this priceless relic" – had survived in pristine condition.

Then, after it finally sank in, there was probably nothing left for it except for a strange, instinctive form of gallows humor to take over.

When finally I edged nearer the wreckage, and could bring myself to look, I saw a splinter of limestone, about two centimeters (or just under one inch) in length – with perfect cross-sectioning through both matrix and patina – lying directly on top of the pile. I could see immediately that it would fit precisely within the dimensions of my sample vial. This time, I collected the sample.

About this same moment, the attendant had decided that he would load the pieces into a wooden crate, nail the crate shut, and forklift it away for eventual repair. Simcha and I insisted on gently wrapping each piece, individually, in soft paper before seeing them lowered into the crate – and by then, of course, I was trying to keep back tears. The room was silent again when Simcha discovered that the entire "Jesus, son of Joseph" inscription had survived perfectly intact, without so much as a scrape. It chilled me when he pointed out that the only damage to the section of stone that bore the inscription involved the parting of Jesus's name from the cross.

A little strange, yes. But not inexplicable. I have reviewed my own pre-shatter footage of the Jesus ossuary, dating back at least two hours before the implosion. It reveals a hairline fracture in the stone, following a path down from the ossuary's rim, between the cross and the word JESUS. There is little question in my mind that this crack was the fault-line from which the initial breaking-in-two of the ossuary began. No mystery here.*

---

* As of this writing, the ossuary has been completely restored by the experts at the IAA.

So here's *another* thing you don't see every day. On Wednesday, December 14, 2005, we entered the tomb itself.

The iron and concrete lid was moved aside again – and the air, of course, was very bad. All those tons of decaying books have replaced the *terra rossa* mud – essentially to the same depth recorded in Shimon Gibson's original drawings. The air is full of their decay products, and the moment the lid was pulled open wide enough to allow ingress, the particles of paper dust appeared to be driven out to the antechamber on gusts of freshly expelled air. A few broad, flat flecks glinted like snowflakes in the first rays of sunlight, and something else moved down there in the bottom – spiders as large as walnuts. Not a great many of them, but enough.

The large antechamber symbol was easy to see, but I thought I noticed a smaller symbol, below the wide circle. It may originally have been a triangle with a doughnut-sized circle in its center. I'm not sure.

Recent rains had percolated into the ground, and everything inside the tomb was sheathed in beads of moisture, yet tiny paper flakes, moist yet ultra-light, were floating everywhere. To me, this was a firsthand look at and feel of what it must have been like throughout the wet seasons of the past two millennia, except that those periods were marked by low levels of oxygen, as when Simcha first broke the seal in September and felt like he was choking.

Then as now, the paper flakes were floating, and for a moment Simcha had thought the low oxygen levels might be causing hallucinations and that they'd have to pull him out through the antechamber on a tether. What else was he to think when letters of the Hebrew alphabet were floating suddenly before his eyes? To his sudden relief, he understood that the letters were real.

For me, there was no time for awed silence, or for thoughts about touching history. Before I went in, I had been told that the neighbors were getting restless about the "intrusion" and that we should expect the religious authorities to arrive on the scene, and to shut us down, at any moment.

My primary concern was simply getting inside for ten minutes, for just long enough to get my patina samples from the tomb wall. I had rehearsed, with my eyes closed, the location of every tool and container inside my bag and the use of my two video cameras (one as backup, in case the first malfunctioned) for recording context shots of each sample. Without evidence verifying whether or not the patina on the walls recorded the same chemical history as the patina on the tomb's ossuaries, there was no determining whether or not tombs and ossuaries had patinas as distinctive as a fingerprint. My hunch was that they did, but this had to be tested.

At one point, I was actually in the bottom of the shaft that enclosed the antechamber – only moments from sliding down on my back into the tomb itself – when one concern or another got me called back to the surface. Simcha was inside the central chamber with the cameras and photographer Steve Quayle. The air was intermittently getting into the red zone and needed time for recirculation. This caused nearly an hour's delay, and a bad sense of "go fever" held dominion over my thoughts. Soon people would be arriving home from work, more neighbors would be crowding around, and all that was necessary to shut the operation down before I could obtain my samples was for only two or three onlookers to start getting twitchy. Ten minutes inside: this was all I wanted, and needed.

By 4:00 P.M., the air was safe again; videotaping, underground, was almost "in the can," and I was inside.

Within two minutes of my arrival in the central chamber, we could hear muffled shouts on the surface. As it turned out, the shouts had nothing to do with us, but fearing that we might be called out at any second, I went straight to work, collecting and documenting samples.

Within ten minutes my primary samples were all "in the bag."

About this time Simcha and Steve, who were setting up lighting angles with their backs turned to me, glanced across the chamber and asked, "Charlie, what on earth are you doing?"

"Finishing my samples," I said quickly, and continued sampling.

"But I wanted to film you *doing* that!" said Simcha. He sounded almost as heartbroken as I would have been if I'd never gotten a chance to go inside.

"Sorry about that," I said. "It's okay, though. I won't likely be running out of things to sample. Don't worry. There's more sampling to film."

But already I was worried that the dark brown patina over the walls and ceiling – and the smell of bacteria and mold working on the paper – had penetrated everything and perhaps reworked the patina all the way down to its roots. Shimon Gibson had told Simcha that when he entered the tomb in 1980 the walls were chalky white and, in places, reddish-tan. As it turned out, the microbes in the air merely settled on the outer surface of the tomb patina, and the patina itself, when dry, was a very light shade of reddish-tan.

I was still brooding over the possibility of a ruined patina that would no longer match the tomb's ossuaries, and Simcha was still worrying about missed reaction shots during my first actual collection of a sample, when a new problem surfaced.

The limestone itself was so saturated with moisture as to be barely more substantial than modeling clay and Swiss cheese. No rock hammer had been necessary – in fact, no hammering of any sort. No chisels either. Most of my samples were cut from the wall and arch of the tomb's north-side burial ledge. Nothing more than a plastic butter knife was necessary. And that was the problem.

By the time Simcha's camera was ready for me, I had realized that something about the ceiling, in the middle of the central chamber, just did not look right. The chisel marks in the rock were as old as Jesus, and yet to all outward appearances they looked brand-new ... until I pressed my knife to the ceiling. The blade sank all the way in, with almost no resistance at all.

"Guys, I think we have to be more careful about how we move around in here."

"What do you mean?" Simcha asked.

I probed again with the blade, more gently this time.

Steve let out a low whistle. "So what's your diagnosis, doc?"

"I don't know," I answered, with a trace of anxiety. As one might have anticipated in a tomb that bore the names of so many saints and prophets, not everything was quite as it appeared. There was something fundamentally disquieting about a roof that was simultaneously freshly chiseled and two thousand years old, about a place that looked rock-solid but was softer than clay.

"To be honest, I'm not sure what's holding the ceiling up," I said. "I'm estimating more than two cubic meters of soggy cheese hanging over our heads. How many metric tons do you suppose that amounts to?"

"Is it safe to move around down here?"

"Unsure," I said. "At a guess, the cheese goes up about a hand-length into the ceiling. You'd probably survive (with just a few aches) if a soft slab of the stuff peeled away and whacked your shoulder. Not as bad as the whole thing caving in, or a hunk of solid rock falling down, but I do think we need to consider this place a hard-hat zone." Trailing off into thought, I supposed that the tomb had become equally damp and "cheesy" once or twice every year ... up to 3,900 times over the course of the last 1,935 years. And yet the ceiling had survived without even a single large chip falling away in one of the planet's most notorious earthquake zones, with dynamite and pile drivers working the hill from 1980 to the present, and with a wide, truck-bearing road barely more than fifty meters away. Add to the usual terrestrial din the chopping away and moving aside of a iron and concrete slab, at close range, and –

"And?" Steve pressed.

"And it's plain that we don't know everything there is to know about this Jerusalem chalk. I can't tell you what's kept this roof intact under these conditions for two thousand years, but I do believe that if a couple of tons of Swiss cheese really were waiting to clobber us, our life insurance policies would have become fully activated by now."

13

GATTACA:
The DNA Story

The seventeenth century had come and gone. The eighteenth century had come and gone. The march of conquering armies resumed and seemed bound never to go away, while underfoot, a silent, geological process was bridging past and future. Were someone to descend upon the Jesus ossuary with a sufficiently advanced microscope, he or she would have seen a tiny forest of apatite crystals and mineral glass, as beautiful as any microscopic landscape of snowflakes. Beneath the crystal bed – cocooned by it – lay shreds of cloth, or shroud, "woven" from a plain, paperlike pulp. Slicked with DNA and mingled with internal body fluids and chips of human bone, most of the fibers had supported colonies of black mold before the crystals overgrew them, and forestalled dissolution.

*   *   *

The **"Mariamne"** and **"Jesus"** bone fragments had been cocooned in the cores of mineral concretions in the bottoms of their ossuaries. The largest fragments were no wider than the crowns from human teeth.

> IAA 80/503: "Jesus, son of Joseph"
> IAA 80/500: "[The ossuary] of Mariamne also known as the 'Master'"

If these two ossuaries truly belonged to Jesus of Nazareth and Mary Magdalene, DNA tests would reveal that the two people buried within were *not* related. All scriptural records – whether canonical or apocryphal – were clear on one genealogical point: Jesus of Nazareth and Mary Magdalene, if their DNA could be read, would be two individuals who had no family ties. But what are the alternatives? People buried in the same tomb were related by either blood or marriage.

Thunder Bay, Ontario, is not a tourist destination.

During winters, the temperature drops to -30 degrees Fahrenheit. And yet students flock to Lakehead University because, even though it lacks some of the benefits of sunnier climes, it boasts one of the five best paleo-DNA labs in the world.

Paleo-DNA labs specialize in getting DNA from "human residue" that would stump any regular DNA facility. James Tabor is friends with Dr. Carney Matheson, who is one of the directors of the Lakehead lab. Carney is an Australian who left Sydney's beaches for Thunder Bay's snowdrifts because of the opportunity to work in the Lakehead DNA lab.

The samples were not identified by their name, but by two numbers: "80-500" and "80-503." Simcha and Tabor wanted a "blind result" from the testers. For this reason, they told Dr. Matheson only that the accretion bed and the bone samples had come from an ancient Jerusalem tomb. Of course, this was not the whole story, but it was the absolute truth.

"We are trying to reconstruct the family relationships of a royal lineage," Tabor had said. For his part, Matheson was up for the task of attempting to extract DNA from bits of ancient residue taken from the bottom of the ossuaries. The idea was to create a DNA profile of each of the two individuals so as to establish any familial relations between them. The samples were sent by courier, and everyone waited anxiously for the results.

Days turned to weeks, and weeks to months, before Matheson, who doesn't own a cell phone and rarely checks e-mails, called Tabor back. They had successfully extracted DNA. Simcha and Tabor gave him an unprecedented response: "Don't tell us the results over the phone. We're coming up as fast as we can. We're coming with a camera crew. Tell us then."

"Whose bones *are* these?" Dr Matheson asked.

"You'll know soon enough," said Simcha. "In fact, if they turn out to be who we think they are, you'll know as soon as we know."

Paleo-DNA

That is how the story started to draw toward a conclusion.

"The samples you sent up," Matheson began, "were consistent with bone material that was centuries old. These people were of Middle Eastern stock."

In an effort to limit contamination by anyone who had handled or sneezed on the concretions in modern times, the samples had to be broken, freshly, in a lab, with the hope that relatively pristine material could be found beneath the surface of each fragment.

"But when we first examined your samples," Matheson explained, "they did not look very good: Very dry. Very desiccated. Very small and very fragmentary."

"And so, for that reason, we knew it was going to be very difficult for us to do the analysis," Matheson continued.

He explained that they broke open the bones in a "cleanroom," where the technicians worked in "space suits," and then extracted fresh samples and began to process them, trying – at each stage – to assess and understand the quality of the DNA. In this particular case, Matheson explained, and indicative of their true antiquity, the DNA samples turned out to be quite degraded (which was, of course, quite the antithesis of what would be found in a modern contaminating sneeze).

Degraded and fragmented. Tabor gave Matheson an expression that asked, *So how bad is this?*

"Well," Matheson said, "the damage occurring to the DNA, over time, limits what type of work we can do."

Simcha said: "There was a question as to whether or not the samples contained enough material to create a significant profile."

"Well, I think we can answer that now," said Matheson. "You see, because we specialize in ancient DNA, we've got equipment and methods that are really sensitive – very, very specific to damaged DNA, such as the material from your tomb."

Matheson then explained that after extraction the *nuclear* DNA in the bones – the broader genetic blueprint copied in the nucleus of every cell – had proven extremely difficult to recover. Impossible, in fact, given 2006 technology.

"However," Matheson said, "we did not quit. Instead, we shifted our focus to the *mitochondrial* DNA – which is, of course, the DNA inherited *maternally,* from mother to child. This means that we can identify maternal relationships. Meaning, we can only address questions such as: 'Are these two individuals – one male and the other female – mother and child? Are they brother and sister? Or are they two unrelated individuals?'" Carney fell silent.

After a moment, Tabor broke the silence: "Well?"

"We successfully extracted mitochondrial DNA," Dr. Matheson announced, smiling.

Over the course of centuries, periodic intrusions of water were bound to be unfriendly to chromosomes. Yet in each ossuary sample, the bacteria-like organelles known as mitochondria had survived relatively intact. Protected by their own bacteria-like membranes, the mitochondria in fact live inside all animals, just like bacteria – which had evidently infiltrated the remotest ancestors of us all and managed to stay aboard. Reconstructing a complete Jesus genome appeared to be beyond human reach. In the mitochondria, however, nature had preserved just enough information. Just enough ...

The mitochondrial DNA of every race on earth has been passed down by women only, beginning about 100,000 B.C.E. with a small tribe in Africa, passing next through an African-Asian branching of lineages near 76,000 B.C.E., and then through an Asian-European branching about twenty thousand years later. Certain rapidly changing regions on the mitochondrial genome had recorded all of the branching lineages through all the generations of all the races and tribes and families – beginning with the tribe of one woman in Africa (known to science as "Mitochondrial Eve").

Through such changes, it has been possible to map out a kind of "mitochondrial clock" and to actually watch how, for example, Greek and Semitic tribes-people begat a lineage that branched off to become Germans and Britons.

In 1980 young Shimon Gibson neither imagined nor dreamed that words such as "we've been able to access the mitochondrial DNA" would be heard in his lifetime – much less that they would be spoken in specific reference to the "Jesus" and "Mariamne" from his tomb. From a 1980 perspective, only a writer of science fiction could have imagined the likes of what Carney Matheson was able to achieve as part of his everyday work routine.

"So we've got the mitochondrial DNA," Matheson continued. "Now, since it was very fragmented, the amounts I'm talking about were very small. But we were able to amplify it and able to sequence it. We then went on to clone those sequenced DNA fragments. And by cloning DNA, we were able to compare many, many copies – which increased the validity of the work when we tried to compare sequences from one individual with sequences from the other. That's essentially what we've done, and I can show you the results, here, today."

Simcha and Tabor held their breath. A positive match would mean that this Mariamne and this Jesus were, say, brother and sister and that this Mariamne could not have been Mary Magdalene, sister of the apostle Philip. In such a case, the Jesus of IAA 80/503 and the Mariamne of IAA 80/500 could *not* possibly have been who they appeared to be. The "Jesus equation" would have been instantly invalidated, and the entire tomb assemblage would have fallen apart.

"I'm ready to hear the results," said Tabor, with a deep breath.

"Okay," said Matheson. "Here it comes."

He called two graphs onto a computer monitor, one above the other.

80-503; Marker 140: CTACCC ...

80-500; Marker 140: ACCTAG ...

Each resembled an electrocardiogram, except that instead of representing a pulse-beat, each peak on the graph represented the signal of a specific nucleic acid base: adenine (A), cytosine (C), guanine (G), and thymine (T). Genetic information was stored in the DNA molecule as a linear code made up of A, C, G, and T – somewhat analogous to the binary code used in twenty-first-century computer software, but only "somewhat" analogous, because the genome's quadnary code offered infinitely greater (and more elegant) variation than could be found in any binary jump-drive.

Matheson pointed alternately to the "120" markers, displayed on the two parallel graphs. "What we have here," he said, "are some of the variations between the two individuals. Now, the top one is known to me as 80-503, and the bottom one is what I know as 80-500."

80-503; Marker 120: CCAGTAGGAT – "Jesus, son of Joseph"

80-500; Marker 120: ACCCACTAGG – "Mariamne, also known as Master"

"Put simply," the paleo-geneticist said, "we have a 'polymorphism' here, that is, a genetic variation, beginning with this 'C' and this 'A,' in which we can see a clear mismatch. We're looking at a variation between two individuals, along the same marker on the same gene sequence. And this polymorphism shows only *one* difference between these two people. There are others, including this example at the '130' marker point."

80-503; Marker 130: ATCAACAAAC – Jesus

80-500; Marker 130: ATACCAACAA – Mariamne

"So," Matheson continued, "when we see a number of polymorphisms between two sequences, we can then conclude that these two individuals are not related – or, at least, not maternally related."

Simcha and Tabor were now both smiling broadly, though Dr. Matheson did not yet know why.

"And," said Simcha, "this means – ?"

"That this man and woman do not share the same mother," Matheson said quickly and conclusively. "They cannot be mother and child. They cannot, maternally, be brother and sister. And so, for these particular samples, because they come from the same tomb – and we suspect it to be a familial tomb

– these two individuals, if they were unrelated, would most likely have been husband and wife."

*   *   *

The woman known to every reader of the King James Bible as Mary Magdalene was, according to the Gnostic Gospels, "the companion of Jesus." In these texts, as in the Church-approved Gospels, it is to Magdalene that Jesus first reveals himself after the Resurrection. In fact, in the Gnostic Gospel of Mary Magdalene, it is she to whom Jesus appears a year and a half after the Crucifixion, and to whom he entrusts his final revelation of the world to come. Mary Magdalene is also identified in the Gospel of Mary as the woman whom "the Savior loved more than the rest of women … Surely the Savior knows her very well."

In the biblical world, to "know" had a very special and very intimate meaning: "Adam knew Eve his wife; and she conceived, and bore Cain" and "Cain knew his wife; and she conceived, and bore Enoch" (Genesis 4:1, 17).

Jesus of Nazareth and Mary Magdalene?

It seemed impossible to Carney Matheson when they told him the rest of the story.

Impossible. But the details extracted from the tomb so far had failed consistently to negate the conclusion and were in fact adding up, one positive indicator after another, in support of it. They had begun to read the DNA of Jesus and Mary Magdalene. Unimaginable. But there it was.

Jesus's mitochondrial DNA seemed typical of the Semitic tribes-people who had inhabited the Jordan Valley region in the time of Pilate and Herod. There were traces of genome from as far away as Greece and India, but the mitochondria mostly reflected what might today be called a "Semitic" ancestry, with all hereditary roads leading southward into Africa.

No one could yet say exactly what Jesus and Mary Magdalene looked like, but Matheson could be fairly certain that their hair and eyes were dark. Jesus's hair in fact was probably curly, even what might be called "wooly." In any case, Jesus probably did not resemble the light-skinned, straight-haired, blue-eyed man depicted in almost every church in the world since the time of the Renaissance painters.

Simcha wanted few things more in the world now than to have a DNA sample from "Judah, son of Jesus." But sadly, despite repeated efforts, his path to a sample from IAA 80/501 appeared to be irreversibly blocked. No one was being particularly clear with him about what had happened to the bone material. By one account, the accretion bed had been scoured out of the Judah ossuary as part of a cleaning in preparation for a museum display of a random collection of ossuaries with typical New Testament names. By another account, DNA work might be possible in the future by swabbing stains on the ossuary walls.

It did not seem to matter. As the ossuary inscriptions told it, if Jesus was the son of Joseph, and if the younger Judah was the son of Jesus, then of course (if Jesus's and Mariamne's mitochondria are proper and truthful guides) the mother of young Judah and the wife of Jesus could have been no one except Mariamne ... "also known as Master" ... also known as Mary Magdalene.

If these ideas were correct, they were only the twilight before the dawn, merely a pathway into the "rose earth" that had left its geochemical signature on the tomb walls and inside every ossuary, providing clues that might yet resolve a mystery more fantastic than any fiction writer could imagine.

14

Charlie:
A Crime Lab's Jesus

January 1, 2006
From Simcha J. to Charlie P.
cc: Jim Cameron, James Tabor, Shimon Gibson

Hi Charlie:

*As things stand, we have a provenanced tomb;
ossuaries found in situ; inscriptions that match the
New Testament narrative, i.e., "Jesus, son of Joseph,"
"Maria," "Jos'e," "Mariamne aka 'the Master'" ...
and now the DNA.*

*But we also have a "missing ossuary" from the Tal-
piot tomb. The mysterious "James, son of Joseph,
brother of Jesus" ossuary suddenly appears on the*

antiquities market at about the same time that the "missing" ossuary goes missing.

James Tabor checked the James ossuary dimensions in Shanks's book, and it's a virtual match to the missing ossuary as cataloged by the IAA.

If we could demonstrate that the James ossuary is Talpiot's "missing ossuary," the case for the Talpiot tomb being the Jesus family tomb would be closed.

To that end ... how are your patina tests going? Have you "fingerprinted" the Talpiot ossuaries? Do they match James? Do all ossuaries match each other from a patina perspective? Need to know asap.

Simcha

* * *

My idea about patina fingerprinting rests on the fact that each soil type and rock matrix possesses its own private spectrum of magnesium, titanium, and other trace elements.

In theory, the patina inside a tomb or on the surfaces of its artifacts should develop its own chemically distinct signature, depending on a constellation of variable conditions, including the minerals and bacterial populations present at any specific location and the quantities of water moving through that specific "constellation."

If such a chemical "fingerprint" existed, scanning patina samples on a quantum level with an electron microprobe would reveal a chemical spectrum that could be matched to a specific tomb and to any objects that come from it.

In Israel, the geochemists Amnon Rosenfeld and Shimon Ilani had already performed an electron microprobe analysis on a patina sample from the James ossuary. At Simcha's request, they sent me their results, along with the requisite microscopic sample. A second James sample was delivered from Vincent Vertolli, a curator at the Royal Ontario Museum in Toronto, where another electron microscope test had been performed.

If the samples I took from the walls of the Talpiot tomb and from its ossuaries all displayed matching elemental spectra, then we could compare these to the scans of the James ossuary and look for a match. If there was a match, we would have to make sure – by testing against random samples – that the match was meaningful. If, however, the walls and the ossuaries of the Talpiot tomb scanned with wildly varying spectra, that would mean that no patina fingerprinting was possible. It would mean that localized habitats *within* tombs produced their own individual patina chemistry, with levels of variation so great that the idea of distinguishing one whole tomb from another would be rendered impossible.

From Charlie P. to Simcha J. and Jim C.
January 27, 2006

Dear Simcha, Jim:
   We are ready to start on the patina samples collect-
ed last month from the walls of the tomb – a patina
that owes largely to the distinctive terra rossa soil that
seeped inside, sometime after 200 c.e.
   It is possible that the wall patina will match the
"Jesus," "Mariamne," and "Matthew" patinas – and
that these in turn will match the "James" ossuary
patina. But only after I have results from the tomb
walls and from our IAA 80/500–509 ossuary samples
(assuming that discernible results are obtainable),
will I actually open the Israeli Geological Survey
package and look at data from the "James" ossuary
patina. I do not want to risk being even unconscious-
ly influenced by the James data. It should, for me, be a
blind study. See you later.
                                          – Charlie P.

In 2006, Bob Genna was director of the Suffolk County
Crime Laboratory in New York. When he began in this field,
he avoided mentioning what he does for a living because the
usual response was a flinch or a slight cringe, followed by
the question, "How can you stand seeing dead people?" He
still avoids mentioning the job, but the reasons have

changed, owing largely to the wildly popular television show *CSI*. These days the first question people ask Bob, when they learn he is a CSI, has become: "What's the most gruesome case you've ever worked on?"

Bob was approximately the thirteenth person to be "brought into it." He and I had come within a gnat's breath of first meeting much earlier, in July 1996 during the investigation of the TWA flight 800 explosion. At the time, the Northrop-Grumman Aerospace engineer George Skurla had called me to look at metallic debris and provide what would have been a three-hundredth opinion on how the aircraft broke apart and fell into the Atlantic. However, I could not bring myself to touch the wreckage. What Skurla did not know was that a sudden family crisis had turned out to be all that kept me from being among the many souls lost in the disaster. I was supposed to be on that flight. Had it turned out differently, Bob Genna would have met me, for the first and last time, as one of the victims whose DNA his crew identified. Instead, years later, we were looking for the chemical fingerprint of the Jesus family tomb.

For Bob, the tomb project had begun simply as planning for a new scientific challenge: could it really be shown that every burial site is chemically distinct and that any object excavated from the ground at the site (be it an ossuary, a piece of jewelry, a murder weapon, or a scrap of skull) can be "fingerprinted," by the chemistry of its patina? The theory, if it tested well, might have wide-ranging applications in crime-scene investigation. A tarnishing piece of metal or a broken chip of china might record changing cooking styles or the types of paint used throughout a generation in a single home, just as the patina on the Statue of Liberty has recorded the history of air pollution in New York City. This technique might be applicable for connecting, say, a murder weapon with the chemistry of a particular backyard.

Closer to the laboratory – and to the tomb project – the scientific challenge was already dovetailing with Oded Golan's criminal case overseas. The collector Golan had been charged with acquiring an ossuary inscribed "James, son of Joseph" from the antiquities market and adding to it the words "brother of Jesus." Allegedly, he did this in order to enhance the value of the artifact. Golan denied the charges. A patina match between the James, son of Joseph and the Jesus, son of Joseph ossuaries would be powerful evidence indicating that, in fact, no crime had been committed.

"Do any of these tombs belong to people I might know from history?" Bob had asked.

"Yes," I had said. "Yes," and nothing more.

On the afternoon of January 30, 2006, by the time the first sample vial was opened, Bob knew the rest of the story. Over the past thirty years, he had examined thousands of objects under the microscope. He had to admit, however, that examining accretion beds from the bottoms of the Mariamne and Jesus ossuaries – and scanning a micro-landscape that

included pearl-like layers of patina growth, sometimes associated with fragments of fiber – felt strange and unprecedented. Before long, the forensic analyst in him took over, and his
interest focused, not on who these people might have been,
but on the patina samples themselves and the attempt to link
them scientifically to each other.

The first "pings" of the electron microscope were of isolated "chalk" matrix and patina collected from the tomb's
northeast wall, inside a primary burial shelf. "Pinging" the
samples was a naval term that I borrowed from my family's
long history of seafaring. The electron microprobe – which
charged atoms and excited them until their electron shells
radiated specific signals – always reminded me of "pinging"
with sonar a deep-ocean target until it radiates back a discernible signal.

The "chalk" matrix from which the tomb walls and
ossuaries were cut had been formed primarily from calcium
carbonate shells of ancient microscopic animals – the same
fossils that were a major constituent in the White Cliffs of
Dover and in most brands of toothpaste. The results (as, for
example, ping number 8) agreed with what one would have
expected from a calcium carbonate matrix, whose formula
was $CaCO_3$: Calcium, carbon, and oxygen signals dominated, followed by barely detectable traces of aluminum, silicon, phosphorus, and iron.

As expected, the patina from the walls mirrored the loud

calcium (Ca), carbon (C), and oxygen (O) signals observed in the stone matrix, but (as suspected) differed from the underlying matrix.

On the monitor screen, the elemental spectrum resembled the breaking up of colors by a prism, converting a shaft of sunlight into a rainbow. Beams of electrons fired through magnetic lenses had very much the same effect on chemical compounds, spreading each of the elements out into distinct vertical bands. In the elemental spectrum of the tomb's patina, the silicon signal was quite loud, as opposed to the general limestone properties that Bob and I had already observed in the chalk matrix immediately below the patina. Bob had expected the two materials to be more similar. But the spectrum also displayed, in what began to resemble an elemental fingerprint, the signatures of magnesium, aluminum, phosphorus, potassium, and – oddest of all – prominent spikes of titanium and iron.

"Iron," I said. "At least we now know what gives the *terra rossa* its name. It's full of rust."

Twelve more pings of different tomb wall and ceiling patina samples demonstrated that the result was reproducible – that is, that future IAA 80/500–509 patina samples would yield the same spectrum in any lab anywhere in the world.

We now turned to the Jesus ossuary patina and obtained the same result. The "Matthew" patina, too, was consistent with "Jesus" and the Talpiot tomb walls. This seemed particularly important, because I had feared that the decay of the holy books buried in the tomb for a quarter of a century might have created a new bacterial and fungal environment that would have differentiated the tomb from the ossuaries that had been removed years earlier. The tomb patina might have been chemically reworked, perhaps even to its very roots, while the Jesus ossuary and its companions had been stored in the dry and bacterially quiescent environment of the IAA warehouse. If this had happened, the Jesus ossuary patina (from the warehouse environment) would have presented a signature very different from the wall and ceiling patina from the tomb. And the test, in essence, would have had to be aborted. But the bacteria had *not* brought about a significant change. In terms of elemental spectra, the patina signatures *matched*.

I began to feel optimistic: by separating the ossuaries from the tomb, Shimon Gibson and his colleagues had performed a great service. In essence, what had now been demonstrated was that even after being subjected to vastly different environments for nearly three decades, the integrity of the tomb's chemical history, as recorded in the two-thousand-year-old patina, had been preserved.

Before time ran out that day, Bob and I pinged the Mariamne ossuary patina. And again, we demonstrated a match. All the while, we didn't look at the results obtained four years earlier from the electron microscope probes of the James ossuary.

When at last I opened the envelope from Dr. Amnon

Rosenfeld and read the electron microprobe spectrum report from the "James" patina, the result was again ... a match, right down to the titanium and iron spikes, which appeared to be a signature of the *terra rossa* soil. A mismatch would have meant that the James ossuary probably originated from a different tomb and could not possibly have been the "missing tenth."

The match appeared to signal the opposite.

The evidence was still very far from conclusive. For all anyone really knew, *every* tomb and *every* ossuary in the Jerusalem hills exhibited a perfectly matching elemental spectrum. The "patina fingerprinting" method might still turn out to be useless if every grave for miles around Jerusalem was coated with the same chemical signature and the real reason "James" matched "Jesus" was because there was only one local patina fingerprint and any two ossuaries could not possibly have failed to match.

And yet, it seemed that we were on the verge of exonerating the James ossuary as an archaeologically significant artifact, clearing collector Golan from the charges against him, and ushering in a new era of "patina fingerprinting" as a valid scientific method.

From Charlie P. to Simcha J. and Jim C.
January 30, 2006

Dear Simcha, Jim:

This was a good day. We were able to "ping" twenty different points of matrix and patina ... yielding only one distinctive patina spectrum for wall, ceiling, and ossuary surface. Interestingly (but not unexpectedly), the bed of semi-fossilized organic debris from the insides of the "Jesus" and "Mariamne" ossuaries produced the same elemental spectrum.

I had expected much more variation from different parts of the tomb and even from different layers of the same patina sample ... As it turns out, the variations between different layers of patina are, chemically, very slight (roughly within the range of 5%); the individual layers differ more by such features as crystal morphology than they do by elemental spectra. An apt analogy would be the rings of a tree, seen in cross-section: the layers look different, yet under an electron microprobe, we would see essentially the same ratios of carbon, oxygen, and iron – much as we would find similar amounts of calcium carbonate in the layers of a pearl.

NEXT STEPS: We need to expand the patina data base. The next phase is to see if we can explain away our tomb patina and the James patina match as a common occurrence (i.e., can it be true that any tomb patina is likely to match any other tomb patina?). If our Talpiot tomb patina can withstand the attempt to explain it away, then we're on to something ... We

*need to begin by comparing ossuaries from other
tombs. No patina sample needs to be more than 1
mm in diameter. Indeed, the samples can be literally
microscopic – meaning, no significant damage at all
to the artifacts.*

   See you later.

   – Charlie P.

*   *   *

Bob Genna was having a very strange month. First, a small
box of rock samples brought to the lab for "a closer look at
how patinas form" in tombs and other places turned out to
be part of an ongoing investigation into what might turn out
to be the Jesus family tomb. And now James Cameron's asso-
ciates were planning to film the next patina test. The experi-
ment was turning out to have broader implications than what
had begun as a spare-time study in patina fingerprinting.

   The next session took place on February 7, 2006, with
cameras rolling – science in a fishbowl.

   This time Amnon Rosenfeld joined us. Four years earlier,
with Dr. Ilani, he had performed the electron microprobe
analysis on the James ossuary patina in Jerusalem. He was
intrigued to learn from Simcha that preliminary results from
the Suffolk County Crime Lab pointed toward the possibility of tracing the James ossuary to a specific tomb. According to Rosenfeld, the titanium and iron spikes could not be
a very common result. In 2002 he had concluded indepen-

dently that the James ossuary patina had formed, at some point during its long history, under a condition of partial submergence in the presence of one of two reddish soil types – *redzina* or *terra rossa* – known from the hills south and east of Jerusalem. The *terra rossa* was the rarer and redder of the two soils and was now known to display a higher iron content (almost 2 percent). This was all consistent with the patinas on the James and Talpiot tomb ossuaries.

Today was mostly a matter of proving that the previous results were reproducible across different patina samples from the Jesus and Mariamne ossuaries. If time permitted, we would also search for bone fragments and other biological remains in the accretion beds sampled from the bottoms of these two ossuaries.

The first ping of the "Jesus" patina matched the previous wall and ossuary patina samples. Ping 22 also matched. Ping 23 matched. Ping 24 matched.

"What's interesting – and key – are the small trace materials that we're locating here," Bob Genna told the camera, pointing to ping 24 on the monitor. "We're noticing iron, titanium, potassium, phosphorous, and magnesium. So far, the elemental composition that we analyzed with this particular section of patina is consistent with the trace materials that Amnon Rosenfeld found in the James ossuary."

"The signature is the same," I affirmed. "It matches."

Ping 25 probed a sample from the accretion bed that had formed inside the Mariamne ossuary, on its very bottom.

The bedding plane had been glued together by waterborne silica, apparently of *terra rossa* origin, over the course of several centuries. The mineral bed's elemental spectrum was a near-perfect match with patina samples from the outer surfaces of the ossuaries and from the walls of the tomb. There was a small deviation, however: the sodium, sulfur, and chlorine levels appeared to be elevated ever so slightly.

Under the microscope, the reason for this was discovered: trails of tiny nematode worms revealed that the debris field on the bottom of the ossuary had been rendered, at least occasionally, as soft as wet silt. Mud-dwelling nematodes are very good at dismantling debris fields of mostly deteriorated bone, and their fossilized trails indicated that, from time to time, the worms of the *terra rossa* had feasted.

The surge and crash of nematode populations easily explained traces of phosphorous and sulfur from bones, and it explained the sodium chloride as well: NaCl is salt. Simply salt. Bone marrow and blood always contain it. In fact, blood plasma, minus its cells, is chemically indistinguishable from seawater.

There were other substances on and in the accretion bed. Some were more or less mundane; others were the opposite of mundane.

A fiber clinging to the surface of the accretion bed turned out to be less interesting than the salt: modern airborne contamination – which probably took place in the IAA warehouse, where the Mariamne ossuary, unlike the Jesus ossuary, had been stored with its lid off. A fragment of insect wing appeared to be more ancient. It came from the forewing of a beetle, and it had grown a silica-rich patina. Probably this and a few similarly preserved insect remains (including the mouth parts of a fly) dated back to the time of primary burial, pre–70 C.E.

Most people believe that worms are the engines of decomposition and dissolution, but in reality the "worms" are the wormlike larval stages of *insects*. Over the course of the past eight million years, the carbon atoms coursing through the veins of every living human have been cycled through the digestive tracts of insects at least twenty times. In death it is the beetles and flies that come after everyone. The nematodes get only the scraps that are left behind. Interestingly, when we next tested the Jesus ossuary, it appeared like a nematode desert compared to "Mariamne," perhaps confirming our suspicion that the larger bones and/or the skull had been removed long ago, say, by the crusading Templars.

Pings 26 and 27 turned out to be more interesting than the rest. In the bottom of the Mariamne ossuary, an actual mineral concretion had built up around a micro-fragment of wood, not quite a millimeter across. Under the microscope, its edges showed signs of decay, indicating that it might have been part of a larger piece (thumbnail-size in diameter, or larger) that simply disappeared in the grave.

There were many sources of wood fragment contamination in ancient ossuary workshops. It did not have to be a family memento related to *that* wood. But, I have to confess, the thought crossed all of our minds.

At this point, Bob and I were ready for a patina sample from the James ossuary, provided from the Israel Geological Survey. The IGS results had matched the Talpiot tomb's patina, but the next order of business was to prove that the results were repeatable in New York. Under the electron microscope, hundreds of tiny fiber fragments could be seen on the sample. They had been torn loose from a large rag and snared on the outer surface. Someone in modern times had given the James ossuary a hard scrubbing with a piece of cloth soaked in a chlorine- and phosphate-based detergent.

Pings 33 and 34, aimed directly at the fibers, revealed a large chlorine peak, combined with a phosphorus peak that was literally off the charts. This was consistent with the phosphate-spiked detergents that were in common use during the 1970s and early 1980s (until they were phased out internationally for the stream- and river-destroying algal blooms they were causing).

Bob and I looked at each other. We were sure that this was evidence that collector Oded Golan would want to know about. After all, the IAA's "isotope test" had suggested that either the "James" inscription was forged or it had been *cleaned*. The police said forged. Golan said cleaned. And here was scientific evidence corroborating the latter.

The tale the fibers were telling suggested that the James

ossuary had been cleaned after it showed up on the antiquities market, with a detergent that was last in common use in Israel around 1980, the time ossuary number IAA 80/509 became the "missing tenth" ossuary from the Talpiot excavation.

Pings 31, 32, 35, and 42 continued to probe the patina of the James ossuary. The detergent contaminants could be clearly seen on the elemental spectra. When these were removed – as modern contaminants – the "James" patina itself was identical in every way to the patina samples from the walls of the Talpiot tomb and from the Jesus, Mariamne, and Matthew ossuaries.

Ping 36 probed the rock matrix below the "James" patina: it was the same as the other rock samples, except for signs of penetration by detergent.

Pings 37–41 produced elemental spectra of a second James patina sample provided by the Royal Ontario Museum. The patina turned out to be a twin of the IGS sample – right down to contamination by cloth fibers and phosphate-based detergent.

From: Charlie Pellegrino
To: Simcha Jacobovici

The next step is to prove whether or not each tomb patina is really unique. Without a broader sample base, a match between the James patina and the patina from our tomb is meaningless. And just to make the proof more difficult, I am asking your contacts in Israel to give a priority to sampling patinas from tombs that are most similar to our tomb – which is to say, ossuaries with a reddish patina indicative of a local soil similar to the terra rossa. If we can see subtle differences even in other terra rossa intruded tombs, then we will know that "patina fingerprinting" really works.

*   *   *

Back in Israel, Shimon Gibson helped Felix Golubev, Simcha's associate, in the collection of a broader sample base for the patina fingerprinting study. As requested, a disproportionately high percentage of the samples were nonrandom. I had wanted the tests to be made particularly grueling by focusing on patinas that showed reddish or reddish-yellow staining similar to the Talpiot tomb ossuary patinas and consistent with ossuary caves that had been situated under or near the relatively rare *terra rossa* soils. A thoroughly random sample might include no patina chemically similar to the Talpiot tomb, but I wanted to see how deeply the unusual exceptions to the rule actually *probed* the rule. White, yellow, and gray patinas were the rule. Reddish patinas were likely to have strong iron signatures and other *terra rossa* similarities. These would be the true test of whether or not individual tomb chemistries were unique.

On July 31, 2006, the first series of tests was conducted on random (but not so random) ossuary samples collected in Israel. The samples were now fed into the Suffolk County Crime Lab's electron microprobe.

Pings 43–46 were directed at the yellowish and slightly red patina of Shimons and Felix's sample 14. The differences between this and the James and Talpiot signatures were immediately identifiable. The reddish coloration was confined to a slight iron signature (associated with a powerful sulfur spike and significantly increased silicon) in the thinnest, outermost (and therefore youngest) layer of the patina. Evidently, sulfur-rich water vapor had condensed on the ossuary, probably within the past century or two. Below this layer, the strong iron signature, as in the Talpiot tomb, was either a barely detectable trace or altogether absent. Titanium was absent throughout. The strong aluminum and potassium peaks seen in the James and Talpiot samples were also absent. Clearly, this patina had formed in an environment chemically distinct from those of both the James ossuary and the Talpiot tomb. No match.

Pings 47–50 were directed at samples 19 and 20, two samples collected from one tomb. This was a more challenging patina type: reddish brown from top to bottom through every layer of its patina, which, in cross-section under light microscopy, was *visually* indistinguishable from the Talpiot tomb patina. In terms of elemental composition, both were very similar to the Talpiot tomb patina – right across through the high peaks of aluminum, silicon, potassium, and iron, with a slight trace of titanium. As with the Talpiot tomb, someone had evidently started a farm over this tomb, for water passing through *terra rossa* soil appeared to have been involved in the formation of the tomb's patina.

The most important contribution of this sample was in the differences that could be seen. The most prominent of these was a sulfur signal that, in most layers, soared above the strongest "James" and Talpiot iron peak samples. This patina also appeared to be more variable from layer to layer, including episodes of sodium enrichment combined with relatively depleted levels of carbon. As might be expected of two samples from the same tomb, numbers 19 and 20 were more similar to each other than either was to the James, Mariamne, Jesus, or Matthew ossuary patinas or the Talpiot tomb wall patina. No match.

Sample 30 yielded a "James"-like signature of high phosphorous and chlorine – indicative, again, of phosphate detergent having been used in cleaning at some point in this ossuary's past. There – as revealed by pings 51–53 – all similarities ceased. In the absence of aluminum, iron, and other trace metals, it was certain that the patina had formed in an environment quite distinct from that of the Talpiot tomb. No match.

Sample 28 (pings 54 and 55) was also different from the "James" and Talpiot samples – and from all the rest. The titanium spike was absent, except for a micro-nugget of essentially pure titanium struck by ping 54. The rest of the elemental signature was completely alien to the Talpiot tomb spectrum. This was so different from our tomb that it might just as well have formed on Mars. No match.

The patina of sample 15 (pings 56 and 57) *seemed* to the naked eye similar to those of the "James" and Talpiot samples, but it was relatively depleted in silicon, aluminum, titanium, and iron, and it had a high sulfur content rivaling the ossuary's own carbon peak. This was a very distinct patina that had definitely formed somewhere other than Talpiot. No match.

Sample 23 (pings 58 and 59) was another sample chosen for its challenging appearance – in this case, for being perfectly indistinguishable visually from the "James" and Talpiot patinas. Here the signature was similar: aluminum, titanium, and iron peaks occurred in the right places ... but not to the right heights. Along with an iron peak that was relatively depleted, lower levels of oxygen and silicon stood out in sample 23. Once again, an ossuary that had formed its patina in or near groundwater that had percolated through *terra rossa* soil had produced an elemental signature easily distinguishable from that of the Talpiot tomb. In fact, sample 23 was more similar to samples 19 and 20 than it was to the Talpiot tomb patina. No match.

The grayish-white patina of sample 26 (pings 60 and 61) produced a signature that was, among other differences, aluminum-depleted, silicon-depleted, sulfur-enriched, and titanium- and iron-depleted. No match.

Pings 62 and 63 probed the white patina of sample 29,

which, like the others, was distinct from the "James" and Talpiot patinas, beginning on the left side of its spectrum with its anemic levels of carbon and oxygen. The patina was almost entirely calcium and silicon – a glaze of white glass. No match.

In conclusion, it seemed that, compared to other patina samples from ossuaries found in the Jerusalem environment, the Talpiot tomb ossuaries exhibited a patina fingerprint or profile that matched the James ossuary and no other.

At the time of our tests, Israeli antiquities collector Oded Golan remained under house arrest for more than a year and was facing trial in criminal court for allegedly forging the second part of the James ossuary inscription.

The police, on the basis of the IAA's investigation, noted that there were distinct layering patterns in the "James patina," and they (correctly) interpreted this to mean that the patina had formed under varying conditions of geochemistry and temperature. They combined this interpretation, however, with evidence of iron-rich soil and running water to assert that the patina was artificially created so as to mask the forged portion of the inscription. The unique layering and chemistry were attributed to conditions so improbable as to preclude the possibility that the "James" patina was produced naturally in a tomb environment. According to the patina fingerprinting investigation that Bob and I conducted in the Suffolk County CSI lab, the "James" patina –

right down to its tree-ring-like pattern of layering – had been produced naturally and perfectly matched the ossuaries found in the Talpiot tomb.

About this time, Wolfgang Krumbein, one of the world's leading experts in geochemistry and geomicrobiology, had conducted his own investigation on micro-samples of patina from inside the inscribed letters of the first and last sections of the "James, son of Joseph, brother of Jesus" inscription. Whatever the conditions under which the James patina had formed (whether outdoors, partly outdoors, or in a tomb whose seals had been breached), Krumbein's lab concluded, "we can state with certainty that a period of 50 to 100 years – *at least* [and more probably a period of centuries] – was necessary for the formation of the specific composition of patina whose traces were identified *inside* the ossuary inscription."

Combined with the New York patina-fingerprinting data, Professor Krumbein's analysis of the patina encrustations that had resided inside key letters of the "James" inscription now made a "beyond a reasonable doubt" case that the ossuaries inscribed "James, son of Joseph, brother of Jesus" and "Jesus, son of Joseph" had once resided together inside the same tomb, for millennia.

Statistically speaking, adding "James, son of Joseph" to the Talpiot cluster would essentially prove that the Talpiot tomb was the tomb of Jesus of Nazareth. "The additional probability factor that the James ossuary inscription would offer," Feuerverger had suggested, "would drive our probabilities down to *extremely* small numbers: into the one-in-thirty-thousand zone. And that would be very, very remarkable."

The evening of May 15 had turned out to be another banner day at the Suffolk County Crime Lab. Forensic scientist Clyde Wells had joined the team (though it would be November before he knew whose accretion beds he had examined that day). There was, because the "Mariamne" lid was off for many years, a lot of contamination in the ossuary, including synthetic fiber dust from modern clothing. Clyde was a fiber expert, so the synthetics were quickly isolated. Modern cotton fibers also stood out – as constituents of airborne warehouse dust that stood apart from ancient fibers in being surface debris and in not having been exposed to oxidation, mineralization, or assault by microbes.

After the "overtly moderns" were weeded out, the interesting particles stepped up to the front. They were too small and too precious to destroy in a process of carbon-14 testing, but they did appear to be ancient. These included plant fibers so deeply penetrated by mold that they appeared to be black, though originally they must have been white. The fibers themselves, too wide to be cotton, appeared to be a form of flax (or linen) – diluted, or cheapened, with what appeared to be a paper-based pulp fiber.

From: Charlie Pellegrino

To: *Simcha Jacobovici, Jim Cameron*

*I think it likely that today we looked at material
from an actual burial shroud, from the "Mariamne"
ossuary. We also found traces of deeply mold-pene-
trated cotton fiber, suggesting a second sheet of
shroud made out of a different material. The cotton
fibers (and also the fibrous stems of reproducing
mold) had been covered in a thin precipitate of mineral patina – meaning that it was semi-fossilized and
probably ancient. Two types of cloth appear to have
been used in the burial, including flax that appears to
have been made even more cheaply, more plainly, by
this odd interweaving of "paper" linen. In some of
these fibers, I really do believe we may be witnessing
the shroud of Mary Magdalene.*
  Charlie P.

Then we found fibers in the Jesus ossuary as well. At first, the
meaning of the unusual fibers from the Jesus ossuary did not
become immediately apparent. They were observed on
Monday afternoon, May 15, 2006. My reaction time seemed
curiously slow that day. What I had seen needed a few hours
to sink in, before finally bubbling up from somewhere deep
in my subconscious.

The fibers from the "Jesus" accretion bed were much
less degraded than those extracted from the "Mariamne"

samples – which seemed consistent with the lower levels of post–*terra rossa* biological activity, compared against the other ossuaries. At first, Clyde Wells did not know what the strange plant fiber could mean. It was not cotton, and it was not flax. Neither was it consistent with anything presently being used in any fabric in the world. It appeared to be a fiber pulped and woven (or pressed) from a straw base – probably the plainest, the cheapest fabric of all, for its time. Because Clyde did not know, as yet, whose name had been inscribed on this first-century ossuary, it was easy for him to suppose that this might have been part of a burial shroud.

For several hours, I did not give the fibers more than a passing, skeptical thought. And so what seemed to be shreds from a shroud might have remained forever explainable as ancient contamination by an ordinary shred of vegetable fiber that only *looked* like fabric and had no connection at all with Jesus's burial.

For several hours, I had managed to maintain some distance from the words "What if?"

About 7:00 P.M., I arrived in New York City and was heading home for supper, timed to the latest episode of a TV program called 24. On my way to a bus stop, I passed a familiar street preacher who ministered to the homeless and who had always called out to me the same greeting: "Have you found Jesus, brother?"

I nodded to him and gave the usual reply: "I'm working on it."

Several times before, I had strolled under the lights near Broadway and Times Square with samples from the Talpiot tomb in my carrying case. This night, for the first time, it occurred to me that no one walking by me on the sidewalks of Manhattan would have believed that the most secret (and perhaps most sacred) artifacts in the world were passing within just a few paces of them. The most deeply hidden secret of military think-tankers was more widely known than the fact that DNA and apparent remnants of Jesus's shroud had come to New York.

An hour later, the magnitude of what had appeared to be an insignificant shred of straw-based fiber suddenly dawned on me. Simcha had told me on many occasions that the Jesus ossuary was the plainest he had ever seen. I had once commented that the plainest ossuary seemed so like a blank coin, without the final stamp of detail put upon it, that perhaps IAA 80/503 had never been completed. However, Simcha had been quick to point out that the Jesus ossuary had in fact been completed. He pointed out that the lid fit perfectly into its grooves, forming a very snug seal – which also explained why there appeared to be relatively little airborne contamination after a quarter-century in the IAA facility.

The plainest ossuary. A shroud of straw fiber.

The plainest ossuary, and the plainest shroud.

I do not like to think of myself as a man who cries easily,

but suddenly I was weeping. Seemingly out of nowhere, the plainest fabric had connected with everything Simcha had said to me about the plainest ossuary, undecorated except for "Jesus, son of Joseph," and a cross. This connection touched everything I had been reading, both canonical and noncanonical, about Jesus's philosophy and about his lesson of traveling lightly through life.

If in fact 80/503 was the ossuary of Jesus of Nazareth, then he, and those who buried him, had practiced as he preached.

Here, really for the first time, the cumulative evidence was not just statistical, or chemical, or biological. Here, for the first time, I saw scripture reaching forward into time and actually ramming head-on into a collision with archaeology. Up to that moment, it had been easy for me to imagine that what Jesus had said was either invented or enlarged by his chroniclers beyond what he actually preached; that Jesus's sermons and parables were also enlarged in death beyond what he had said in life. Now I wondered: *What if* ... I'd gotten him wrong ... all along?

Simcha: A Conclusion

The tomb lay *empty now. The ossuaries that had rested in its bowels for nearly two millennia were no longer there. The guardian skulls were gone and the* terra rossa *that had seeped, almost imperceptibly, for a thousand years, leaving its improbable patina on the tomb and its occupants had been hauled outside into the daylight. Apartment buildings from whose rooftops you could see Jerusalem and Bethlehem lined brand new streets that had yet to be named.*

A young municipal official stopped to wipe his brow directly opposite the tomb's entrance, and at that moment decided on a name for the street that ran above it. The road would memorialize a thirty-five-year-old Jew who fought an empire and was hanged just after Passover, 1947. At the time, some fellow Jews had called him a brigand. Now, his

*time had come. The street would be called "Dov Gruner"
after the underground fighter who had opposed Great
Britain in the struggle for modern Israel's independence.*

*   *   *

In the first week of December 2006, I screened my film *The
Tomb* for a group of executives representing the Discovery
Channel in the United States and Vision Television in Canada, two of the three broadcasters that funded our film (the
third being C4 in the United Kingdom). After it was over,
there was stunned silence in the edit suite. To break the ice,
one said: "Let's see ... what's our lead line on this film?
'Jesus's bones found!' Or how about, 'DNA proves Jesus and
Mary were married!' Or 'Entire Holy Family found!' Or
should we just stay simple: 'They had a kid!'"

There was nervous laughter in the room, and then the
executives fell back on executive-type talk: *How close to
Easter should we play this? How long should it run?* And
my favorite: *We should adopt a skeptical tone throughout.*
As the discussion turned to things like the number of com-
mercial breaks and bumpers and the lightning speed at
which our credits had to whiz by, my mind returned to the
story.

After all is said and done, what did our sleuthing really
turn up?

The fact is that in 1980 bulldozers uncovered a tomb in
Talpiot, Jerusalem, halfway between the Old City of

Jerusalem and Bethlehem. On its facade was a unique symbol. Inside, there were ten ossuaries. Six had inscriptions.

The fact is that no one challenges the provenance of the ossuaries. There is not now, and there never will be, a dispute about the authenticity or the legitimacy of the inscriptions. They were found *in situ* by archaeologists. The tomb was mapped, the ossuaries cataloged, and the inscriptions verified.

The most dramatic of the six inscriptions boldly states: "Jesus, son of Joseph." Out of thousands of ossuaries that have been found and cataloged, this is one of only two ossuaries that have this particular combination of names on it. Interestingly, the box is extremely plain. It has no ornamentation whatsoever – none of the "rosettes," the circles or designs that are usually found on ossuaries. This isn't "proof" of anything, but it is consistent with what we know of "Jesus, son of Joseph" from the New Testament and other, noncanonical, writings. Perhaps the plainness of the ossuary speaks to the character of the man who was buried in it, or maybe it speaks to the fact that his followers didn't want to draw attention to the box-that-dare-not-speak-its-name. But the undisputed fact is that one of the plainest ossuaries ever discovered also bears what may be the most famous name in history: "Jesus, son of Joseph."

Of all the inscriptions found in the Talpiot tomb, the "Jesus, son of Joseph" is the hardest to read. That's also a fact. It's not that deciphering it is controversial; everyone, from the noted epigrapher L. Y. Rahmani to the legendary Frank Moore Cross of Harvard, agrees that the inscription on the ossuary must be read "Jesus, son of Joseph" and no other way. But the fact remains that the inscription is written in such a fast and cursive hand that it is, in a sense, hiding in plain sight.

Also, there is a clear "X" mark in front of the name, incised at the very time that the inscription was scratched onto the box. At this point, I have to admit that I've "crossed," so to speak, a controversial line. In Israel, no one is allowed to mention cross-marks on ossuaries in polite archaeological company. Most archaeologists, especially Israeli archaeologists, assume – wrongly – that the cross as a Christian symbol begins with the Roman emperor Constantine in the fourth century C.E. At that time, Constantine legalized Christianity, positioning it as the next official religion of the Roman Empire. Prior to that, say the historically uninformed, fish, not crosses, were the only symbols used by Christians. But as *any* New Testament scholar can attest to, crosses predate Constantine by decades, if not centuries. In the writings of Tertullian, for example, the cross is already explicitly mentioned as a Christian symbol one hundred years *prior* to Constantine.

So where did the symbol of the cross really come from? Can it be that the early followers of Jesus adopted the instrument of his death as a religious symbol? Had the Romans hanged Jesus from a tree, would his followers have walked around with tiny ornamental gold nooses around their necks? Father Jerome Murphy-O'Connor of the École Biblique in Jerusalem believes it is unlikely that anyone would have worn a cross as a religious symbol at the outset of the Jesus movement. It was a symbol of torture, not redemption.

And yet, in Herculaneum, sister city of Pompeii, a cross *was* found in the context of a religious shrine. It dates to the eruption of the Vesuvius volcano in 79 C.E., only forty-nine years after the Crucifixion. Instead of trying to explain what this cross is doing there, scholars have tried to explain the cross away. "It's not a cross, it's a shelf," they say. After all, crosses cannot be religious symbols for the followers of Jesus prior to Constantine. And what about the hundreds of crosses on ossuaries dating back to the time of Jesus? "They're not crosses, they're mason's marks," is the conventional wisdom.

"Mason's marks" on ossuaries are marks that stonemasons made so as to let their clients know how to align the ossuaries with their lids. To this end, they made crosses on ossuaries *and* on their lids. By definition, ossuaries with single crosses on them don't qualify as ossuaries with mason's marks. This is not to say that a cross is never a mason's mark. It is to say that every cross-mark prior to Constantine cannot be automatically dismissed as a mason's mark. And if they're not mason's marks, they must mean *something*. For example, in the Talpiot tomb there is a clear cross-mark on the back of one of the uninscribed ossuaries. Why is it there next to the ossuary of Jesus, son of Joseph? Also, there is the unexplained "X" that, according to L. Y. Rahmani and Frank Moore Cross, forms part of the "Jesus" inscription. Since there is no corresponding "X" on the lid, there is no reason to conclude that it's a mason's mark. So what *does* the "X" in front of the word "Jesus" mean?

As we've argued, the answer to that question is not that hard to track down. The fact is that since the time of Ezekiel, over five hundred years *prior* to Jesus, the "X" and its rotated form, the cross, was a mark signifying righteousness. For example, Ezekiel 9:4 states: "And the Lord said to him [Ezekiel], go through the midst of the city, through the center of Jerusalem, and set a 'Tao' on the foreheads of the men that sigh and cry because of the abominations that are done in the heart of the city." The "Tao," also know as the "Taw," is the last letter of both the Hebrew and Aramaic alphabets. It's called "Taf" in Hebrew, "Tao" in Aramaic. The name literally means "mark"! It signifies the end of the road, and perhaps also a new beginning. In the plain meaning of the Ezekiel text, this *mark of the righteous* is a protective symbol that differentiates the ones marked for redemption from the ones marked for destruction. Why then do archaeologists dismiss the "Tao" in the "Jesus, son of Joseph" inscription as nothing more than a mason's mark?

If all this seems esoteric or far-fetched, just remember that Jesus calls himself a living "Tao." In Revelation (22:13),

Jesus utters his now-famous words: "I am the Alpha and the Omega" – I am the beginning and the end. (Alpha and Omega are the first and last letters of the Greek alphabet.) But as anyone with a basic knowledge of the New Testament will acknowledge, Jesus spoke in Hebrew and Aramaic, not Greek. If he said what the New Testament says he said, he would have used the first and last letters of the Hebrew and Aramaic alphabets and said it this way: "I am the Aleph and the Tao." Some scholars may argue that by Jesus's time the Hebrew "Taf" had already evolved beyond "X" marks and cross-marks. By the first century it was written differently, they will say. But this ignores the fact that for nearly six hundred years the last letter – the "Tao" – had served as the sign of the righteous. By the first century, the sign of the "Tao" had almost six centuries of history behind it. As a religious symbol, it must have been depicted as it always had been – as an "X" or a plus sign ("+").

I realize that not every "X" on an ossuary can be identified as a "Tao," but neither can every "X" be dismissed as nothing more than a mason's mark. The fact is that whether we look at Tertullian, Herculaneum, Ezekiel, or Jesus's own description of himself as a "Tao," Taos and crosses cannot be dismissed out of hand. The fact is that the ossuary inscribed "Jesus, son of Joseph" most decidedly does *not* have a mason's mark on it. But it *does* have a deliberately inscribed Tao.

The idea that the cross of the Gentile followers of Jesus

evolved from an earlier symbol of the Jews and the Judeo-Christians is not new. In the third century, Origen, one of the Church fathers, wrote:

> Jews were being questioned as to whether they had anything in the traditions of their forebears to illustrate the letter *taw*. The response was as follows. One said the letter *taw,* one of the twenty-two used by the Jews, is the last in the received order. Yet, though the last, it has been chosen to symbolize the perfection of those who, because of their virtue, bewail and mourn the sins of the people and pity the sinners. A second person said that the letter *taw* is the symbol of those who observe the Law since this, called by the Jews Torah, begins with the letter *taw*. Finally, a third, belonging to the number of those who had become Christians, said that the Old Testament writings show that the *taw* is a symbol of the cross and was a foretype of that sign which Christians are accustomed to make on their foreheads before beginning their prayers or undertaking the reading of prayers and sacred readings. (Origen, *Selecta in Ezechielem,* PG 13, 799–802)

Clearly, at least as early as Origen, Christians were aware that the "Tao" preceded the cross as a symbol of perfection and observance of the Law. Why then should we be surprised that "Taos" are found on Jewish and Judeo-Christian ossuaries? Why should we minimize the fact that a "Tao" is inscribed on the "Jesus, son of Joseph" ossuary, right in front of the inscription itself?

In 2006 I traveled to Naples to the Commissariato di Terra Santa to meet Father Ignacio Mancini. Father Mancini is old and his feet ache. He walks with a shuffle, aided by a novice. For thirty years he lived in Jerusalem at the Franciscan-run Church of the Flagellation. Mancini worked under the legendary Father Bellarmino Bagatti, monk and archaeologist. He is also the author of *Archaeological Discoveries Relative to the Judeo-Christians*, which was first published by the Franciscan Printing Press of Jerusalem in 1968. In his book, Father Mancini catalogs hundreds of Taos, crosses, and other marks that seem to be connected to the early followers of Jesus. And yet all these signs of early Christianity have been ignored by secular academics and by Mancini's fellow Christians. Why?

Again, the answer is not hard to come by. After all, for millennia, the Judeo-Christians, or Ebionites, were an embarrassment to both Christians and Jews. They were an embarrassment to Jews because, in the midst of their persecution at the hands of Christians, they were a reminder that Jesus had a Jewish following hundreds of years before Christianity became a Gentile movement. Conversely, the Ebionites were an embarrassment to Christians because they bore silent witness to the fact that the people who knew Jesus, broke bread with him, and listened to his teachings directly from his lips, kept kosher, observed the Sabbath, circumcised their males, and rejected the idea of both virgin births and trinities.

As a result of all this, the Judeo-Christians have fallen into a black hole in publishing called the Franciscan Press. Simply put, outside a small circle of academics, hardly anyone knows that the Judeo-Christians existed. And yet, as Mancini told me sitting among beautiful and fragrant flowers high above the port of Naples, "you can't dismiss all the evidence all the time. These people existed, and they left behind archaeological evidence of their existence. Christianity didn't emerge out of theological and social nothingness."

Mancini is not alone in his beliefs. Scholars such as Charles Simon Clermont-Ganneau, Father Sylvester Saller, Eleazar L. Sukenik, Father Bellarmino Bagatti, Claudine Dauphin, Jack Finegan, and others have been pointing out archaeological evidence for Judeo-Christians since 1873. Again, one can dismiss some of their evidence some of the time, but you can't dismiss *all* of their evidence, *all* of the time. And yet, with respect to the early Jesus movement, that is exactly what the academic community has been doing for almost 150 years.

The result of this neglect is that when a truly paradigm-shifting discovery comes along, such as the Talpiot tomb, it seems impossible to take it seriously. But it only seems unbelievable if we imagine the discovery emerging from an archaeological vacuum. If, however, we understand that the

Talpiot tomb exists in an archaeological *context* made up of hundreds of first-century artifacts attesting to the early Jesus movement, then the tomb starts coming into archaeological focus.

This speaks to another point, namely, some people might draw the conclusion that the entire exercise of attempting to link specific ossuaries to specific individuals in the New Testament story is silly from the get-go. But again, the fact is that scholars *do link* specific artifacts to specific people in the New Testament. For example, as we have seen, according to the Gospels, Joseph, son of Caiaphas, was the high priest who prosecuted Jesus and turned him over to the Roman authorities as a dangerous troublemaker (Matthew 26:57). In December 1990, outside the Old City of Jerusalem, construction workers uncovered a first-century burial cave. Inside the cave were eleven ossuaries. Two of them bore the name Caiaphas. One of them, the most ornate, now on permanent display at the Israel Museum, had the inscription "Joseph, son of Caiaphas" carved into it twice. Without much fanfare, most New Testament scholars now consider the ossuary at the Israel Museum to be the bone box of Joseph, son of Caiaphas, the New Testament high priest who sent Jesus to his death. Why is it possible to find the prosecutor but not the prosecuted? Clearly, this is not a scholarly position but a political one.

But there is more. According to the Gospels, en route to the Crucifixion, Jesus stumbled and fell. He was helped to carry his burden by a Jew visiting Jerusalem for the holidays from Cyrene, a great Jewish Diaspora center in what is today Libya. Simon, a Cyrenian, as he is known in the Gospels (Mark 15:21), seems to have been deeply affected by his encounter with Jesus. So much so that the Gospels report that both he and his son Alexander became early followers. In 1941 an ossuary was found that has on it, drawn in green chalk and carved in stone, the words "Alexander, son of Simon," "Simon," and "Cyrene." As we have shown, scholars agree that the combination of names indicates that either one or both of these individuals were laid to rest in this ossuary. Scholars also generally agree that the Simon and the Alexander mentioned on the Cyrene ossuary are the very same people described in the New Testament.

For decades, the Simon of Cyrene ossuary has been sitting under a desk in a storehouse at the Hebrew University in Jerusalem. Ironically, each year, tens of thousands of visitors file past the "Simon of Cyrene" chapel on the Fifth Station of the Via Dolorosa, the route that Jesus took to the Crucifixion. None of them is aware that Simon's ossuary may very well have been identified. Why? Because his ossuary falls between the theological and archaeological cracks. It appeals to neither Jews nor Christians ... nor, for that matter, to archaeologists of any political or religious stripe.

But the most unheralded discovery, besides the Talpiot tomb, involves the ossuary of Shimon bar Jonah. According to Christian tradition, the first pope was none other than

Peter, one of Jesus's original twelve apostles. Many historians of the early Church record that after the Crucifixion, Peter was one of the leaders of the Jesus movement and, according to some, an opponent of Paul's version of Christianity. Tradition says that he was martyred in Rome and buried in a cemetery underneath what is now the Vatican. The fact, however, is that there has never been a single shred of archaeological evidence attesting to Peter's having been buried under St. Peter's Basilica in Rome, and it's not for lack of trying. Excavations have been mounted. Bones have appeared and disappeared. Monuments have been found. Pagan cemeteries have been identified. But no Peter. Not even a single Jewish or Christian tomb to show for all those years of effort. Certainly no ossuaries. In other words, Roman traditions notwithstanding, the brutal fact is that there has not been one shred of credible evidence that Peter, or *any* of the original followers of Jesus, is buried under the Vatican.

In 1953 Bellarmino Bagatti excavated what he called a "Judeo-Christian necropolis," or cemetery, on the Mount of Olives. The necropolis is situated in a Christian holy site called Dominus Flevit. According to tradition, it is here that Jesus looked at the Holy Temple and wept for what he foresaw as its upcoming destruction. In the necropolis of Dominus Flevit, Bagatti unearthed dozens of first-century ossuaries. One may have belonged to Peter.

As every Christian child knows, "Peter" is not the apostle's real name. It's a nickname given by Jesus to "Simon son of Jonah." According to the Gospels, Jesus dubbed Simon "kepha," or "rock" in Aramaic. "Petrus" is the Latin translation of "kepha." It's an ancient version of Rocky. Among the ossuaries of Dominus Flevit, written in black chalk, Bagatti found the name Shimon bar Jonah – Simon, son of Jonah.

Shimon was the most popular name of first-century Judean males. But the biblical name Jonah had fallen totally out of fashion by Jesus's time. Out of hundreds of ossuaries that have been cataloged, the Simon, son of Jonah ossuary is one of a kind. It should have made international headlines. In fact, had this one-of-a-kind inscription been found under the Vatican, the ossuary would immediately have become an object of veneration and pilgrimage. But it wasn't found in Rome. It was found in Jerusalem, in a Judeo-Christian context. As a result, to this day it sits abandoned in a tiny museum in the back of the Church of the Flagellation.

The point is that the Jesus family tomb does not emerge out of nothingness. It is only the latest example of discoveries related to Jesus that seem to have been ignored because they involve archaeological artifacts that people would rather not find.

At the end of the day, had the Jesus, son of Joseph ossuary come to light in some private collection, it would have been archaeologically and statistically irrelevant. The name, the plainness of the ossuary, the cursive nature of the inscription, and the deliberate "Tao" in front of the inscription might have made for interesting dinner conversation among a very tiny group of people, but that would have been all. It would not have amounted to much. The fact is, however, that the Jesus ossuary, unlike so many others, did not emerge mysteriously out of the antiquities market. It was found *in situ* by archaeologists. As a result, the question of whether this is or is not the box that once held the mortal remains of Jesus of Nazareth *can* be scientifically investigated. The obvious first question is: who else was buried with him? If this is indeed the Jesus family tomb, the ossuaries found alongside Jesus should correspond to the historical data that can be gathered on the family.

As we now know, in the same tomb as the Yeshua bar Yosef (Jesus, son of Joseph) ossuary, Yosef Gat, Amos Kloner, and young Shimon Gibson discovered an ossuary on whose side was written, in big unmistakable letters, the name Maria. Maria is a Latinized version of the biblical name Miriam. In first-century Judea, perhaps as many as one-quarter of all women were called Miriam, Mary in English. This led to confusion then and now. That's why the Gospels often have various nicknames or explanations following the mention of a Mary, as in "Mary, the wife of so and so," "Mary, the mother of so and so," "Mary, the sister of so and so," "Mary from this or that town," etc. With 25 percent of the women in ancient Israel called Mary, you always had to qualify which Mary you were talking about.

Anyone who has listened to "Ave Maria" – the haunting

Catholic liturgy in praise of the mother of Jesus – knows that in Church tradition the Mother of the Lord is referred to in one way and one way only: Maria. The veneration of Mary, mother of Jesus, is one of the things that differentiate Catholics from Protestants, with the former much more likely to focus on the mother, seeking her intercession and congregating in places where she is reported to have made miraculous appearances. And it's always Maria – never Miriam, or Mary the Nazarene, or Mary, the wife of Joseph. It's always "Maria."

Forgetting the Talpiot tomb, if somewhere there was an ossuary inscribed with Jesus's mother's name, what should we expect to find on it? Since there is no indication that she was anything other than a first-century Jew, we would expect to find her name written in Hebrew or Aramaic. It wouldn't surprise us, therefore, if it was rendered as "Miriam." And it would delight us if it said something like "Wife of Joseph," or "Mother of the Master." But it would be equally dramatic if we found an ossuary that used four *Hebrew* letters – "Mem," "Resh," "Yud," and "Hay" – to record the *Latin* version of her name, Maria, as it has come down to us over two thousand years.

Again, out of all the ossuaries cataloged by scholars, only a handful have been found that have the Latin version of "Miriam" written in Hebrew letters. One of them comes from the Talpiot tomb, where for two millennia it kept a silent vigil next to the ossuary of Jesus, son of Joseph.

Does the Maria inscription on an ossuary in the Talpiot

tomb provide us with final and indisputable proof that this ossuary once held the mortal remains of the woman called the Virgin Mary in the New Testament? Of course not. Any number of interpretations can be provided for the same phenomenon. But the fact is that we now have three Jesus-related names clustered on two ossuaries: Jesus, Joseph, and Maria. Back in 1980, the discovery of these three names in a single tomb should have invited a flurry of scientific activity: statisticians should have been drawing up probability studies, and DNA should have been extracted – at the very least – from the Jesus and Maria ossuaries to determine whether there was a familial relationship between the two. But that's not what happened. Archaeologists with zero training in statistics decided that the names Jesus, Joseph, and Mary were so common in first-century Judea that the entire cluster was not worth looking at.

And that's not all. The undisputed fact is that next to the Maria and Jesus ossuaries was yet another ossuary with four clear – one might even say fancy – Hebrew letters chiseled on its side: "Vav," "Yud," "Samech," and "Hey," spelling Yosa. Coincidentally, according to the Gospel of Mark, Yosa, or Jos'e, just happens to be a nickname for Joseph, brother of Jesus.

The Gospels (Mark 6:3 and Matthew 13:55) state that Jesus had four brothers: Shimon (Simon), Yehuda (Judah or Judas), Ioseph (Joseph), and Yacov (James). The Gospel of Mark mentions at least two sisters. According to early Christian tradition (Epiphanius, *Panarion* 78.8–9), they were called Shlomit (Salome) and Miriam (Mary). Using textual and archaeological inscriptions as a database, scholars agree that Simon was the most popular name in the first century (21 percent), Joseph was the second most popular (14 percent), Judah the third (10 percent), and Jacob (Yakov) the fourth (2 percent). But the earliest source, the Gospel of Mark, gives us an important piece of information about one and only one of the brothers. Joseph was known by his nickname, Joses (Jos'e) or Josi, possibly a Greek version of Yose, or Yosa in Hebrew. Perhaps this Jos'e was named after his deceased father Joseph, or perhaps after an earlier ancestor. Whatever the reason, unlike the father of Jesus, he was known by the diminutive of Yosef/Joseph, a kind of Hebrew Joey.

The amazing thing is that in Talpiot we have the only version of the name Yosa *ever* found on an ossuary. So, while it's true that if you stood in a crowded first-century Jerusalem marketplace and shouted, "Yosef," fourteen out of one hundred Jewish males would probably put up their hands. If you shouted, "Yosa" on the other hand, only one would answer. You would then have to ask him the following question: "Are you the brother of Jesus of Nazareth?" Odds are that he would answer in the affirmative.

Again, "Yosa" by himself does not clinch the probability that the Talpiot tomb is indeed the Jesus family tomb. Unfortunately, we have almost no information about Jos'e, the brother of Jesus. But if we are in the right tomb, we now know that he didn't stay behind in Nazareth. Along with Jesus and his mother Maria, he ended his days in Jerusalem. Furthermore, we now have four Jesus-related names on three ossuaries: Jesus, Joseph, Maria, and Jos'e.

But other than the Jesus, son of Joseph ossuary, to use Feuerverger's term, the most "surprising" of all the ossuaries in the Talpiot tomb is the one inscribed "[the ossuary] of Mariamne also known as Mara." From the beginning, we focused on this particular ossuary because it seemed to be the key to the whole story. Everything depended on this unique artifact. Nonetheless, we did not learn its secrets right away. They were revealed slowly over time.

James Tabor, using other ossuaries as precedents, pointed out that the "Mariamne" inscription should be read: "[the bones] of Mariamne also known as 'Mara.'" For our part, we learned that, independent of the Talpiot discovery, leading Mary Magdalene experts have concluded that the woman known in the Gospels as Mary Magdalene was actually called by the Greek version of her name: "Mariamme," [Mariamene, or Mariamne]. The information comes, in the first instance, from the Church father Origen, who calls Magdalene "Mariamme," and then from the writer Epiphanus and noncanonical texts such as the *Pistis Sophia*. But the clincher is the Acts of Philip.

The Acts of Philip record the evangelical mission of Philip, brother of Mary Magdalene. Extracts from this noncanonical text have been available for millennia. But it was only in 1976, when searching in the library of the Xenophontos monastery on the island of Mount Athos in modern Greece, that Professors François Bovon and Bertrand Bouvier found an almost complete text of the Acts of Philip. It came in the form of a fifth-century text, probably copied from an even earlier manuscript. To this day, the manuscript has not been translated into English. It only appeared in French in 1996. So even among scholars it has pretty much gone under the radar.

The Acts of Philip tells the same story as the Mariamne ossuary from the Talpiot tomb. For example, the Acts of Philip call Mary Magdalene "Mariamne" and Jesus's mother "Maria." And in the Talpiot tomb, there is a "Mariamne" and a "Maria."

According to later Christian traditions, after the Romans crushed the Jesus movement, Mary Magdalene escaped to France. If this tradition is true, her ossuary couldn't be in Jerusalem. But the earlier tradition recorded in the Acts of Philip states that, after accompanying her brother to Asia Minor, Mary Magdalene returned to Jerusalem and ended her days there. Clearly, the Talpiot tomb is consistent with this tradition.

Whereas later Christian tradition identifies Mary Magdalene with an adulteress whom Jesus saves from being stoned and with an unnamed woman who washes his feet and dries them with her hair, the Gospels themselves give absolutely no indication that Mary Magdalene is the adulteress or the foot-washing sinner. In fact, all we know from the Gospels is that Mary Magdalene always seems to be at the center of Jesus's life, including his death and subsequent Resurrection. According to the Gospels, she's at the foot of the cross, she is the first to discover the empty tomb, and she is the first to encounter the risen Messiah. It is to noncanonical texts such as the Gnostic Gospel of Mary Magdalene and the Acts of Philip that we have to turn for a more complete profile. There she is a beloved apostle, a healer, a preacher, and a master in her own right. In the New Testament (1 Corinthians 16), Jesus too is referred to as "Mara" or "Master." In mirror fashion, in the Talpiot tomb the Mariamne inscription ends with the words: "also known as Mara."

According to the New Testament, Philip was the apostle to the Greek-speaking Jews of ancient Israel. Since we know that Mariamne, his sister, accompanied him on his ministry, she probably also spoke Greek. Incredibly, the "Mariamne" inscription from Talpiot is the only Greek inscription in the tomb.

I guess it's possible that a Jesus, son of Joseph other than Jesus of Nazareth could be buried next to a Maria and a Jos'e and another Mary known as "Mariamne the Master." But can any reasonable person imagine that there were two Jesuses in first-century Jerusalem with a father called Joseph, a close male relative called Jos'e, and two Marys in their lives – one called Maria and the other a Greek-speaking woman known as "the Master"?

The Gospels are also clear that Jesus is *not* related to Mary Magdalene, the one called Mariamne in the Acts of Philip. In theory, it's possible that the second Mary in the Talpiot tomb, even if it *is* the Jesus family tomb, is Jesus's sister Miriam, although we have no references to her as a "master" or to a Greek version of her name.

In 2005 producer Felix Golubev, working together with scholar Steve Pfann and forensic archaeologist Steven Cox, removed human residue from both the Jesus and Mariamne ossuaries. The tiny fragments were then shipped to Dr. Carney Matheson of the Paleo-DNA Lab at Lakehead University in Ontario. Dr. Matheson and his team were not able to extract nuclear DNA from the degraded samples. However, they were able to extract mitochondrial DNA from both the Jesus and Mariamne ossuaries. This allowed them to confirm that these were indeed Middle Eastern people of antiquity and that they were *not* related.

Forgetting for a moment that we are talking about Jesus of Nazareth, the only reason two unrelated individuals, male and female, would appear together in a *family* tomb in first-century Jerusalem is if they were husband and wife.

In the post–*Da Vinci Code* era, the idea that Jesus had a wife and children is part of the popular imagination. There is also no question that various secret societies have subscribed to this belief for centuries, if not millennia. But can this belief be grounded in canonical and noncanonical texts dating back to the period immediately after the Crucifixion and prior to Christianity emerging as the dominant religion of the Roman Empire?

As we have seen, it seems that Thomas, the "twin," may in fact have been Thomas the son. But the references to him are primarily noncanonical. What about the New Testament itself?

Clearly, the Gospels harbor a deep secret. The Gospel of John, for example, purposely obscures the identity of someone who was loved by Jesus above all others: the Beloved Disciple. No one knows why this individual is identified not by name but by reference to Jesus's feelings for him. In the plain meaning of the text, and *The Da Vinci Code* notwithstanding, he is a male. But what else do we know about him?

At the Last Supper, in the Gospel of John, the Beloved Disciple is depicted as "leaning against Jesus's chest." Again, sticking to the plain meaning of the text, what does it tell us about this "beloved" male? Unless your eating habits are very different from mine, at my dinner table only my kids cuddle with me and lean against my chest. The Beloved Disciple, therefore, is clearly very young. He's not a baby or a toddler, but he is also not a full-grown man. He's a kid, a young boy. This interpretation is not new. In fact, Albrecht Dürer, the famous German painter, in his masterful depiction of the Last Supper on a woodcut, has a young boy sitting in Jesus's lap. Simply put, it's what the text says.

But the cuddling incident is not the only enigmatic event involving a young man recorded in the Gospels. Mark 14:51

states that when the officers of the high priest came to arrest Jesus, a "young" lad followed them. He had nothing on but a "linen cloth." They tried to seize him, but he slipped out of the linen cloth and "fled from them naked." Is Mark talking about a grown man? Obviously not. In fact, it is explicit in the text that the disciples *all* deserted Jesus and "ran away." Only this lad, dressed in nothing but linen, followed the arresting party. In first-century Jewish circles, grown men did not walk around stark naked except for light linen shirts. But a boy of ten or thirteen might.

It appears that Mark is telling us the sad story of an unnamed boy in his linen pajamas who followed Jesus as he was being led into the night. When the soldiers tried to grab the lad by pulling on his "linen," the boy literally gave them the slip and ran away naked. Why is Mark giving us this curious detail? Obviously, it involves an important figure. So why aren't we told his name? Clearly, embedded in the text is the hint that Jesus had a son.

The mysterious Beloved Disciple appears again at the foot of the cross. It seems that, protected by his youth, he is the only male mentioned in any of the Gospels as accompanying Mary Magdelene and Mary, mother of Jesus, to the Crucifixion. According to the Gospels, the Romans had placed a crown of thorns on Jesus's head and above him they had written "King of the Jews." Obviously, the official Roman message was that this was what happened to anyone claiming descent from King David. Simply put, if Jesus had a son, a male heir to the Davidic throne, the son would have had to be hidden for fear that he too would soon be wearing a crown of thorns and hanging bloodied from a Roman cross.

The point is that the Gospels invite us to speculate about the secret identity of the Beloved Disciple and the young lad running naked through the streets of Jerusalem the night Jesus was arrested ... and the fact also is that the most compelling reason to hide the identity of a young boy in Jesus's most intimate entourage would have been that he was Jesus's son.

Furthermore, John records that Jesus saw his mother with the Beloved Disciple at the foot of the cross. He then says to her: "Woman, behold thy son!" Turning to the Beloved Disciple, he states: "Behold thy mother!" (John 19:26–27). From then on, John tells us, Mary shared the same home as the Beloved Disciple. Clearly, they're family. Most probably, grandmother and grandson.

Alternatively, isn't it also possible, as some scholars have suggested, that Mary Magdalene is often replaced in the Gospels by Mary, mother of Jesus, in order to obscure her role in Jesus's life? If this is the case, the incident at the cross can be reinterpreted as a dying man's last words to his wife ("woman"), not his mother, asking her to overcome her grief and protect their son from imminent danger.

Whatever our interpretation of the Gospels, the fact is that in the Talpiot tomb we know the young boy's name from the inscription on the box: "Judah, son of Jesus." Is Judah the

Beloved Disciple? Has the millennias-old mystery been solved? Did Judah follow his father on the night of the arrest? Did he run desperate and naked to his mother, telling her the terrible news?

Taken together, the Gospels, the noncanonical texts, oral traditions, the DNA tests, and the archaeology all seem to be telling the same story. There *was* a son, and he found his final resting place beside his father, mother, uncle, and grandmother in a family tomb halfway between their ancestral home in Bethlehem and Jerusalem, where they had hoped to establish their dynastic throne.

In British common law, there is the principle of the "reasonable man." Basically, when you look at the evidence you are not obliged to come up with every possible sci-fi scenario that might explain it. You simply have to be reasonable. And when you bring brother James into the equation, it seems that the case can be closed.

The James ossuary is what launched me on this journey. At first, the inscription "Yakov [James], son of Joseph, brother of Jesus" was hailed as the greatest archaeological find of the millennium. Then several Israeli experts announced that "brother of Jesus" was cynically added to "James, son of Joseph" by a brilliant forger. The fact is that this argument has never been proved to anyone's satisfaction. On the contrary, as recently as 2006, Dr. Wolfgang Krumbein of the Oldenburg University geology department published an online paper arguing for the authenticity of the entire inscription. But let's for a moment allow that "brother of Jesus" was added in modern times. Where does that leave the James ossuary? After all, everyone agrees that the ossuary is authentic. And what do we make of the inscription "James, son of Joseph," which everyone also agrees is authentic?

Here's where the plot thickens. The fact is that ten ossuaries were found and cataloged at the Talpiot site, but only nine made it to the IAA. One went missing between Talpiot and the headquarters of the IAA. What do we know about the missing tenth ossuary? What we know is that it disappeared – was misplaced or stolen – before it could be photographed or properly inspected. In the first instance, it seemed to the excavators to be "plain," much like the James ossuary appears at first glance. From the IAA records we do, however, have preliminary measurements of the missing tenth ossuary. According to Amos Kloner's report, IAA ossuary 80/509 – the missing ossuary – is 30 centimeters high. The James ossuary is 30.2 centimeters high. Ossuary 80/509 is 26 centimeters wide. The James ossuary is 26 centimeters wide. Finally, the missing ossuary is 60 centimeters in length. The James ossuary is 56.5 centimeters in length, a 3.5-centimeter discrepancy. It's possible, as has been suggested, that, because the James ossuary broke en route to Toronto and was then reglued, its original length changed slightly. But we don't even have to go this route. Given the preliminary nature of the inspection and the fact that the numbers of the missing ossuary are rounded to even numbers across the board, it may very well be that the initial measurements are off by 3.5 centimeters on one side. So, the missing ossuary and the James ossuary may be one and the same after all.

Oded Golan, owner of the James ossuary, has a black-and-white picture of his ossuary, dating back to the time when he claims he bought it. The photograph was sent to a Washington, D.C. lab that determined that it had not been doctored and that it was printed on Kodak paper that was discontinued in 1980, the exact year of the Talpiot discovery.

But there's more. When Charlie tested the patina of the Talpiot ossuaries under an electron microscope, he found a chemical signature that matches the James ossuary and – so far – no other.

If the James ossuary can be traced back to the Talpiot tomb, the statistical case is closed. In Andrey Feuerverger's words, it would be a statistical "slam-dunk." The Talpiot tomb would have to be acknowledged as the Jesus family tomb. But what if it can't be definitively traced back to Talpiot? Well, even if we exclude the James ossuary from the Talpiot cluster; and even if all of Charlie's numbers are discounted; and even if we totally discount the "Matias" inscription, which preserves the lineage of Maria, mother of Jesus; and even if we discount the Judah, son of Jesus ossuary because the connection with the Beloved Disciple is too tenuous; and even if we give no statistical weight to symbols such as the chevron and the "Tao"; and even if we divide all our numbers by four allowing for unintentional biases; and even if we then divide the whole thing by one thousand so as to take into account *all* possible first-century tombs in the Jerusalem area – even tombs that have not been found and may not exist – we are still left with what statisticians call a "P factor" of one in six hundred. Meaning that the odds are six hundred to one that the Talpiot tomb is the resting place of Jesus of Nazareth. In other words, it now seems clear that the tomb of Jesus, son of Joseph and five members of his family, including his wife and son, has been discovered.

As I left the edit suite and emerged into the Canadian cold, far from Jerusalem and the secrets beneath its soil, my mind wandered to many unanswered questions: Can DNA be retrieved from the other ossuaries? What is the true meaning of the chevron and the circle? Why exactly were skulls placed in ritual fashion to guard the kokhim in the tombs? Are there any as-yet-unseen inscriptions in the tomb, hiding beneath the accumulated patina on the walls? But then my thoughts somehow settled on the lid of the Jesus, son of Joseph ossuary.

Numbers 24:17 states that "a Star shall come out of Jacob; a Sceptre shall rise out of Israel." For millennia, that has been seen as a reference to the promised Messiah. The second-century Judean warrior Simon bar Kosiba, who fought the Romans from 132 to 135 C.E. and was hailed as Messiah by Rabbi Akiva, the greatest sage of the Talmudic period, had coins stamped with the Star of Jacob on them. It was his way of laying claim to the throne of David and announcing his status as Messiah. In fact, to this day, Simon bar Kosiba comes down to us as Simon bar Kochba, or "bar Kochva" – the "Son of the Star."

Jesus did not raise an army, nor did he strike any coins. But he and his followers clearly believed in his Davidic and messianic claims. Finely etched on the lid of the Talpiot ossuary of Jesus, son of Joseph, is a symbol. The mark was most probably made by whoever went through the heart-wrenching process of inserting Jesus's bones into the ossuary and then covering the box with the lid. It was probably a last act of love, loyalty, and respect executed just prior to pushing the ossuary into its burial niche, where it was destined to remain for two thousand years. There on the lid, that unknown kin of Jesus, son of Joseph, carved a simple but unmistakable … star.

Selected Bibliography

Adkins, L., and R. A. Adkins. *Handbook of Life in Ancient Rome*. Oxford: Oxford University Press, 1994.

Bellarmino Bagatti, B. and Milik. *Gli scavi del Dominus Flevit: An account of the excavations, 1953–55*. Studio Biblicum Fransicanum, 1968.

Berry, P. *The Christian Inscription at Pompeii*. London: Edwin Mellen Press, 1995.

Bovon, F. "Mary Magdalene in the Acts of Philip" *In Which Mary? The Marys of Early Christian Tradition.*

Ehrman, B. D. *Lost Scriptures: Books That Did Not Make It into the New Testament*. New York, London: Oxford University Press, 2003.

Eusebius. *The Church History*. Translated, with commentary, by P. M. Maier. Grand Rapids, MI: Kregel Press, 1999.

Figueras, P. *Decorated Jewish Ossuaries*. Leiden, Netherlands: E. J. Brill, 1983.

Finegan, J. *The Archaeology of the New Testament*. Princeton: Princeton University Press, 1992.

Gibbon, E. *The Decline and Fall of the Roman Empire*. New York: Heritage Press, 1946.

Goodenough, E. R. *Jewish Symbolism the Greco-Roman Period*. New York: Pantheon, 1964.

Greenhut, G., and R. Reich. "The Tomb of Caiaphas." *Biblical Archaeology Review* 18 (1992): 28–57.

Hachlili, R. "Names and Nicknames of Jews in Second Temple Times" *Eretz-Israel 17*. Israel Exploration Society, 1984.

Ilan, T. *Lexicon of Jewish Names in Late Antiquity, Part 1 Palestine 330 b.c.e.–200 c.e.* Tests and Studies in Ancient Judaism 91. Tubingen: Mohr Siebeck, 2002.

Jonas, H. *The Gnostic Religion: The Message of the Alien God and the Beginnings of Christianity*. 2nd ed. Boston: Beacon Press, 1963.

Josephus, F. *The New Complete Works of Josephus*. Translated by W. Whinston, with commentary by P. L. Maier. Grand Rapids, MI: Kregel Press, 1999.

Jones, F. Stanley, ed. *Which Mary? The Marys of the Early Christian Tradition*. Society of Biblical Literature Symposium Series 20, Brill Academic Publishers, 2002.

Kasser, R., M. Meyer, G. Wurst, and B. Ehrman. *The Gospel of Judas*. Washington, D.C.: National Geographic Press, 2006.

King, K. L. *The Gospel of Mary Magdala: Jesus and the First Woman Apostle.* Santa Rosa, CA: Polebridge Press, 2003.

————"Why all the Controversy? Mary in the Gospel of Mary." *Which Mary? The Marys of the Early Christian Tradition.* F. Stanley Jones, ed. SBL Symposium Series 20. Atlanta: Society of Biblical Literature, 2002: 53–74.

Kloner, Amos. "A Tomb with Inscribed Ossuaries in the East Talpiot," *Atiquot* 29 (1996): 15–22.

Mancini, I. *Archaeological Discoveries Relative to the Judeo-Christians.* Jerusalem: Franciscan Printing Press, 1968; reprint, 1984.

Meyers, E. M. *Jewish Ossuaries: Reburial and Rebirth.* Rome: Biblical Institute Press, 1971.

Pagels, E. H. *Beyond Belief: The Secret Gospel of Thomas.* New York: Random House, 2003.

Pellegrino, C. R. *Ghosts of Vesuvius.* New York: Harper-Collins, 2004.

Pliny. *Letters and Panegyricus.* Translated by Radice and Loeb. Cambridge, MA: Harvard University Press, 1969.

Pritz, R. A. *Nazarene Jewish Christianity.* Jerusalem: Magnes Press, Hebrew University, 1988.

Rahmani, L. Y. Ossuaries and Ossilegium (Bone Gathering) in the Late Second Temple Period. *Ancient Jerusalum Revealed: Reprinted and Expanded Edition.* Hillel Geva, ed. Jerusalem: Israel Exploration Society, 2000: 191–205.

Rahmani, L. Y. *A Catalogue of Jewish Ossuaries in the Collections of the State of Israel.* Jerusalem: Israel Antiqui-

ties and Israel Academy of Sciences and Humanities,
1994.

Robinson, J. M., ed. *The Nag Hammadi Library.* New York:
HarperCollins, 1990.

Scarre, C. *Chronicle of the Roman Emperors.* London:
Thames and Hudson, 1995.

Schaff, Philip, ed. *Eusebius Pamphilius: Church History,
Life of Constntine, Oration in Praise of Constantine.* New
York: Christian Literature Publishing Co., 1890.

Shanks, H., and Ben Witherington III. *The Brother of Jesus.*
Biblical Archaeology Society. San Francisco: Harper-
Collins, 2003.

Suetonius, G. *The Twelve Caesars.* Translated by R. Graves.
London: Penguin, 1957.

Sukenik, E. L. *The Earliest Records of Christianity.* Rome,
1952.

Tabor, J. *The Jesus Dynasty.* New York: Simon & Schuster,
2006.

Acknowledgments

We Thank:

Elaine Markson, our agent, Gideon Weil, our editor, Carney Matheson (Lakehead University Paleo DNA lab), Robert Genna, Linda Parisi, Clyde Wells (Suffolk County Crime Laboratory, New York), Alberta Nokes (Vision Television), Billy Campbell, Jane Root, Clark Bunting, Phil Fairclough, Steve Burns, David McKillop (Discovery Channel), Simon Andreae, Ralph Lee (Channel 4), and Robin Mirsky (Rogers Telefund).

Special Thanks To:

James Cameron, James Tabor, Shimon Gibson, Andrey Feuerverger, Nicole Austin, Karen Dougherty, Andrea Gallagher Ellis, Felix Golubev, Chelsea Johnston, and Ric Bienstock, Associated Producers staff.

311

Charlie Thanks:

Father Mervyn Fernando (Subhodi Institute), Father Robert McGuire, Rabbi Zuscha "Mel" Friedman, the Cameron boys, "The Don" (Peterson), Mary Leung Young, Omar Cedeno, Bill Schutt (American Museum of Natural History), Reverend Jill Potter, Doug McClean, Giuseppe Mastroloren-zo, and Pier Paolo Petrone (forensic archaeology, Vesuvius). Thanks also to Ma and Pa Pellegrino, who, with the input of five incomparable teachers – Adelle Dobie, Barbara and Dennis Harris, Agnes Saunders, and Ed McGunnigle – helped a child who was judged forever unable to read books, to grow up and write them. A special thank-you also to Captain Paddy Brown and to his late great friends in Ladder 4 and Engine 54 – who know why.

Simcha Thanks:

My father Joseph, mother Ida, sister Sara, children: Ziva Esther, Nava Hana, Iosefa Liza, Adin Hananya, Michaela Sashi, and my wife, Nicole.